CW00689176

# BOLDNESS BE MY FRIEND

## *Remembering Bob Cryer*

An Anthology of Memories and Tributes
by the Family and Friends of
Bob Cryer, MP
(1934–1994)

Bradford Libraries

© Copyright Contributors, 1996

Published by
Bradford Libraries
Central Library
Prince's Way
BRADFORD
West Yorkshire
BD1 1NN

ISBN 0 907734 48 0

Typeset and printed in Great Britain by Alden, Oxford, Didcot
and Northampton

## *Dedication*

For my grandchildren Conor James, Robert Calum and Ciaran Patrick Kilduff, and Hirun Robert and Anchal Cryer, so that they know who their Grandpa was.

"Boldness be my friend!
Arm me, audacity, from head to foot!"

Shakespeare, *Cymbeline* (Act I, Scene VI)


Bob used this quotation during the 1992 General Election to illustrate his view that the Party leadership should follow Mrs Thatcher's example and pursue policies that would benefit 'our' people unambiguously.

# CONTENTS

# CONTENTS

# FOREWORD

## RICHARD WHITELEY
*Yorkshire Television*

Bob Cryer was a man who liked to say 'yes'. As such, he was a delight to me and my colleagues who toiled daily to fill a nightly news programme with topical comments.

For years Bob was a regular on Yorkshire Television. An appearance was never too much trouble – although Bob didn't oblige so readily because he liked the colour of our collective eyes. No, Bob was a passionate man, a man of opinions and causes, and sharp enough to grab any chance to preach that message to a wide audience.

When the news about Bob Cryer's death broke that Tuesday afternoon, our newsroom was stunned.

Newsrooms, by their very nature, are used to bad news suddenly breaking – and our Calendar news team, like those in all the Yorkshire-based media, have had their share of shocks.

Flixborough, Bradford City, Hillsborough. All terrible tragedies, with appalling loss of so many lives.

Yet news of this one single death was different. It was personal. Each member of the team felt affected, each in a different way. Some had known Bob Cryer for years, many others for a lesser time. Some had known him from phone conversations or interviews, others hadn't actually met him or known him at all.

But everybody felt they knew him. That is why the huge crowd at a triumphant Odsal that night stood so silent, in tribute to a man that few would have actually known personally, that you could hear a pin drop.

How many other politicians could have earned such a sincere silent tribute? Not many, I guess.

People respected Bob. Not everybody agreed with his views – especially many members of his own party. Respect is a scarce commodity when it is being distributed among Members of Parliament. Theirs is not a profession which generally attracts a large amount of it.

So why did Bob earn his? Everyone will have their own reasons. But it's fair to say that he showed total commitment to causes great and small. He made no compromises, he led by example and he redefined the meaning of the word 'work'.

Those better qualified than me have written their tributes in this book.

But what did Bob Cryer mean to us in television?

Quite simply, he was the dream politician. Consider why.

He answered messages. He rang back. He turned up at the right time at the right studio. He was happy to stand on the freezing and windblown Green outside Westminster waiting for a two-minute insert into a live programme. If there was a technical cock-up he would understand. If he had to stand in as second choice, he wouldn't mind.

If a 20-second soundbite was required, he'd give it, word perfect. If the question was daft he'd answer it sensibly. If a half-hour studio debate was called for, he would deliver.

Because his views were unfashionable, he took a lot of flak. He took it with good humour, a boyish grin and unfailing good manners.

There were some classic encounters. I remember Cryer versus Mitchell – when young Austin was one of us. These two lads had grown up together in Shipley – both had great intellects and were devilishly articulate. Or the great Cryer versus Fox confrontations. Constituency neighbours, from similar humble backgrounds, but different parties.

Bob and Sir Marcus would exhibit a ducking and diving skill of great speed, wit and charm. Wonderful wordplay . . . the cheeky chappie, against plain Bob, the people's friend.

Or put him against a more traditional enemy – a Tory grandee, a knight of the Shires. Here you would have a jousting match – elegantly fought as they tilted at each other, both obeying the rules, each one seeking to topple the other in grand style.

Bob had no fear. We once gathered 200 of his constituents who didn't vote for him in a hall in Keighley. The programme was called 'Cryer's Critics'. At the beginning, a show of hands revealed that no one liked him. Bob faced them and, by the end, he had made a lot of friends.

I remember the memorial meeting at St George's Hall on the Friday. Bob had so many friends, I could only find space at the back of the balcony. It is fitting that so many of his friends should now contribute to this book which will ensure that both he and his work will be remembered, long after the transient images of television and the fickleness of day-to-day politics have vanished. This book reminds us of Bob's principles, his interests, his hobbies and, of course, his family.

Bob Cryer, right, and Shipley-born MP Austin Mitchell, centre, talk to John Watcham, left, and Arthur Mosley, chair and vice-chair of the Sutton Ward Labour Party, March 1978.
(*Keighley News*)

# ACKNOWLEDGEMENTS

Rory Hegarty, freelance journalist, for the Alice Mahon interview.

Malcolm Hoddy (*Keighley News*) and Frances Wood (*Telegraph & Argus*) for photographs.

Bob Jones for the recording of the St George's Hall Memorial Service, and to Joyce Williamson and Janet Ostrowski of Bradford Libraries Access To Print Unit for transcribing the tape.

Diane Tempest of Bradford Arts, Museums and Libraries for transcribing the Westminster Hall recording.

Messrs Putnam for permission to quote *For Johnny* by John Pudney.

William Heinemann (publishers) for permission to quote from *Bright Day*.

The Clarendon Press, Oxford, for permission to use the poem *Adlestrop*.

Her Majesty's Stationery Office for permission to quote from Parliamentary Debates.

*The Independent* for permission to reprint Tam Dalyell's obituary of Bob Cryer.

Parliamentary Profile Services for Andrew Roth's Parliamentary Profile.

PHOTOGRAPHS. Unless indicated otherwise, all photographs are the property of Ann Cryer.

EDITORIAL NOTE. Throughout this book many mentions are made of money orders and money resolutions. Norman Wilding and Philip Laundry, in their book *An Encyclopaedia of Parliament*, 4th edition, define a Financial Resolution thus:

> In addition to the ordinary annual expenditure as embodied in the Estimates and authorized by means of Supply resolutions, the House is sometimes called upon to consider new or extraordinary expenditure which is unrelated to the regular business of Supply.... In the case of a Bill containing expenditure clauses which are incidental to its main purpose, only those particular clauses, which are printed in italics, require preliminary authorization by means of a financial resolution. The committee stage of such Bills may not be taken until the financial resolution has been agreed to. The debate on the committee stage of such Bills is limited to three-quarters of an hour or 10.45 p.m., whichever is the later.

# INTRODUCTION

## ANN CRYER

Had Bob survived to retirement he would have written a quite fascinating autobiography. The many and extremely varied facets of his life, his ready wit and elegant turn of phrase would have guaranteed it.

In his fifty-nine years Bob achieved so much, and yet he had two major regrets, in his view imperfections: he never directed a feature film and he never played cricket for Yorkshire! Given these two 'grave omissions', I still felt that his had been a life worthy of recording. Following discussions with my family I decided that I really must somehow produce a book for people to remember him by. More particularly, I wanted something for our grandchildren. Since no one person had the time or knowledge to encompass the many areas of Bob's life, I approached family and friends who could go into the details of one period or an area of activity or enthusiasm. Then other volunteers came forward, some quite unexpected.

This collection of memories and comments, therefore, is a substitute for the autobiography that will not now, alas, be written. It is not an objective or detailed account and could not be described as a biography; the contributions overlap and display a variety of styles and points of view. I have supplemented the reminiscences and tributes with photographs which may help plug a few gaps. I trust, therefore, that you will find this book a reminder, an interesting record, and a celebration of a very singular life lived to the full.

I would like to record my thanks and appreciation to all who found the time in incredibly busy lives to contribute to this book, the speakers at the Bradford Funeral Meeting and the Westminster Memorial Meeting, also the organisations who have provided memorials to Bob. Thanks are also due to Bob Duckett and the staff of Bradford Libraries without whose help this book would not have been published. I would also like to convey my appreciation to the hundreds of people who wrote such warm, encouraging letters following Bob's death. May I also use this opportunity to put on record my appreciation of the support and care generously given by John and Jane who, despite their own enormous loss, helped me through the black months. Lastly, very special thanks indeed to our wider family and close friends whose kindness and consistent friendship helped me to survive.

# BRIEF CHRONOLOGY OF
# THE LIFE OF BOB CRYER

1934   Born in Great Horton, Bradford
1958   Joined CND and the Labour Party
1960   Joined the Co-operative Party
1960–1961   Contested (unsuccessfully) the West Ward of Shipley in the West Riding County Council elections and Shipley Urban District Council elections.
1962   Called the first meeting of the Keighley and Worth Valley Railway Preservation Society and became first chairman
1963   Married Ann Place of Darwen
1964   Birth of John Robert Cryer
       Contested Darwen, Lancashire, in October General Election
1965   Appointed Lecturer in Law and Government at Keighley Technical College
       Birth of Jane Ann Cryer
1968   Re-opening of the Worth Valley Railway
1971   Elected to Keighley Borough Council
       Selected as Parliamentary Candidate
1974   February General Election. Won Keighley with 878 vote majority
       Death of John Arthur Cryer (father)
       October General Election. Retained Keighley with 3,081 vote majority
1976   Appointed Under Secretary for Industry
1978   Resigned as Under Secretary for Industry
1979   Retained Keighley at General Election with 78 vote majority
1979   Chairman, Joint Parliamentary Select Committee on Statutory Instruments
1983   Lost Keighley at General Election by 2,774 votes
1984   MEP for Sheffield, Chesterfield and NE Derbyshire
1987   General Election. Won Bradford South by 209 votes
       Chairman, Joint Parliamentary Select Committee on Statutory Instruments
1989   Ceased being MEP
1989   Select Committee on Members' Interests
1990   Death of Gladys Evelyn Cryer (mother)
1992   General Election. Retained Bradford South by 4,902 votes
       Birth of Conor James Kilduff (grandson)
       Appointed Governor, British Film Institute
1994   Died in motorway accident

# CHAPTER 1

# THE ROOTS OF BUDDING INTERESTS

"... Lost in its smoky valley amongst the Pennine hills, whistling with tall mill chimneys, with its lace of blackened stone, Bruddersford is generally held to be an ugly city; and so I suppose it is; but it always seemed to me to have the kind of ugliness that could not only be tolerated but often enjoyed: it was grim but not mean. And the moors were always there, and the horizon never without its promise. No Bruddersford man could be exiled from the uplands and the blue air, he always had one foot on the heather; he had only to pay his tuppence on the tram and then climb for half an hour to hear the larks and curlews, to feel the old rocks warming in the sun, to see the harebells trembling in the shade ..."

J. B. Priestley
from *Bright Day*

This extract is used on the statue of J. B. Priestley in Bradford. On reading it Bob was clearly moved by how close Priestley's words were to his own feelings for Bradford. It was quoted in the programme for the funeral meeting.

---

## 1

### JOAN PETFORD
*Sister of Bob Cryer*

On 12 April 1994, a devastating and sad event occurred which stunned his family, relatives, many, many friends, and even some Conservative Members of Parliament. Bob Cryer, MP, was killed in a car accident whilst returning to the House of Commons after the Easter recess.

He was born on 3 December 1934, at 18 Kelsall Terrace, Shepherd Street, Great Horton, Bradford. As a rather dreamy seven year old sister it was not an event I was anticipating – very little in the way of hatches, matches or despatches was discussed in my youthful presence. Mother was a very talented and very enterprising dressmaker and I can scarcely remember a time when she didn't have two or three assistants in the workroom. That particular day I was taken by my father to the home of one of them, Blanche, and given tea there. This was a rare treat as we only went out to tea very

Bob Cryer, aged 18 months. This photograph won a Farley's Rusk competition and won Bob a box of baby food.
(*Walter Scott*)

occasionally to mother's brother, Harold or father's sister Mary. Early that same evening father returned with the news that I now had a brother and off we went back home, walking from Lidget Green to Great Horton.

In the thirties babies were highly decorated individuals surviving very successfully in a froth of lace and muslin pillows, satin ribbons and elaborately decorated wicker cots. In the middle of such a froth I saw, that evening, a tiny crumpled pink face belonging to a very sleepy small person. He developed into a placid, cheery baby thriving on Allenbury's Baby Food Nos. 1, 2, and 3 and had ginger hair which, to mother's delight, was curly. My ginger hair was, by contrast, dead straight and subjected each night to the then current fashion of being twisted in rags to induce a few curls.

As mother was of a religious nature and a keen church-goer Bob was christened George Robert Cryer at St Columba's Church, Grange Road, Great Horton. George Robert Chester, after whom he was named, was a dressmakers' supplier who had a business just off Darley Street in Bradford. Mother never went anywhere else for all the zips, cottons, silks, trimmings and buttons she needed. Often I was sent to collect an order and climbed two flights of rough wooden stairs to the shop where there were thick wooden counters with inlaid brass tapes along the edges and shelves crammed with boxes each advertising its contents by means of a sample stitched on the front. Mr Chester and his wife Rose were a childless couple who took a great liking to Bob and myself. After we had moved from Great Horton to Saltaire we often visited them at their house in Baildon Green. For me, this was a paradise as they had a wonderful walled garden; for Bob, by that time seven or eight years old, a Mecca, because he could sit in the driving seat of the Chesters' Morris 8 car which was confined to the garage by wartime petrol restrictions.

During Bob's early childhood we continued living at Kelsall Terrace. The house was rented from a local butcher who had electricity installed not long before Bob was born. Previously all lighting was by gas mantles which didn't give a very good light. The living room at the back had a large cast iron range at one end. Mother used the fire-oven for baking bread but most meals were made on a huge, old gas cooker. The only other downstairs room was at the front and was used for fitting the clothes mother made. There were three bedrooms, one of which was used as a workroom. There was a bathroom with wash basin and bath but the toilet was outside. One of the highlights of

'Bobby' aged 3 in Roberts Park, Saltaire, wearing a coat made by his mother.

each week was the visit of the organ grinder. For a few coppers he would stop by the back gate and play a few tunes. He always had a small monkey attached by a chain to the organ. The monkey used to sit on the top and chatter away wearing a bright red coat. I remember Bob being held up to see the monkey and being very delighted about it all.

Father worked intermittently as a painter and decorator at that time. Sometimes when he went back to the customers to collect payment or ladders he would take me along. Once, just before bonfire night, I remember one customer giving me sixpence to spend on fireworks. Bob missed out on such events as by the time he was old enough to enjoy 5th November it was wartime and in the blackout there were no such things as bonfires or firework displays. In spite of the Thirties depression mother's dressmaking business thrived. She always managed to keep a good clientèle, and by dint of hard work and thrift in 1936, when I was nine and Bob aged two, she had decided to buy a house as opposed to renting one. For a time there was a great deal of discussion as to where we should move.

Father's family had lived in Shipley: 182 Bradford Road, to be precise. His father, whom we never knew as he died in 1924, was successively a schoolmaster, a schools inspector and eventually a deputy director of education in Bradford. He was also a very keen and knowledgeable amateur botanist (once visited by the well known Druce of Oxford). In order to botanise more easily he rented a cottage first at Yarnbury above Grassington in the Yorkshire Dales and later one at Linton down by the Falls. Father could remember that they and the family in the cottage next door would rent a cart, a driver and horse for the day to drive up to Buckden. The hire

Bob having an exciting afternoon at the farm at Hawksworth. (*May Davey*)

charge was six old pence ($2\frac{1}{2}$ pence in today's currency). This was in the early 1900s. Thus father had had a middle class existence along with three sisters and one brother all but one of whom lived in the Shipley, Bingley, Baildon area. Although in the Thirties father earned a living by painting and decorating he was originally an engineer, apprentice trained. In the 1914–18 war he had joined up at the age of seventeen and was always proud of the fact that he was one of the first 50,000 to volunteer. By contrast, mother was a pacifist and her views must have influenced Bob profoundly, as in his political life he became well known for his CND activities. After the armistice in 1918 father left the Royal Flying Corps where he had worked as a fitter and set up an engineering business in Bingley designing a lathe. The business fell through but all this added up to the fact that father had very strong links with both industrial and agricultural Airedale and Wharfedale. Mother was born in Halifax but had lived all her life in Bradford, but father's preferences carried the day, and in December 1936 we moved to 15 Albert Road, Saltaire, just one mile from Shipley. Curiously, although father's work was spasmodic and mother was the chief breadwinner, father had to sign as a guarantor when it came to applying for a mortgage. A good example of the entrenched views of the patriarchal society in the 1930s. Incidentally, in 1936 the house cost £450.

No.15 Albert Road was an attractive stone-built house with two reception rooms, three bedrooms, a long narrow kitchen with a tiled Airedale range (no more black leading) and a bathroom complete with toilet. It had a small front garden, a stone flagged path, a long side border and a stone flagged yard at the rear with washhouse and coalhouse. I can remember even at the age of nine infinitely preferring it to the house at Great Horton and much preferring its situation. The house was one of the Salt estate, some of which were beginning to come on the market at that time. It was on the edge of the village built in the 1870s by the philanthropist and mill owner Sir Titus Salt for his workforce. The upper end of Albert Road consisted of houses built in blocks of four or two for the mill executives. This meant that it was more expensively constructed than

Bob and Joan Cryer photographed in March 1943.
(*Photo: Walter Scott*)

the remainder of the village. The front room had a wooden floor for instance, as opposed to stone flags which was the more usual flooring material, and the inside toilet was a great advance. There were cellars but no attics and being south facing and with a skylight over the stairs it was surprisingly light in spite of a very solid exterior. It says a great deal for mother's stamina, powers of organisation and ability to keep her clientèle that the move went smoothly. I think the only useful part I played was in 'singing' Bob off to sleep in the evenings as, at the age of two, he didn't settle into a strange bedroom at first. We both went across the road to Albert Road Junior School as it then was. Bob of course attended the infant and primary classes but after a year and a half I won a County Minor Scholarship and moved to the Salt High School. I only knew one year of 'normal' school life before war broke out on 3rd September 1939. We had been for one of our rare holidays at St Anne's which mother liked very much. The weather had been superb and I can remember the anti-climax of seeing coachloads of khaki-uniformed and tin-hatted soldiers as we returned home. These forbidding signs didn't affect Bob, by then a cheery blue-eyed, ginger-haired five year old. We had the unpleasant experience of being fitted for gas masks, as did all

Bob Cryer at the front door of 15 Albert Road, Saltaire. (*Joan Petford*)

civilians. This took place across the road at the junior school and the familiarity of both the place and the ARP warden – our neighbour – made it a slightly more bearable experience. After the declaration of war Britain was zoned so that some areas were to have their children evacuated (town and city centres), some were classed as neutral (e.g. Saltaire – no movement of children – we were six miles from Bradford) and the remainder were reception areas for children – the rural areas. Hence for us life went on much the same as usual in some respects. We were never separated from our family, we attended the same schools and we lost none of our friends through evacuation. We had air raid practices at school and some broken nights with air raid sirens, though luckily nothing materialised and the all-clear siren soon sounded. When Bradford was bombed though, and we could see fires in the distance, that was quite frightening. Everyone had some form of air raid shelter. Ours was in the small cellar under the hall and council workmen were sent to install the reinforcements. This they did so well that after they left we found the hall floor had been slightly raised and we couldn't open the front door. Back they came the next day to ease off the jacks. Drapers did a roaring trade in black-out material and all curtains were lined with this. If the curtains weren't completely drawn and a chink of light showed there would be a tap on the door from the local air raid warden during his rounds at night.

One of the constant worries of wartime on the home front was food rationing. Mother performed miracles with the small amounts allowed on ration books. I can remember going to the local butcher's before school one morning for one ration of meat. The only thing on the butcher's block was a large tin of corned beef so we had one shillingsworth. This had to make a meal for the four of us. We were always hungry in the sense of having a good appetite and Bob, always tall for his age and growing rapidly ate everything put before him. Fish wasn't rationed though supplies were very spasmodic, but usually once per week we had fish of some sort and on another day sausage. At week-ends we had a joint, either sirloin or lamb, which spun out for three days. Meals were all eaten in the kitchen during the week. This was rather cramped as, at the end of the table where Bob sat, father had one or two radio cabinets piled up as he was keen on making radio sets as a hobby. On Saturday, and certainly on Sunday, we had tea in the dining room, a large, pleasant room with windows on two sides. We had a large, oval polished oak dining table and I can remember after mother died the pleasure it gave Bob to see the table installed in the equally pleasant Victorian house in Halifax belonging to my elder son.

Oddly enough wartime brought us some financial relief. Father, who had worked spasmodically, became a machine tool training instructor at a Government Training Centre in Kirkstall Road, Leeds. This provided a steady income until the end of the war. Mother continued with the dressmaking and tailoring business but times were difficult. One of the girls who worked for her came from a farm at Hawksworth and left to work on the farm, driving a tractor – something that was unheard of for women before the war. She had worked for us for many years and

Bob Cryer with sister Joan and mother.

was very much missed. We visited the farm sometimes – an event we always enjoyed. I remember before the war taking Bob, when I was ten and he was three years old, on a blackberrying expedition to some fields at the bottom of the farm well-known for excellent blackberry bushes. We set off after dinner on a warm sunny day walking there and back and arrived home at 9 p.m. to panic and consternation. I had carried Bob and the blackberries a good part of the way home but he, poor lad, was so tired he fell asleep as he was carried upstairs. Only the substantial picking of blackberries saved me from being totally in the dog house.

One person who continued as a customer and great friend of mother's was Mrs Grimshaw. Her husband owned a woollen mill in Calverley and she had an obsessional interest in clothes, luckily for us, as she brought in extra income before, after, and during the war. She was very kind and Bob remembered her bringing model engineering magazines and car magazines which her son, who was my age, no longer wanted. She also brought very thoughtful and generous Christmas presents. One was a Brownie Kodak camera given to me when I was fourteen, another was a maroon Triang tricycle given to Bob after he had recovered from a very serious illness, of which more later. We both had great fun with that tricycle. One of the bonuses of the 1940s was that there was very little

With St Peter's, Saltaire, boy scouts, at camp *c.* 1946. Bob is fourth from left.
(*Photo: Arthur Blakey*)

traffic on main roads, and side roads were almost totally traffic free. With some friends on Avondale Crescent in the holidays, we played a game of taxis on an assortment of bikes, trikes and scooters. In wintertime we could use the full length of Albert Road for sledging and it was ideal with a slightly steeper slope to start off at the top and a long steady slope down to the railway at the bottom. I cannot remember anyone ever complaining about either the taxi game or the sledge runs.

Bob began his passionate interest in trains and railways in the early forties. At the bottom of Albert Road was the L.M.S. line and by dashing out of school very promptly at 4 p.m. Bob and friends would be just in time to see the 4 o'clock 'Namer' go past. This was the train running from King's Cross to Edinburgh. Eventually Bob had all the Ian Allen engine lists and would tick off each number or name as he saw the engine, as all train spotters did. On the Friday before he died he came up to visit us in Cumbria driving the Armstrong-Siddeley Star Sapphire. It was an added pleasure for him that we were close by the Settle to Carlisle railway line and I remember the delight with which he saw 'Sir Nigel Gresley' go past that day. It was duly noted down in a small pocket book he kept for that purpose.

When we visited Bob and his wife Ann at their home in Shipley, one of his pleasures was to show us a film. Home movies and the cinema were another of his great interests and it was there that we first saw the 'Titfield

Thunderbolt'. Bob was never really keen on gardening but he would cut the grass and trim the considerable hedges at their Shipley home. As Ann was very interested in gardens they visited some when abroad and his pleasure was to make a film of the visit, so we were entertained with his 'shooting' of such gardens as that at Varengeville near Dieppe – a Lutyens–Jekyll garden – and Monet's garden at Giverny.

Returning to Bob's younger days, in the early summer of 1941 there was an outbreak of diphtheria at Albert Road School. I was thirteen at the time and Bob was six. Several children were taken ill and a friend of Bob's died. There had been a vaccination programme throughout the country but father was opposed to vaccination. Like many people he hadn't the faintest idea what he was talking about medically but was first class at pronouncing a medical opinion. Mother was over-ruled and my opinion simply didn't count and so we were never vaccinated. However during the outbreak Bob developed a very nasty sore throat and I was sent to 'phone the doctor – a kindly man who had been with the family since before we were born. He practised in Great Horton but came over to Saltaire very speedily, took swabs from us all and feared that Bob had diphtheria. This was rapidly confirmed and he was taken to Morton Banks isolation hospital at Riddlesden. I remember it was a lovely, sunny morning when the ambulance came. I was away from school for two weeks in quarantine. As I enjoyed school immensely that was an additional blow. The weeks passed by and each Saturday or Sunday we went to the hospital lodge just to be told that there was no change. This total lack of communication was typical of hospitals at that time. One Sunday morning however, a policeman arrived on a bicycle with a message from the hospital to say that Bob had taken a turn for the worse and would mother and father go to the hospital immediately. Much, much later that day they returned. The crisis had passed but it was many weeks before Bob came home. I remember he couldn't walk and looked a poor thing like something out of Belsen (though that was a word unknown then). Mother gave up dressmaking for the time being and it was so fortunate then that father was working. There wasn't a National Health Scheme in existence and we would not have been able to pay the doctor's bills. The sitting room which normally functioned as a fitting room for mother's customers was turned over to Bob. His bed was brought downstairs to make it easier for mother. Bob had to be fed a little and frequently, calves foot jelly and slippery elm food were the order of the day. Gradually, with great patience on mother's part, he began to recover, and by Christmas that year life for all of us was beginning to return to normal. The single bed which Bob used never went back into the large front bedroom but instead was put in the workroom and made up each night after work was finished

The wedding of Joan Cryer to Ken Petford at St. Peter's Church, Saltaire, on 9 August 1952. Bob and his parents, John and Gladys Cryer, are standing to the right of the bride, Bob's sister.
(*Arthur Blakey*)

there and cleared away each morning. I never remember hearing him moan about the arrangement but then he was always smiling and later developed a lovely sense of humour. After I went to the university in Manchester, at the age of 18, Bob used the small back bedroom, which must have made things easier for everyone.

Another of our benefactors was Mr Chester and his wife, Mr Chester (George Robert) being the aforementioned dressmakers' supplier. Before Bob's illness he used to turn up at about 9 o'clock on Christmas Eve with our presents, one of which was always Tiger Tim's or Teddy Tail's annual. We have them still. They gave us a great deal of enjoyment and we half believed that the donor at that time of night might have been Father Christmas himself. 25th December was the one day of the year when we had chicken. Mother didn't like turkey, and goose and duckling were thought to be too fatty, so, chicken it was. The infrequency of a chicken made it more special, as with many families then. A battery system of production didn't exist. All hens were free range, there were far fewer of them, and so they were much dearer. The balance has tilted the other way now of course. Mother was an excellent cook and so there was always a delicious Christmas pudding of which Bob was extremely fond. Once, just before Christmas near the end of the war, the Chesters brought their

Saltaire Second Eleven, Bradford League, 1952. Bob is seated third from right.

car round and took Bob and myself over to Huddersfield. Bob was ecstatic. We all had tea at Collinson's Café, of which there was a branch then on John William Street. Collinson's always used to have a trio playing at tea time and I enjoyed listening. I think that passed Bob by as he wasn't musical at all. To a certain extent after his illness Bob was spoilt, understandably so. If a consignment of oranges came into the shop and I queued for our share as I did most of the shopping, Bob was given them as it was felt his need was the greatest. Gradually mother re-instated the dressmaking business. Customers anxious for first class dresses, costumes etc. returned and the girls came back to the workroom. As well as running the business mother made all our clothes including suits for Bob, overalls, coats and suits for father and all my clothes. She even managed to find time to coach Bob a little for the 11+ exam. By the end of the war in Europe in May 1945, Bob had passed that exam and so there was double relief all round. Bob was never academically inclined so obtaining a County Minor Scholarship satisfied mother's aim, which was that he should eventually obtain a degree and, as the thinking was then, a good, steady, well-paid job unlike father. Bob's preferences, however, were for a visit to the cinema, looking at cars in Hirst Wood garage, going to the railway or down to Shipley station train spotting or playing with a friend of his who lived further up the road. Raymond, that particular friend, was an evacuee from London staying with his grandmother and he was one of the few boys allowed to play at No. 15. I don't remember ever having a friend in to play myself and though plenty called for each of us, we always played out. With the sitting room in use as a fitting room and the dining room as a waiting room there was only the kitchen left, and that was rather cramped. As I grew older I was occasionally allowed to have a friend or two for tea, which we had in the dining room. All my friends admired mother's cooking as much as her dressmaking and the teas were delicious even on wartime rations. On those occasions we never had tea with mother and father, and looking back I think the real reason was that father's temper was so uncertain and he could be so unreasonable that it was thought easier if we ate separately. Another oddity of father's was that he never acknowledged Bob if he met him outside, and I know Bob was rather hurt about it, but took it in his stride. One thing that father did occasionally on a sunny evening was to walk up to Northcliffe playing fields with us and Bob was coached in the arts of batting and bowling, whilst I acted as a back stop/wicket keeper. Later Bob played for Salt High School and later still, for Saltaire in the Bradford League. I quote from a letter from a school friend of his written to Bob's wife after the fatal accident,

I knew Bob himself for about fifty years. We were at Albert Road School at the same time, though he was a year ahead of me. There he was involved in a big fight with a rather snooty boy who lived up Moorhead somewhere. We moved on to the Salt School. Bob was a good cricketer and an excellent captain of the school team, for which I was the scorer. I recall his elegant left arm slow bowling and his huge old Armstrong Siddeley, in which he took about half the team to away matches. Bob was rebellious and disliked by the headmaster, Mr Parkin. In the 1953 staff match in Roberts Park he obtained a measure of revenge. Parkin has been a reasonable cricketer in his day but overestimated his own abilities. He ill-advisedly opened the batting, and Bob gave the ball to a lad named Scrimshaw, who was not a regular member of the school team but was known to be pretty fast. He bowled Parkin first ball, and two other masters in the first over, when Bob took him off to give the other masters a chance. I caught up with Bob when he stayed on a third year in the sixth form. We studied English with Miss Edwards (with whom I still correspond); she encouraged debate, but was taken aback when Bob argued that Chaucer's *Prioress's Tale* was full of vile race-hatred and sickening sentimentality. I once successfully opposed Bob in another debate, on the Sunday opening of cinemas, of which he was in favour needless to say. Also from those days I remember his performance as Sir Andrew Aguecheek in *Twelfth Night*, especially the comic-pathetic way he spoke the line "I was adored once too".

Bob's interest in cars developed from an early age. First the Chesters' Morris 8, then, helping to deliver groceries in the local van, he learnt to

Bob's childhood home in Saltaire, in 1996.
(*Bob Duckett*)

drive under the instruction of the delivery man. His passion even filtered through to my wedding in 1952. After the ceremony we were to use the wedding car to drive to Shipley Station en route for a train to Scarborough. Could he possibly ride in the front seat with us down to the station? The car was a large and very elegant Daimler, so of course he came too, and saw us off at the station. He didn't achieve many passes in School Certificate exams, the equivalent of GCSE's now. But that didn't bother him. He applied for and was offered an apprenticeship with Jowett Cars of Bradford. They made vans and the much admired Jowett Javelin. Alas! when the offer came mother said VERY FIRMLY that he could write and refuse that. HE was going to university after which he would be able to obtain a very good job. And so with a great deal of reluctance he stayed on into the sixth. Although he never obtained good results he eventually went on to the University of Hull, but he never had a grant, only a loan, so had to work part-time to make ends meet. It was short-sighted as just a little application would have saved all that, he would have had adequate results and a grant, and saved all the hassle. However he did obtain a degree and I was glad he did. He must have had an excellent memory. I can recollect discussing the 1945 General Election with him. Our house at No. 15 was used as the committee rooms, an operation I detested, and voting took place at the school across the road. I was 17 at the time and he was only 10, yet he remembered far more about the day's events than I did and had obviously thoroughly enjoyed the whole affair. Father of course was a keen Labour Party man and in a dictatorial fashion, which certainly never savoured in the least of democracy, laid down the rules about politics.

And so whilst for me P stood for plants and I became a botanist, for Bob P stood for politics and he eventually became a very able politician. But throughout all his interests and an exceptionally busy life he always managed to find time to visit me and later the family, something which was always very much appreciated and very much missed by us all.

---

## 2

## JIM MORTIMER

*Former General Secretary of the Labour Party*

The tragic circumstances of the death of Bob Cryer took from the Labour movement an outstanding representative. He died at an age when, as a Member of Parliament, he had still a distinguished future before him.

I remember Bob for his Socialist commitment, his keen intellect, his diligence, his identity with the interests of common people and his wide interests. He knew that the strength of his Socialist commitment and his readiness to give voice to it would not necessarily commend him for parliamentary promotion to those who led the Labour Party. The criticism for such a situation should not be directed against Bob. To put it simply: he was a human being with principles and he adhered to them.

Bob came from West Yorkshire and he was well aware and proud of the part played by the area in the development of the Labour movement. It was fitting that in his life he represented parliamentary constituencies in Keighley and then in Bradford. When he served as an MEP in the European Assembly it was as the representative of the neighbouring area of Sheffield and North Derbyshire.

Bob's association with the industrial areas of Yorkshire influenced his thinking. Bradford was, after all, the city in which the Independent Labour Party was formed in 1893. Half a century earlier it had been a Chartist centre, when for the first time in British history – and some would argue for the first time in world history – the industrial working class entered the political struggle as an independent force.

The formation of the ILP represented the convergence of three separate industrial and political currents. All were present in the outlook of Bob Cryer. He inherited this tradition in the development of his political ideas.

Wedding of William and Elsie Mortimer, parents of the author Jim Mortimer. Seated to the right of the bride is Gladys Corney, who was later to become Bob Cryer's mother, 1920.

The first current was that of identity with the interests of working people and organisational ties with trade unionism. The immediate catalyst for the formation of the ILP was an industrial dispute at the Manningham Mills in Bradford. The dispute lasted for about 19 weeks and the workers were eventually defeated. It was a bitterly fought dispute and at one stage the Riot Act was read in Bradford with the introduction of troops against street demonstrators. It is not an exaggeration to say that eventually the workers were starved into submission.

Nevertheless the Manningham Mills dispute had a deep and lasting effect on the consciousness of many Bradfordians, particularly among sections of the working class. They came to understand that their interests had to be defended by both industrial and political action. The leader of the workers at Manningham Mills, Willie Drew, argued that workers' political representation on the Bradford Council was essential to bring the police under democratic control. By the end of 1892, just before the formation of the ILP, two independent Socialist councillors had been elected from Manningham to the Bradford Council. One of them, Fred Jowett, a textile worker, was many years later to become a Labour Cabinet Minister.

The second current was that of socialism. In the 1880s there was a Bradford branch of the Socialist League, an organisation associated with the name of William Morris. One of its members was Fred Jowett. It also included a number of Germans who had come to Bradford to work in the textile industry, particularly in the dye houses. German chemical technology was said already to be ahead of that of Britain. Some of these German artisans brought with them the ideas of Marx and Engels from the early socialist movement of their own country.

There was also in Bradford a growing Co-operative movement. The early co-operators in the city were influenced by the traditions of the pioneers of co-operation and the ideas of Robert Owen that commerce should be conducted not for private profit but for the welfare of all.

The essence of the socialist case was that the emancipation of the working class and the ending of exploitation of one class by another depended upon changing the economic basis of society. The private ownership of the principal industries and financial institutions had to be replaced by social ownership under popular and democratic control.

The third current was the demand for independent parliamentary representation for working people. By 'independent' was meant independence from the Conservative Party, which was seen as the party of the aristocracy and the squires, and from the Liberal Party, which was identified, certainly in West Yorkshire, with the interests of the textile manufacturing employers.

It was recognised, of course, that within the then two big parties there were minority voices. Within the Tory Party there were a small number of factory reformers who were appalled at the exploitation of women and children, particularly in the textile industry. Bradford's record of shame was second to no other city in Britain. In the Liberal Party, there were a number of radicals, who articulated democratic and progressive demands in many different areas of life. Nevertheless both the main parties remained, in the main, tied respectively to landed interests and the interests of manufacturing employers.

The argument for independent labour representation was, therefore, a very radical demand at the beginning of the 1890s. It probably had wider support in Bradford at that time, even though it was still minority support, than in any other city in Britain.

When Keir Hardie was first elected to Parliament in the 1892 General Election he had to face only a Conservative opponent. The Liberal withdrew in his favour. In contrast, in Bradford at the same General Election Ben Tillett, standing as an Independent Labour candidate against both a Tory and a Liberal candidate, came within 557 votes of victory. It in no way diminishes the significance of Keir Hardie's victory to suggest that the Bradford result was even more indicative of the progress of the notion that Labour should seek its own representation, independent of both the Conservative Party and the Liberal Party.

Bob Cryer never lost sight of the currents that converged to form the ILP in Bradford. They remain as relevant as ever to this day. They are: the day-to-day struggle for the interests of working people, expressed through trade unionism, legislation on the social services and employment rights, municipal power and a range of single-issue causes; the objective of socialism, with democratic control and accountability, as the means to end class exploitation; and the constant campaign for independent labour representation in Parliament and in local authorities.

Readers of this short essay may ask what is the evidence of the importance of the history of the labour movement of West Yorkshire on the development of the outlook of Bob Cryer. I have two pieces of evidence. The first is of my personal reminiscences of conversations with him. I met him from time to time over many years when we discussed political issues and exchanged views on experiences that shaped our views.

Secondly, we shared a close family background. My parents and I were born in Bradford and when I was a schoolboy in the city my parents always regarded John and Gladys Cryer – Bob's parents – as their closest friends. Indeed, my parents met through John and Gladys Cryer. Before their marriage my father was a friend of John and my mother a friend of Gladys. One of my father's brothers also married John's sister.

My mother remained a friend of Gladys to the very end, years after my parents had left Bradford because of unemployment in the depression of the early 1930s. She was still in communication with Gladys even when my mother was in her nineties.

My mother regarded Gladys Cryer as the most talented women she had ever known. She never ceased to tell me of her admiration for the woman she always regarded as her best friend. My mother, who was interested in music, spoke of Gladys's natural ability as a pianist and she spoke in the highest terms of her talents as a dressmaker. I think my mother once told me that Gladys had made her wedding dress.

I do not know how my mother first met Gladys. Perhaps it was through her work. My mother started work as a doffer in the spinning shed of Tankard's mill in Bradford as a half-timer at the age of 12 years. She later became a spinner, a weaver and then a burler and mender. She was always interested and knowledgable about the quality of worsted cloth and this, I think, may have given her a common interest with Gladys.

The wedding of John Arthur Cryer and Gladys Evelyn Corney, 1926.

My mother was also active throughout her life as a Methodist. Gladys was also, I think, a church-goer. My mother's religious views were inseparable from her politics and probably this too gave her a common interest with Gladys.

My mother's view of Christianity was that it was the religion of common purpose and human co-operation. Christ, she believed was a reformer, even a revolutionary, who sided with the poor and the disadvantaged. He was put to death because his ideas and activities threatened the power of the ruling class of his time.

My mother saw the church not as an hierarchical religious institution to prop up the secular power but as an organisation to conduct a crusade for good behaviour both in personal and social terms. My mother opposed all forms of hereditary privilege and was always a republican. When Gladys and my mother were young women and their views were being moulded by experience perhaps they discussed some of these ideas. They would later be passed on to Bob. My mother took great pleasure in the progress of Bob as a Labour representative and spoke warmly of his frequent appearances on Yorkshire television (by this time my mother as a widow had moved back to Bradford).

My mother also had a lifetime's interest in music. As an adolescent her ambition was to be accepted as a member of the Bradford Festival Choral Society and to sing in the big subscription concerts, led by world famous conductors, held at that time in St George's Hall in the centre of the city. She achieved her ambition. This enthusiasm for music also gave her a common interest with Gladys.

Unfortunately I am also unaware how my father first met John Cryer. Undoubtedly, however, their close friendship as young men rested upon a community of ideas and an interest in the labour movement. I assume that John Cryer shared many of my father's views. My father always spoke of John in warm terms and enjoyed exchanging ideas with him. He considered it a social outrage that such a talented man as John Cryer, skilled in engineering, should have suffered long periods of unemployment.

I have no proof that John Cryer's politics and my father's politics were identical but given their mutual strong interest in politics I cannot imagine that their close friendly relationship would have survived fundamental disagreements. I never heard my father criticise any of the views held by John. On the contrary, he always spoke appreciatively of John's political and social understanding.

My father was no 'moderate' social-democrat. His early twenties were in the years of the 'great unrest' before the First World War. He strongly

The Cryer family shopping in Bradford, 1935.

supported the struggles of workers in a succession of industries for trade union recognition and better pay and conditions. He was influenced by the syndicalism of the time and these convictions remained with him throughout the 1920s. He was convinced that progress towards socialism would be determined mainly by workplace militancy.

In 1912 some 23,000 textile workers in Lawrence, Massachusetts, USA took part in a bitterly fought industrial dispute. It attracted international attention. Some of the textile workers were immigrants from West Yorkshire and from Bradford in particular. The strike was led by the American organisation known as the Industrial Workers of the World. The leader of this organisation was Daniel de Leon. The IWW had a syndicalist programme which emphasised the importance of industrial struggle.

Efforts were made in Bradford to win sympathy for the Lawrence textile workers. Leaflets were distributed explaining their case and collections were organised to help the strikers and their families. A pamphlet by Daniel de Leon, entitled 'Strike', was circulated in the city.

My father participated in these efforts at workers' solidarity. It is possible, indeed probable, that John Cryer also participated. Perhaps that is where they met or where their friendship was strengthened.

The syndicalist outlook of the IWW, or the 'Wobblies' as they were more familiarly known, remained with my father for many years afterwards. He often used the phrase 'Labour fakkirs' to express his opposition to the leaders of right-wing social democracy. His opposition was transformed into bitterness after the betrayal of the top leaders of the Labour Party in 1931 when MacDonald, Snowden and Jimmy Thomas joined with the Tories to form a National Government.

In Britain before 1914 there was one political party, the Socialist Labour Party, that was close to the IWW in its outlook. Unfortunately I do not know whether John Cryer and my father were members of the SLP or only sympathisers. My father died nearly 50 years ago but I wish now that I had questioned him more closely about his organised political activities. I remain grateful to him, however, and to others in the family, for their explanation of their socialist convictions.

The Socialist Labour Party was one of the organisations that helped to form the Communist Party. My father did not join the CP and, as far as I am aware, neither did John Cryer. My father, in a manner typical of the IWW, was suspicious of all forms of bureaucracy. The theory of 'democratic centralism' would have no appeal to him. Beware, he said, 'of the official with a peaked cap'. For the rest of his life he would not join either the Communist Party or the Labour Party. In the 1920s he sympathised with the Minority Movement and he was closer in outlook to the Communist Party than to the Labour Party. In the 1930s, with the rise of fascism, he modified his views and accepted that industrial militancy alone was not an adequate answer to reaction.

My mother differed from my father, though I do not remember them ever arguing about politics. My mother joined the Labour Party and perhaps, ironically, was more sympathetic towards the Soviet Union than my father. My father was not hostile to the Soviet Union but he was never comfortable with an acceptance of any kind of dictatorship, even when it was claimed that the dictatorship was exercised in the name of the proletariat.

I have set down these family reminiscences because they may provide clues to the kind of ideas which Bob Cryer may have heard from his parents as he grew through childhood into adolescence and then into manhood. Bob emerged as an outstanding representative of the interests of working people and of the struggle for socialism.

# CHAPTER 2

# REMINISCENCES OF REDBRICK

## 1

## ALAN A. COULSON

When I began my degree course at Hull University in 1955 it had only recently received its charter and had fewer than a thousand students. The feel of the place was distinctly personal and friendly but there remained a post-war utility air about it, with much of the student and teaching accommodation in huts. Because of the university's small size individuals mixed socially across departments a good deal. The limited scale of the Students' Union meant that it was possible to know almost every one at least by sight and those students who, like Bob Cryer, were vocal and active in the larger Union societies were familiar to all of us.

I was aware of Bob's presence at Hull well before we actually met. His appearance, tall and lean with sandy hair and pale blue eyes behind brown-rimmed spectacles, made him distinctive. Even then he seemed mature, confident and articulate. Like Hull University contemporaries who also became prominent Labour politicians, Roy Hattersley and Kevin McNamara, Bob often spoke in Students' Union debates and on other public occasions. His political leanings and his capacity to speak out about things were exercised in union affairs and a couple of years later he served successfully as President of the Students' Union.

My acquaintance and subsequent friendship with Bob resulted from our shared enthusiasm for cinema. In the mid-fifties the University Film Society (Filmsoc) was one of the largest and most flourishing societies in the University and attracted regular attendance from teaching and administrative staff as well as students. Though I had been a film devotee from early teens, I had never before had the opportunity to see foreign films nor the classics of cinema history I had read so much about. Additionally, Hull itself held many cinematic temptations, for in those days the city had more than thirty commercial cinemas, one of which, the Curzon, specialised in exhibiting foreign films. Viewing films and endlessly talking about cinema with Bob and other kindred spirits was my youthful idea of bliss.

Bob, aged 20, in Hurst Wood, Saltaire, 1955.

In my second year Bob became Filmsoc's chairman and I was elected secretary, a situation which gave us the lion's share of control over the programming. Many of our supporting films were drawn from the then still lively British documentary tradition. Bob was a particularly ardent critic of the 'stagey' home counties/middle class emphasis of most British cinema and the prominence it gave to jingoistic war films and genteel or patronising comedies. We lamented the absence of any social critique and of any realistic portrayal of the lives of working people.

We did not use written programme notes but introduced our shows with mini speeches to explain our choices and give background information about the films and their makers. My introductions tended to be careful, studied and factual whereas Bob tended to speak off-the-cuff, refer a lot to social issues, and be more polemical. My memory of him standing at the demonstration bench at the front of the Physics Lecture Theatre (our 'cinema') is a vivid one. He always began the same: in a raised voice, "Good evening Ladies and Gentlemen," pause for audience conversation to subside, "Our film tonight...". He always ended the same too: with an "O.K. let's start" thumbs-up signal to our projectionist, Mr Lawson, in his sound-proof booth high up at the back of the steeply-sloping rows of wooden seats.

Viewings were often followed by spontaneous discussions among those of us who stayed behind standing around in the lecture theatre until we were eased out by the duty caretaker wanting to lock up. Our desire to exhibit films which depicted a Britain not then shown in commercial features sometimes resulted in an audience backlash against worthy but tedious material. On one occasion we showed a documentary called *Inland Waterways* about two bargemen. It certainly was about working people, but the pedestrian treatment and solemn commentary aroused a volatile mixture of boredom and derisive laughter. Only Bob could find enough merit in the film to defend it. Perhaps though it was our choice of film and our stance which was being defended. For a while this incident was frequently referred to. Indeed, the words 'Inland

Waterways' became shorthand for tediousness and a dismissive phrase in our audience's vocabulary of film criticism: for example, "It's a bit of an Inland Waterways isn't it!"

Given our preoccupations, we followed keenly the newer, more socially-conscious strain of writing and criticism which had recently entered British Film Institute publications with writers such as Lindsay Anderson, Karel Reisz, Gavin Lambert and Tony Richardson, most of whom were former contributors to the magazine *Sequence*. Soon many of these authors turned to film making. Their documentaries such as *Momma Don't Allow* (Reisz and Richardson, 1955), *Every Day Except Christmas* (Anderson, 1957) and *We Are the Lambeth Boys* (Reisz, 1958) marked the emergence of the so-called Free Cinema movement. Bob and I and our friends felt that we shared the moral and social concern with which these films were imbued and they had a freshness and vitality we admired. As a consequence, and to great anticipation, Lindsay Anderson was invited to the University to give a talk. At the last moment, however, Lindsay couldn't come and David Robinson, later the film critic of the *Financial Times* and a well-known film historian, took his place. During the evening he mentioned that he and some of his colleagues at the British Film Institute had been reading and enthusing about Richard Hoggart's recently published *The Uses of Literacy*. Fortunately, Richard, then in Hull's Adult Education Department, was in the audience and the two were introduced. After the talk was over, Bob invited them and me to the Students' Union President's office for a drink. I don't remember the conversation but I do remember that it went on long enough for David to miss the last train from Hull back to London. However, as Bob was one of the few students with a car, David Robinson was driven to Doncaster to catch another train. En route he gave us an account of his recent visit to the Soviet Union. Of particular interest was the fact that he had met the widow of one of our 'idols', the great director Sergei Eisenstein. On another occasion Bob extended similar Students' Union hospitality following a lecture by Marie Seton, Eisenstein's biographer.

Though none of our work reached the screen, a number of us in Filmsoc, including Bob and myself, toyed with the idea of making films ourselves. Ever practical, he knew a good deal more about the technical side of things than most of us. He deeply regretted the decline of 9.5 mm films and film-making, a system which gave larger frame size and better quality projected images than the more heavily marketed 8 mm 'home movie' equipment which came to dominate the pre-camcorder years. To him it was an example of craftsmanship and quality giving way to something admittedly cheaper but very inferior in value.

Each November in the 1950s and early 1960s Hull University's Adult Education Department, in collaboration with the Northern Group of the Federation of Film Societies, arranged a residential film study weekend at Cober Hill near Scarborough. There in a narrow, sometimes poorly-heated hall with creaky floorboards, Bob and I and other devotees perched on canvas-seated tubular steel stacking chairs to listen to and quiz film makers, critics and film historians. Among many others I recall Michael Denison, Karel Reisz, Clive Donner, Roger Manvell, John Halas, Ivor Montagu and Jacques Brunius. Each weekend had a theme or themes: French cinema, film acting, Italian neo-realism or animated film, all of them illustrated by films and film extracts. These were projected by the reliable Mr Lawson. He never said much but was unflappable during the not-infrequent technical crises and no doubt welcomed the overtime.

Bob and I and companions from the University Film Society attending this annual film feast travelled to Cober Hill in Bob's Armstrong-Siddeley. The Armstrong was Bob's pride and joy and seemed to be under more or less constant maintenance from him. He was renowned for his lack of punctuality and the car was often given as at least one of the reasons. Frequently his greasy hands testified to some adjustment made en route. Once on board, passengers would from time to time be given a discourse on the merits and virtues of the real car as compared with the mass-produced 'tin box' and were warned never to slam coach-built doors.

Bob's love of the coach-built quality car was part of a broader appreciation of and respect for a tradition of good solid craftsmanship which pervaded his whole outlook. To an extent unusual in a person in his very early twenties he showed a concern for things with enduring, solid, perhaps rather old-fashioned qualities. He nourished a special affection for things under threat or about to be lost: the coach-built car, the steam train, 9.5 mm film, plain English cooking. He could be intolerant or disdainful of the 'modern', the fashionable, the shoddily-made or insubstantial. I'm sure he preferred steel and wood to plastic; wool and cotton to nylon and, most definitely, steam locomotives to diesel or electric. He seemed proud of being a Yorkshireman and from time to time would tease me about my Kentish accent and being 'a southerner'. In addition to his down-to-earth, plain spoken approach to life and his practicality with mechanical things, he enthused about cricket and vigorously supported the Co-op. He embodied qualities very different from my own, qualities which as well as being personal to him I perceived as very 'northern'. We were different in so many ways but I felt we always had fun together and I was enriched by his friendship.

He was a truffle-hound for any hint of pretentiousness or snobbery, some-thing which we occasionally encountered at Cober Hill. If he scented a *poseur* he was inclined to indulge in coarsely exaggerated imitations of what he took to be a falsely 'posh' accent or to caricature the gestures of a cigar-smoking or martini-sipping companion. This game usually gave him gleeful amusement. However, his voice was not a quiet one and his very individual, gurgly way of laughing often entailed rather a lot of head and body movement making his antics rather conspicuous. I admired his brash self-confidence on these occasions. At the same time being, unlike Bob, a shrinking introvert, I sometimes felt embarrassed.

The Cryer antipathy to pomposity and hypocrisy was strongly evoked when the City and University of Hull received a Royal visit. Never a follower of fashion, Bob did not wear the jeans and pullovers adopted by most students of the mid-fifties. He normally wore a sports jacket, flannels and strong laceup shoes, and he usually wore a tie. This ensemble seemed to him a perfectly suitable outfit for a Students' Union representative to wear for presentation to Royalty. Apparently, however, his everyday garb caused consternation among some university officials who tried to persuade him to change clothes with another student who was wearing a suit. I don't remember now if the Queen, if it was she, was saved from the ordeal of shaking hands with a sports-jacketed Bob. I don't like pomp and show either and stayed well away from the event.

A Filmsoc duty Bob and I enjoyed carrying out was attendance at the National 16 mm Film Viewing Sessions. Here once a year representatives from Film Societies all over Britain previewed possible films for their forthcoming seasons. These viewings were held in the film theatre of the Prudential Assurance Headquarters, a strange reddish Gothic building in Holborn. Long sessions in the magical darkness were punctuated by earnest discussions in snack bars. Bob's socialist leanings were evident in his attitudes to most things but he was definitely a conservative where food was concerned. At a time when a greater variety of restaurants and cuisines were beginning to become accessible to a wider public, Bob always preferred familiar and traditional English fare over any of that 'foreign stuff'.

I have never been much interested in the political scene and my only participation in an election campaign was due to Bob's persuasion. It also involved the treasured 'Armstrong'. In the Hull City Council elections Bob was working for the Labour group in the ward where I lived. He inveigled me into helping. The help consisted of being driven round the streets by him in the 'Armstrong' whilst through a loudspeaker

27

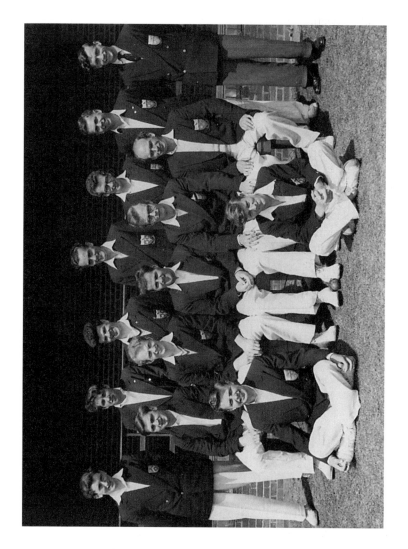

Hull University 1st XI, 1955(?). Bob Cryer, seated, second from left.

precariously attached to the roof I regularly intoned, "Vote for Mrs Nellie Walker, your Labour candidate". I was even allowed to drive the car for a bit though I am not sure who was the more nervous about it, Bob or I. Our escapades fixing up the broadcasting equipment and getting it to work, which it did sporadically, were reminiscent of Laurel and Hardy and our political conviction frequently gave way to hilarity.

I don't remember Bob ever talking about his undergraduate studies at University though we spoke freely about most other matters. However, I knew a good deal about his postgraduate year of educational studies. I followed the same course the following year and to spare me the inconvenience of having to attend all the lectures Bob passed on his, rather incomplete, notes.

After we left University our lives and careers took different paths and though we kept in touch Bob and I met infrequently. Apart from his developing political career and time spent with his family, he continued to indulge his enthusiasm for steam trains with his active participation in the Worth Valley Railway Society. As usual his interest was practical and 'hands-on'. I regret now that I never got round to accepting his invitation to ride on the footplate with him. I know, however, that the selection of 'Bob's Railway' as the principal location for the film *The Railway Children* brought together two of his most enduring interests in a most enjoyable way. That gave him, and me, a lot of pleasure.

In later years Bob and I stayed in contact but rarely met. In one of the last notes I received from him he excitedly informed me that a wish he had held for some time, and which he knew I would share, was to be fulfilled: he was to join the board of the British Film Institute.

---

**2**

*Extracts from a letter to Ann Cryer from Mike and Nancy Houston of Kendal*

You do not know us, although we did meet briefly when Bob came to speak to the local Labour Party group at Kendal some 10 or 15 years ago.

My wife and I were exact contemporaries of Bob's while at university at Hull. It is natural that one should follow the progress of one's colleagues over the years and so, although never being in direct contact with Bob, we have followed his career in politics with interest and great admiration. To a degree this was because we were both of the same political persuasion as Bob, but I believe it was more as a result of what we came to realise as the basic sincerity of the man. I suppose this was first brought home to us at the time he resigned (we always interpreted it as a matter of principle) from his post as a junior minister in Jim Callaghan's Government. I recall asking Bob about this when we had a chat after his talk at Kendal and he pointed out to us as lay persons that he was not a little disillusioned with things he discovered once he was involved in the inner ring of politics. Some of the stands Bob took over the years must have required great courage and there will be thousands like us who admire him for doing so.

At the end of March my wife and I returned to Hull to mark the 40th anniversary of the granting of the University's Charter. Our own year was well represented with about a dozen or so students. The event was organised by Terry Smith who was President of the Students' Union the year before Bob. It was inevitable that conversation among us would come round to the triumvirate of Bob, Roy Hattersley and Kevin McNamara, and we all had our tales to tell. There were two incidents which we would like to tell you.

Like Bob, I was a resident of Camp Hall, Cottingham. I think Bob was in hut 3. I was in hut 19. My wife Nancy and I both hailed from north Northumberland and for Nancy to arrive just south of Berwick by bus in a single day required an early start. It also required a taxi to Paragon Station to catch our bus; Nancy would be picked up at Thwaite Hall on the way. Standing outside the gates at Camp Hall, I realised that the taxi which was already 5 minutes overdue would not arrive. The only person I could think of with a car was Bob and before I realised what was happening I had sprinted to hut 3 and was banging on Bob's window – Bob, whom at that time I barely knew. Clothes were half pulled over pyjamas and in a half-daze Bob sped us down to the station. When asked how much, he said ten bob, so we gave him a quid as the bus was actually pulling out of the station. I am sure to this day that Bob was at the station before he had realised what he had undertaken. I cannot remember if we ever thanked him properly, but perhaps the extra ten bob said it all.

The other incident refers to the last few days I spent at Hull. I was a soccer player and, although a great lover of cricket and a player, I never played at Hull. Rather unexpectedly the university did well in the U.A.U. matches and reached the quarter-finals. Everyone had gone down from university when the quarter-final's match was arranged at Manchester, and the team was without a dog's body to carry bags, help with scoring and tend to any injuries. In a rash moment I agreed to help. I say rash, because Manchester were beaten and the semi-finals were at Durham. It was Bob's car again and two other hired cars. Durham were beaten and the finals were at, of all places, Aberystwyth. What I cannot recall is how we managed to pay for it all – I suppose it came from the students' or athletics' union funds. I can recall as if it were yesterday travelling across the heart of England and Wales in the middle of the night to Aberystwyth – Bob's car again – where, helped to a considerable extent by the bowling of Barry Laughton, Jack Lucas and one Bob Cryer, they overcame the Welsh on their own ground.

I hope you will excuse all these mental meanderings, but I felt we had to put pen to paper if only to let you know of the high esteem in which Bob was held by a great many people. The anecdotes were by way of demonstrating the generosity and integrity which Bob obviously retained throughout his life. He was a man true to his principles and who will be greatly missed. There are children not yet born who will live to suffer from the legacy of Thatcher, and Bob was one of the few with the courage to prick the over-inflated balloons.

# CHAPTER 3

# THE SCHOOL TEACHER

## 1

## JEFFREY T. DUFFIN

*Head of Physical Education, Holycroft School, Keighley*

I first met Bob in the early sixties at Holycroft School, a very large Secondary Modern with its fair share of the disadvantaged, disruptive and downright awful! I warmed to Bob immediately for his zeal and his humour. Armed with these qualifications Bob captured the children's interest and enthusiasm. Whatever the subject he taught he brought to it a kind of freshness and honesty which often invoked from the children their highest compliment, "Mr Cryer's real!".

The staff room, however, was his natural platform. Here he bemoaned the plight of the working classes, the under-privileged and the like. I recall a wonderful exchange between us when I accused him of claiming the Berlin Wall was to keep out Westerners! He infuriated the staid and the comfortable on the staff simply by his honesty (plus a little rhetoric).

Never missing an opportunity he organised a petition against J. F. Kennedy and his blockade of Cuba. Not all signed it but all were required to explain why. The Head at the time rebuked him for using the office typewriter for the petition. Bob and I agreed we could rest peacefully when Heads had such priorities. Bob played for the staff versus boys at cricket with his usual skill and enthusiasm. The only mistake I made was not making him captain right away because within minutes he certainly was. I listened with ever increasing respect to his views on things from the Worth Valley Railway to Armstrong Siddeleys to the future of Western Democracy.

Bob was a very fine teacher and would have become a gifted one. His passion and compassion allied with burning enthusiasm made him an ideal person to be at 'the chalk face'.

I was better in every way for knowing him and was privileged for being his friend. Along with people of quality everywhere, I miss him.

## 2

## BILL HENSMAN
### *Highfield School, 1956–1979*

Bob joined the staff of Highfield School in Keighley about 1961 or 1962. At that time Keighley was known as an 'Excepted Area' which meant that though it was part of the West Riding Education Authority, Keighley had its own Director of Education (Mr Frank Pedley), and an Education Committee with a degree of autonomy, though Wakefield controlled the purse strings. The general arrangement in Keighley at that time was that each school for pupils aged 11–15 had special facilities loosely connected to careers, and parents had a good deal of freedom to choose a school. Highfield School was to provide courses in Commerce and Typing, and Bob joined the staff to teach commerce as his main subject, though as I remember, there would not be enough such lessons to take up all his time, and he filled in the rest of his timetable with some English etc. Since he was hoping for a parliamentary career, he only accepted a temporary post.

Bob had his own particular sense of humour. He always brought a copy of the *Morning Star* (a left-wing newspaper of that time) into the staff room which he would ostentatiously leave for other staff members to read. Quite often at morning break he would mischievously ask the Headmaster if he had read a particular article, knowing full well that he was a staunch member of the Conservative club who invariably read the *Telegraph*. For all the difference of political view, several people have told me that Bob had a great respect for the Head whom he regarded as a true 'Gentleman'.

In the staffroom he would sometimes make outrageous statements, simply to stir up an argument, often prefacing them with "Of course it is true to say..." and several times said that if you repeat something like that often enough and with enough conviction, people will believe it, true or not.

His aversion to formal religion is of course well known, and he never attended the school morning religious assembly, but sent the rest of the staff along with remarks like "Go on to prayers you Christians, I'll stay here and be a Heathen". It was said in such a way that no one ever took offence.

His commitment to his pupils was absolute. At that time the school offered courses leading to Royal Society of Arts exams in commerce and many stayed beyond the legal leaving age to take these. Another teacher recently

Highfield School, Keighley. Staff photograph 1961. Bob is standing in the middle of the back row. The author, Bill Hensman, is seated on the far left.

told me that when he had set English essays to his class, Bob would offer to let the commerce pupils type them up for extra practice and even went to the trouble of getting the needlework mistress to machine sew one edge to bind them into booklets. That teacher also told the the that me only time he had ever voted socialist was for Bob.

My only big argument with Bob arose because another teacher and I on dinner duty were eating our lunch in the commerce room – the only one available since the dining hall and kitchen were still being built. I sent out pupils who came in whilst we were eating. Bob was unhappy that I had prevented his pupils from getting in extra typing practice in their own time. He was very popular with the pupils, and even persuaded one or two of the boys to help out on the Worth Valley Railway.

On a personal level, some years after he had left Highfield there arose a misunderstanding with the local Rector who was sure that the Church Authorities were to take over the running of Highfield as a Church School. As a Union Representative I contacted Bob, and within two days received a letter from the Ministry of Education, confirming that no such change would take place.

After I retired I had a query with the Inland Revenue in Cardiff where retired persons' tax records are kept. This dragged on for two years, until I threatened to get Bob to take up the matter. Without my having to do so, the query was resolved in my favour within a week. Such was the power of simply mentioning his name as a former colleague.

Though we sometimes disagreed in arguments, I respected his views and commitment, and I am quite certain that many people in Keighley would see him on television, sitting below the gangway in the House, usually trying to catch the Speaker's eye, and would remark with pride, "He used to teach me!"

# CALENDAR
## 1994

The Queensbury Triangle lines

Opened in 1884 the railway linking Bradford, Halifax and Keighley via Queensbury was finally closed in April 1974 though the majority of the line was dismantled well before that date. This calendar is a reminder of this magnificent railway the remnants of which can, in some cases, such as Hewenden and Thornton viaducts, still be seen but most of which is slowly disappearing. It is a reminder that with foresight these lines could have still been serving the public.

Calendar produced by Bob Cryer.
(*Alan Whitaker*)

## CHAPTER 4

# TRANSPORT OF DELIGHT

### ADLESTROP

by Edward Thomas

YES, I remember Adlestrop –
The name, because one afternoon
Of heat the express-train drew up there
Unwantedly. It was late June.

The steam hissed. Someone cleared his throat.
No one left and no one came
On the bare platform. What I saw
Was Adlestrop – only the name

And willows, willow-herb, and grass,
And meadowsweet, and haycocks dry,
No whit less still and lonely fair
Than the high cloudlets and the sky.

And for that minute a blackbird sang
Close by, and round him, mistier,
Farther and farther, all the birds
Of Oxfordshire and Gloucestershire.

Evocative of a time when Bob was a small boy and when there were many country stations served by steam trains. He loved this poem and all that it represented. His nephew, Alan Petford, read it at the funeral meeting.

### ALAN WHITAKER

*Journalist (ex-Telegraph & Argus)*

Britain's railways emerged from the Second World War still providing the backbone of the country's freight and public transport network.

Although very rundown, the system was still able to pay its way because road transport facilities remained limited. But by the early 1950s, this had begun to change and the British Transport Commission, created by nationalisation in 1948, was sharpening its knives in preparation for the pruning of loss-making lines.

Among those on the hit list in the days before Dr Beeching were the former Great Northern Railway Company's routes from Bradford and Halifax to Keighley which converged at a triangular junction below the hill village of Queensbury, home of the world famous Black Dyke Mills Band.

These lines were the most spectacularly engineered in Yorkshire's West Riding, characterised by magnificent viaducts, deep cuttings and tunnels galore – and they held a particular fascination for the young Bob Cryer.

Bob had been born at Great Horton, one of the Bradford suburbs served by the old GN line, but his family moved when he was still a toddler and he grew up at Saltaire, within a stone's throw of another railway – the main line linking Leeds and Bradford with Scotland and the West Coast.

Among his most lucid memories of the war years were the sights and sounds of heavy northbound steam-hauled trains grinding up the gradient near his home.

By the time the British Transport Commission was ready to wield the axe for the first stage of what was purported to be the modernisation of British Railways, Bob was a student blessed with a sharp intellect and keen sense of logic.

Closing railway lines and handing traffic on a plate to road transport which barely had the infrastructure to cope did not seem to him to be particularly sensible. As a student of economics, he struggled to equate the logic of discarding railways, which required comparatively modest investment, to spending a fortune on building new roads to enable them to cater for traffic which had been moved safely and adequately by rail for generations.

But even he never envisaged the scale of decimation of the rail industry which was to contribute forty years later to parts of Britain grinding to a halt in huge traffic jams while derelict railway land was still being sold off to provide space for yet more new roads.

In 1955, word reached him at Hull University that the 'Queensbury Lines', as the old GN routes had become known, were to be closed. Bob was appalled. He immediately penned a letter of protest which was published in the Bradford *Telegraph & Argus* along with other letters of complaint.

A belated anti-closure lobby subsequently emerged with various local prospective parliamentary candidates leaping on the bandwagon as the closure of the GN lines was to take place in the same month as the 1955 General Election.

British Railways' 'last train' excursion at Oakworth, 23 June 1962.
(*Richard Smithies*)

There was much hot air and political posturing and most of the protesters disappeared without trace after the Election. Bob Cryer was not one of them and five years after the line's closure, he was still trying to persuade the powers that be to reopen it to passenger trains, taking advantage of the new cheap-to-run diesel multiple units to reduce costs.

Although his was a lone voice, he would not be swayed. Bob was never afraid to go it alone if he believed in something passionately. His tenacity – some would say stubbornness – were to become familiar hallmarks of his political style in later years.

Having graduated, Bob worked briefly as a personnel assistant for Northern Dairies in Hull before returning to his native West Riding as a supply teacher in the Bradford area. This enabled him to keep a watching brief on the local rail network and he often made weekend expeditions to obscure wayside branch lines, occasionally accompanied by bemused girlfriends.

His wife-to-be, Ann, well remembers various such visits during their early courting period.

In 1961, Bob was teaching at Highfield and Holycroft schools in Keighley when news broke that the five-mile branch line up the Worth Valley to Oxenhope was destined for the chop. With the axing of the Queensbury

The Worth Valley Preservation Society negotiating team at Leeds following a meeting with the British Railways Estates Department, 1965.

lines to passenger trains a few years earlier still fresh in his mind, he was determined that the same fate would not befall the Worth Valley branch.

The line had been on borrowed time since the late 1950s when British Railways accountants began to take a keen interest in its balance sheet.

Closure was staved off, largely thanks to the efforts of local people led by the Mayor of Keighley and the rail users' watchdog – the Transport Users' Consultative Committee.

Under pressure, BR agreed that instead of immediate closure, a diesel multiple unit service should be introduced in an attempt to make the line profitable. But it did not succeed and closure was announced for 30 December 1961.

Bob swung into action and called a public meeting to assess support for the possible resurrection of the Worth Valley branch. In a rough draft for a book he intended to write on the history of the line, he made it clear that his inspiration for the preservation bid was the fate of the Queensbury lines.

No doubt his enthusiasm was fired by the fact that the old GN line had joined the Midland Railway's Worth Valley branch near Ingrow for the final mile or so into a shared station at Keighley.

He wrote: "As a railway, the Worth Valley branch was inferior to the GN route. On the latter, the ballast was stone, there were two tracks, much of the rail and most of the sleepers were in very good order. The Worth Valley branch, in contrast, was laid on ash ballast, the railhead was quite badly worn on the curves and many sleepers were no more than a gesture of solidarity. Nevertheless, the Worth Valley line had fewer engineering features and I thought it would be a much more practicable proposition for preservation than the exciting but unrealistic notion of resurrecting the GN line."

The public meeting was held in Room 14 of Keighley's Temperance Hall on Wednesday 24 January 1962. Bob was not sure how much support his plan would receive so he selected a room he regarded as large enough for a good turnout of 75 to 100 people but small enough to make 30 seem reasonable.

However, any initial fears he may have had that the event would be a flop were soon banished. By the start time of 7.30 p.m., the room was packed and it was standing room only.

The meeting agreed to explore with British Railways the feasibility of preserving the Worth Valley line. A small committee was formed with the remit of reporting back at the beginning of March and Bob Cryer was elected chairman.

Although a rail enthusiast at heart, Bob was astute enough to realise that some potential critics would regard his scheme as little more than a device to enable him and others like him to play trains.

To disarm such criticism, he made it clear from the start that the plan had not been hatched by 'blurry-eyed sentimentalists' and stressed his desire to see the Worth Valley branch revived for genuine public service.

Almost 100 supporters packed into the next public meeting on 1 March 1962 when it was decided to officially form the Keighley and Worth Valley Railway Preservation Society. A membership fee of £1 for adults and 7/6d (37.5 pence) for juniors was fixed and the committee was given the task of negotiating with BR to run a special train from Bradford's Forster Square station to Oxenhope at the earliest opportunity.

This ran on 23 June 1962 and gave the KWVRPS a massive publicity boost. Bob's vision was no longer just a pipe dream.

Bob, in 'dirty duffle coat', watches the newly purchased 'Pug' pull the Gresley
Buffet Car and Director's Saloon at Ingrow, 1966.
(*W. Hubert Foster*)

Securing the Worth Valley line for preservation was by no means easy and
without Bob's determination, dogged persistence and refusal to take no for
an answer, it is doubtful whether the fledgling society would have survived
long enough to create what is now one of Britain's top preserved lines.

Bob took on the onerous task of unravelling BR and legal red tape by leading the society's protracted and complicated negotiations. Railway preservation was still in its infancy in those days so he was very much a pioneer.

A vast wedge of paperwork ensued but he remained undaunted. Each
setback was shrugged off as Bob ground on, brushing aside obstructive
railway bureaucracy with a finely honed mix of diplomacy and disdain.

Six and a half years later, the Keighley and Worth Valley Railway was
secured from BR ownership and approved for light railway operation
after inspection by the Department of Transport. The 'impossible dream'
had become reality.

Another of Bob's passions was the film industry so it was not surprising
that he was keen to welcome television film makers and movie moguls

to the line. Of course, his motivation was not simply based on his own personal interest. There was good money to be made for the society which was vital if its development plans were to progress.

The first approach came sooner than expected – in 1966 – and was from an agency representing a firm of biscuit makers. BR, which still had full legal ownership of the line at this time, kindly agreed to the commercial being made and generously allowed the KWVRPS to keep the fee. Bob's charm had clearly worked wonders. Mytholmes Tunnel was used for filming but, unfortunately, few local people saw the results as it was only screened in the Tyne Tees and Southern Television areas.

However, an approach from the BBC Television drama department in February 1968 was to have a significance which could not have been foreseen at the time.

The BBC was seeking a location for a TV serial of Edith Nesbitt's Edwardian story, *The Railway Children*. A previous effort had been broadcast about ten years earlier but the screen rights had expired and a new production was planned.

Director of the series was Julia Smith, later to achieve fame as the first producer of EastEnders.

The television series proved popular and attracted the interest of Lionel Jeffries, an esteemed actor who wanted to direct his own feature film. He believed *The Railway Children* would make an excellent film so he bought the rights and set about writing the screenplay.

Having seen and liked the location shots in the BBC TV series, Jeffries asked his producer, Robert Lynn, to contact Bob to discuss the possibility of filming *The Railway Children* movie on the Worth Valley line. The trio got on well and subsequently walked the full length of the branch to identify specific locations and the types of rolling stock which would be required for the railway scenes.

Among the stars of the film were Dinah Sheridan, Bernard Cribbins, Iain Cuthbertson and Jenny Agutter and it became an instant hit at cinemas throughout the country. Bob even squeezed in a cameo role as a train guard and his wife Ann and their children John, then aged six, and Jane, aged four, were also featured as extras, suitably clad in period dress.

The success of *The Railway Children* transformed the Worth Valley line from an obscure backwater in the Pennine hills to a railway of national fame and it never looked back. The KWVRPS received £3,130 for its services in making the film – a tidy sum in those days. Bob also received a mention as 'railway advisor' in the credits.

A break during the filming of the BBC's version of 'The Railway Children', winter 1967/68, Bob giving John Vint a cigarette on the Oxenhope Curve. Director Julia Smith has her back to the camera.

After completion of filming in the summer of 1970, Robert Lynn wrote a letter to Bob in which he said: "We have high hopes the picture will be a winner and if it is, then you must know that you and your staff will share a great deal of the credit. It was a pleasure to work with you, your staff and your engines."

The Worth Valley line has since been used as a location for a variety of productions but none has ever equalled the profile of *The Railway Children* and it is that film with which the line will always be closely associated.

Ralph Povey, who was among those who attended the Temperance Hall public meeting in January 1962, had also toyed with the idea of seeking to preserve the Worth Valley line when he learned it was destined for closure. However, he was already middle-aged and was happy to leave the leadership of the project to a younger and more energetic man.

"Bob was still in his twenties and not long out of university. He was the obvious leader and chief negotiator. His vision and enthusiasm and the optimism with which he inspired us ensured the success of our efforts and made the whole enterprise very much his. He was someone we could all follow to the ultimate goal. His total honesty and sincerity meant that no one could be in any doubt where he stood – and where he thought we ought to stand!", said Mr Povey, now the Keighley and Worth Valley Railway Preservation Society's president.

Another member of the audience at that famous public meeting, which has become part of local railway folklore, was a young geography student at Leeds University called Graham Mitchell.

Graham was inspired by Bob's drive and determination and was eventually to succeed him as KWVRPS chairman, a position he still holds.

Paying tribute to Bob's contribution to the success of the Worth Valley railway over the years, he said: "Integrity has always been significant on our railway and no one could ignore or fail to admire Bob's total sincerity. He was always completely honest and straightforward, a man of boundless optimism and enthusiasm."

Bob served as chairman of the KWVRPS for 10 years, creating a unique system of railway management in which 24 democratically-elected members form a council in direct control of all aspects of the railway's operation.

The Society now has 5,000 members and is one of the most successful and acclaimed preserved railways in the world. Without Bob Cryer it would probably never have happened.

In spite of the increasing demands on his time as a teacher, college lecturer, local councillor and later as an MP, Bob always retained his connections with the Worth Valley line. After stepping down as chairman, he remained active in the society as a qualified steam loco driver and a vice-president. He was also editor of the railway's quarterly magazine *Push and Pull* for many years.

Although a keen and astute Parliamentarian, Bob never let his politics interfere with his work on the Worth Valley railway. Long-serving member David Moorhouse once said of him: "The thing is about Bob, he never lets politics get in the way of friendship."

The vast workload associated with the preservation of the Worth Valley railway never caused Bob to lose his interest in the Queensbury lines, which had inspired him at the outset. Most of the old GN route had remained open to goods trains following closure to passengers in 1955 and he still made regular visits with his camera.

The Autumn 1970 issue of the Worth Valley Railway's magazine, *Push and Pull*, published when Bob was its Editor and major contributor.

When tracklifting began on the most scenic section of the line between the villages of Thornton and Cullingworth in 1964, Bob appeared daily, wielding a cine camera to record what he regarded as an act of official vandalism. Many years later this footage was to form the basis of a film entitled *The End of Enchantment* which he showed on a number of occasions to appreciative audiences along the old GN route.

The still photos he took in the early 1960s also provided material for a calendar he published in 1994. In it, he wrote: "This calendar is a reminder of a magnificent railway, some remnants of which can still be seen but most of which is slowly disappearing. It is also a reminder that, with foresight, these lines could still have been serving the public."

Bob's sense of loss at the demise of the Queensbury lines never left him.

Their final closure and demolition in the mid-1960s coincided with a critical period in the progress of the Worth Valley scheme to which his energies were devoted.

His subsequent election as MP for Keighley in 1974 transformed his life and many of his other ideas – including writing a book on the history of the Queensbury lines – had to be put on the back burner. But a chance meeting with myself in 1978 revived his interest in that particular project.

As Keighley district reporter for the Bradford *Telegraph & Argus* newspaper at that time, I was dispatched to the site of a new factory building in the town. As local MP, Bob had been asked to turn the first sod of the development and did so by donning a hard hat and taking great delight in operating a mechanical digger.

After the official business, I interviewed Bob for the paper then mentioned my interest in the Queensbury lines. My father had been the last station master on the lines and, like Bob, I had been planning to write a book about their history for a number of years.

Bob had been a regular visitor to my father's office in the railway goods warehouse at Thornton in the early 1960s and, although I had been too young to be a party to those meetings, I was aware he had a collection of photos which I wanted for my proposed book. With a bit of cheek, I decided to use the *Telegraph & Argus* assignment as an excuse to sound him out about the prospect of including his material.

What followed was a long chat about the form the book would take and he said he was keen to get involved. We agreed to meet for further discussions and, over the next few months, our mutual interest in railways – and in particular the Queensbury lines – cemented a close friendship.

Acting as R.O. (Responsible Officer), Bob Cryer supervises the day's movements out of Keighley's No. 4 platform. 1971.

Our modest 40-page illustrated book entitled *The Queensbury Triangle* was published in July 1979 and 2,000 copies were printed with both of us sharing the cost. It sold out within six months and demand remained so intense that an expanded version was subsequently published by Dalesman Books in 1984 to commemorate the centenary of the opening of the lines. This sold 4,500 copies.

The success of these books renewed our enthusiasm for revisiting the Queensbury lines to document what remained. Although much had been lost, many of the bridges, viaducts and tunnels had survived the ravages of weather and neglect.

In September 1979, we accompanied scientists from Leeds University's Department of Earth Sciences into the disused Queensbury Tunnel. They were using the tunnel for scientific experiments connected with the development of equipment to monitor the effects of lunar and solar pull on the surface of the Earth.

It transpired that they had been working in there for years with the vast majority of Queensbury townsfolk blissfully unaware of what was going on beneath their feet.

'R.O.' Bob Cryer chats to Richard Coulson (Civil Gang), now auditor with the
Vintage Carriages Trust. 1971.

A mile or so inside the tunnel, and almost 400 feet underground, we found
a very badly corroded Great Northern Railway cast iron chain marker
which was subsequently obtained for a new role as Bob's house number-
plate in Bradford. It was an unexpected but welcome bonus.

His position as an MP continued to prove useful in securing artefacts from the old GN line. Often, I provided publicity in the *Telegraph & Argus* which Bob then followed up by exerting pressure on the powers that be to pay heed to the railway heritage of the Bradford area.

Among our successes was the removal in 1986 of the last remaining reinforced concrete station nameboard on the whole of the Queensbury lines. This had stood for years almost completely hidden by vegetation at Horton Park, not far from Bradford city centre, but with contractors about to start a reclamation scheme on the site, the century-old sign was only weeks away from destruction.

Thanks in no small part to Bob's friendship with Bradford Council's then Chief Executive, Gordon Moore, the board was moved intact for preservation in a flowerbed at the entrance to the nearby park bearing its name.

We were, however, thwarted by the Council when attempting to persuade officials to follow the lead of some other local authorities which had resurrected disused rail lines as linear footpaths and cycleways.

Passing as it does through some of the Bradford district's finest scenery, the Queensbury line would have been ideal for such a purpose, although we acknowledged that heavy vegetation clearance, drainage repairs and other works would be expensive. Not quite as expensive as the then chairman of Bradford's Leisure Services Committee claimed, however.

He reckoned that the scheme would cost £1 million, and that the Council could not spare staff time to undertake the necessary preparatory work.

Bob took this rebuff badly. He hated defeatism and remained convinced the idea was at least worth investigating, particularly as it had the backing of the Countryside Commission and the Sports Council, both of which could have contributed funds. To add salt to the wound, Bradford Council's senior countryside officer, Les Morgan, also said publicly that the idea had merit after he, Bob and I walked parts of the old trackbed in April 1987.

The lamentable failure of the local authority to grasp the nettle of what could have been a worthwhile job creation project irritated Bob to the end.

Keeping the old line in the news ensured interest in it was maintained and Bob's screenings of his film *The End of Enchantment* also helped immensely when it came to his next scheme – one which was never fulfilled because of his untimely death.

He was keen to establish a Trust to take over supervision and maintenance for two of the finest railway viaducts in the West Riding. The towering

Driver Bob waits for the 'right away' at Oakworth, August 1974.

17-arch Hewenden Viaduct near Cullingworth and the 20-arch Thornton Viaduct both formed part of his beloved GN line to Keighley and afforded superb views of the surrounding countryside. Sadly, they had to be sealed off to the public following incidents of vandalism.

But Bob firmly believed that if responsibility for these magnificent structures was handed to local people, they would take a pride in them, thereby preserving them for future generations. After meetings with the BR Property Board at York, Bob set about the task of establishing the Hewenden Viaduct Trust.

Harking back to the foundation of the KWVRPS almost 30 years earlier, he called a public meeting at Bradford's Victoria Hotel, a former GNR hotel built in 1867, to gauge support for the idea.

Fifty people attended and Bob explained that he wanted to form a Trust to supervise Hewenden Viaduct and reopen it to the public on several designated days per year. If the scheme was successful he would seek to take on Thornton Viaduct as well.

BR had been sympathetic to the scheme, which received coverage in the national Press, and even paid for a structural survey to determine how much would have to be spent before Hewenden Viaduct could be handed over to a Trust.

But the Government's break-up of British Rail put the spanner in the works and Bob was not quite able to conclude negotiations.

All the rail officials involved in the original talks either retired or moved on and at the time of writing the Hewenden Viaduct project was in limbo. The death of Bob's solicitor friend, Roger Suddards on December 30, 1955, was another blow to the scheme as he had indicated his willingness to assist in resolving the complicated legal aspects of transfer of ownership and public liability.

Bob's love of the Queensbury lines also threw up a catalogue of amusing interludes – one of which is particularly memorable.

It occurred in May 1987 when we successfully sought permission to take a trip through the 1,533 yards long Lees Moor Tunnel near Keighley. It was appallingly wet with no ventilation and curved through 90 degrees in the middle so, for well over half its length, it was absolutely pitch black with no view of either end.

The owner opened the gates fitted to the northern portal and we headed into the dripping gloom in Bob's 1952 Armstrong Siddeley Hurricane convertible, LOX 21. Bob was very proud of this superb classic car but it took the Lees Moor Tunnel trip to persuade him that his pride and joy needed a little more attention.

It soon became clear that the canvas hood leaked and by the time we emerged back into daylight we were, to say the least, somewhat damp.

Les Morgan (left), Bradford Council's Senior Countryside Officer, explains what is required to create a linear cycleway and footpath on the old 'Queensbury Lines' to Alan Whitaker, *Telegraph & Argus* reporter, and Bob Cryer at Hewenden Viaduct, April 1987.
(*Telegraph & Argus*)

"If your constituents could see you now you'd never win another election," I told him, threatening to publish details of our expedition in the *Telegraph & Argus*. "If they found out about this I'd win even more votes, no problem, so print and be damned," he retorted.

Bob was always game if it meant saving transport heritage. In the mid-1960s, he paid the princely sum of £3 to secure a Peckett tank engine withdrawn from service at Darwen Gasworks in Lancashire. The engine became part of the KWVR collection at Haworth and was later joined by a small industrial diesel loco which Bob rescued from scrap. But his first and only foray into bus preservation was destined to end in disappointment.

As a youth, he had had a passing interest in the vehicles of the West Yorkshire Road Car Company which operated a large network of services in the Bradford and Keighley areas. Thus, when he had the opportunity to help save an old 'Westie' for posterity he did not need asking twice. Once again, I must take the blame for getting him involved.

In the spring of 1990, I received a phone call from a local JP and garage proprietor, Albert Taylor, who'd worked for WYRCC as a driver before setting up in business on his own.

He informed me there was an old West Yorkshire double decker in a yard at Crossflatts which was about to be sold for scrap or exported to Asia, never to be seen again. I contacted the owner who said he wanted £1,500 for it.

I immediately telephoned Bob at his London office and he said he would be happy to become a part owner. So in May 1990, Bob, his wife Ann, Albert Taylor and a business colleague plus myself became the proud owners of YDX 221, a 1966 Bristol Lodekka, formerly of the York–West Yorkshire fleet.

When the big day came to move it to a transport museum compound in Bradford, Albert proudly climbed into the driver's cab and set off on the ten-mile journey. But just two miles down the road the veteran vehicle expired, causing rush-hour mayhem.

Unfazed, Bob stood in the road directing traffic before handing over to his wife and heading off to summon a tow truck. Quite a sight, the Honour-able MP for Bradford South on point duty! The omens were not good and things did not improve over the ensuing months. Eventually, after a succession of bills and a failed attempt to get the bus through its MOT, we sold it on, though happily it still remains in preservation.

Bob's unshakeable belief in railways as a vital part of the country's trans-port infrastructure remained throughout his life and he did not restrict his activities simply to preservation and the past.

He was one of the leading campaigners in the long fight to save the Settle to Carlisle railway, about which he had written and filmed a documentary for BBC Look North in 1973. He gave evidence at the public inquiry where he scornfully dismissed BR's feeble case for closure and also bombarded the then Transport Secretary, Paul Channon, with questions about the future of the line in the House of Commons, thereby ensuring the debate remained in the public eye.

Thankfully, the protest lobby proved too strong and the Government refused BR permission to close the route. It was a significant success in which Bob played a major role.

Another high profile rail campaign in which he became heavily involved was that to electrify the Airedale and Wharfedale lines out of Bradford's Forster Square station.

Bob's Armstrong Siddeley Hurricane reposes alongside YDX 221, the former York–West Yorkshire double deck bus purchased by a consortium including Bob and Ann, May 1990.

Bob had actually suggested electrifying the Airedale line from Bradford to Skipton as far back as 1978 when he was MP for Keighley, but his suggestion was not taken seriously. However, severe and worsening road congestion in the 1980s persuaded the West Yorkshire Passenger Transport Authority that something fairly dramatic had to be done to woo more commuters from their cars to trains.

Unfortunately, intervention and procrastination by the Treasury delayed a start on the scheme so long that its costs more than doubled – putting it in jeopardy.

But due to continued pressure from MPs such as Bob, his Labour colleague Max Madden of Bradford West, and the Conservative MP for Keighley, Gary Waller, who had snatched Bob's Keighley seat following boundary changes in 1983, electrification of the lines from Bradford Forster Square and Leeds to Skipton and Ilkley was eventually completed.

Bob's single-minded determination to pursue any cause he believed worthwhile and justified never prevented him from locking horns with those in authority. And it did not concern him too much if the people standing in his way were Labour councillors.

His popularity within Bradford Council took a nosedive when he strongly criticised members for refusing to give the previously mentioned Queensbury line footpath and cycleway project a chance.

But that was nothing compared to the ructions when the Labour-controlled Council attempted to scupper plans for a big transport museum in his Bradford South constituency at Low Moor.

In October 1987, Bob attacked the Council for its 'lacklustre' attitude to what he regarded as a major leisure development which would have beneficial spin-offs for the local community.

Support for the plan had already been well demonstrated when residents of Low Moor and neighbouring Oakenshaw staged a transport gala on the site of the proposed museum which attracted 10,000 visitors. Bob made a guest appearance to show his support, turning up in his Armstrong Siddeley Hurricane. The gleaming vehicle was well received and earned him a small commemorative shield as a prize.

But behind the scenes it became known that the Council wanted the site to be used for light industrial development. Various feasibility studies were produced offering widely differing conclusions about the economic potential of the proposed museum venture.

In typical crusading fashion, Bob cut through all the bluster by pointing out, to the Council's immense chagrin, that the land at Low Moor had been bought by the former West Yorkshire County Council specifically for a transport museum and cash had been held in Trust for that purpose. Councillors should not therefore attempt to hold back any portion of the site for alternative uses as such action would be legally flawed.

Eventually the Council capitulated and the museum was built, although not as Bob had envisaged. Never one for futuristic toys such as computer simulators, he would have been dismayed by some elements of the Low Moor centre, which no longer likes to be regarded as a museum, preferring to be known as 'Transperience'.

Nonetheless, the centre still has transport history as its theme and its existence is another example of Bob's lasting contribution to the Bradford Metropolitan District.

The Keighley and Worth Valley Railway has attracted millions of visitors to the area since its reopening in 1968, and will continue to contribute significantly to the local economy well into the next century.

Hopefully, the Low Moor transport centre will also attract many thousands of visitors to Bradford in the next few years.

Sitting in a locally made Jowett Jupiter car at an Open Day of the West Yorkshire Transport Museum at its old Ludlam Street headquarters, Bradford.

These are just two of Bob's many contributions to the area. There is a strong likelihood that neither would have achieved fruition without his involvement.

Local businesses in Bradford and Keighley and visitors to the area will continue to benefit from his foresight and determination for many years to come.

# CHAPTER 5

# THE KEIGHLEY YEARS

## 1

## ALAN RYE

*Former Secretary of the Keighley Labour Party*

One of my abiding memories of Bob was during the referendum campaign of 1975, when he asked me to help organise a series of meetings
around Keighley at which he spoke, hoping to persuade people to vote
'No' to remaining in the Common Market. One meeting was in an
almost deserted school hall in Silsden, where an over-hopeful caretaker
had set out at least a hundred chairs. It fell to me to introduce Bob
to our audience – three old ladies and a dog. The dog nodded off, the
ladies looked up at Bob in shy admiration, and Bob rose to his feet
and gave the same rousing speech he would have delivered to a crowd
of thousands. He banged the table with his fist to make a point, chopped
the air with his right hand for further emphasis, and now and then
leavened the dough with a mocking story about his political opponents,
some of them Tories, but others in the Parliamentary Labour Party. And
Bob's mocking stories were always very funny: the old ladies' faces lit
up in a smile and Bob's face lit up in a smile (and he'd heard his
stories many times before). Bob's speeches were powerful, arresting,
amusing, and the Silsden ladies obviously loved every minute of his
performance.

When Bob at last sat down, it was my job to invite questions. The ladies
all looked down in embarrassment; the dog sighed wearily; there was an
awkward silence. I repeated the invitation for questions, and one lady
raised her hand hesitantly. "Mr Cryer, I don't know about the Common
Market, but I think you're lovely."

She wasn't the only one. When we lived in Sutton our neighbour over the
road was Mary Pierce, a pensioner in her seventies who'd been in textiles
all her working life and was an ardent Labour supporter. Although Mary
had never met Bob in person, she (like countless of his constituents)
thought of him as almost one of the family: he was always being quoted
in the papers, his voice often came over the radio, and, most important
of all, they watched him frequently on local and national television. He
was immediately familiar to people.

With John, Ann and Jane at home at Oakworth following selection as Keighley
Labour Party's Parliamentary Candidate, 1971.
(*Keighley News*)

So when Bob came to call on us one day it wasn't a minute or more before
Mary came out of her front door and pottered down her garden path,
drying her hands on her pinafore and calling across to us where we stood
talking by Bob's car: "Bob, Bob, I just want a quick word." I hastily
explained to Bob who Mary was and he turned to meet her with a beaming
smile and hand outstretched, every bit the politician.

"Hello, Mary, Alan told me you're a supporter. I'm delighted to hear it!"

"Yes, Bob, yes, but I was just going to tell you that me and our Rita were
watching you on the telly last night, and ..."

"Ah, yes, I was talking about the Consolidated Fund Bill."

Mary's eyes glazed for a moment; "Well, I can't just remember what you
were talking about, Bob, but me and our Rita just want to tell you to get
your hair cut. It looked a right mess. People aren't going to vote for you if
you don't look tidy, you know," she said, patting him affectionately on the
arm.

If Bob was offended in any way he certainly didn't show it. He grinned
impishly: "Do you know, Mary, I'm off to get it trimmed this very
day," he said, patting down the stray hairs blowing around his face.

The Cryer family at their Oakworth home, October 1974.
(*Steve Bingham*)

"You mind you do now, Bob," smiled Mary, and with that pottered back home.

So Bob had a truly personal following. Thousands of Keighley people regarded him with real affection, and even those who didn't like him, or at any rate, his politics, viewed him with marked respect.

Bob really was 'a man of the people' when he was out and about; but he was, by all accounts, including his own, a dedicated parliamentarian. He devotedly attended almost every sitting of Parliament he could get to, and he regularly reported back to the Keighley Labour Party on his attendance record. More importantly, it was the quality rather than the quantity of his presence in Parliament which made an impact. Looking back over my long association with Bob – close family friendship when our respective children were still small; for several years as Constituency Secretary; twice his election agent; for three years his paid assistant – I realise I only once heard Bob speaking in person in the House. I saw him speak frequently outside Parliament, and I knew that his political opponents must have feared and admired his self-assurance, his analytical mind, his grasp of procedure, and not least his cruel, caustic wit. He must have been a formidable presence in the Commons.

Just as remarkable is the fact that Bob anticipated many issues which Parliament, Press and public woke up to only later. Two examples are MP's business interests, and the need for public control and ownership of water. As for MPs who hold directorships, continue running private businesses or work 'on the side' as journalists or lawyers, he never had any time for them, and some, sadly, were Labour members. Bob declared from the time he entered Parliament that he would devote himself to the job full-time. He went further, calling for a register of MP's business interests, long before the House of Commons itself voted to do just that. And he long ago warned of the dangers of corruption and the deceit of Parliament and public by unscrupulous MPs and Ministers who saw that large profits could be made through their association with the area's industry. Bob told the House that if there were a register of MP's interests he would be delighted to declare his – five £10 shares in the Keighley & Worth Valley Railway Company.

As to the water industry, even before the Thatcher Government announced plans to privatise water, Bob was demanding restoration of local democratic control over water services. He believed that the Water Boards should include representatives of local people, democratically elected, and that Board meetings should be open to the Press and public so that the management of the industry was always under proper scrutiny. How right he was to maintain that water should remain under public control and ownership, given the shambolic response of Yorkshire Water to the shortages of 1995.

There was a less public, but perhaps more significant way in which Bob used Parliament, as he might have said, "to further the interests of working people and their families". He was first elected in 1974, when Labour took over from a failed Tory Government, and promptly put his mind to sifting through the small print of the new legislation which Labour soon enacted, such as the Health and Safety at Work Act, and the Employment Protection Act. He joined a little-known all-party group of MPs on the Statutory Instruments Select Committee (with the addition of Peers forming the Joint Committee) whose job it was to scrutinise the rules and regulations by which an Act of Parliament is put into practice or modified. Bob was soon elected to chair this Committee and was so obviously effective that he continued in this role even after the Callaghan Government collapsed and Mrs Thatcher took over.

These days I work as an employment law adviser, helping ordinary people who suffer unfair dismissal, victimisation and discrimination from their

The Cryer family at Keighley Station's Worth Valley Railway platform. Publicity
photograph for the October 1974 General Election.
(*Steve Bingham*)

employers. Frequently they take their cases to an industrial tribunal,
using the legislation which Bob Cryer helped to put on the statute
book, redressing somewhat the imbalance of power between employers
on the one hand and their employees on the other.

If Bob Cryer was such a successful constituency MP and if he was such an
accomplished parliamentarian, why did he never apparently aspire to a
place on the front bench? Why didn't he go for the leadership of the party?
He had a huge appetite for politics and enjoyed it with boyish enthusiasm
and seemingly boundless confidence. Why did he remain, for the most
part, a dogged back-bencher?

Years ago I went round to Bob's house for one of his house film-shows.
We sat in the living room and watched an old print of *Brief Encounter*
or *The Third Man*, and then he showed us a silent film which he had edited
and put together himself from his own shots of British Railways lifting the
track on the redundant Queensbury lines in the mid-sixties. It was a
wistful reminder of a once-busy local railway, soon reduced to weed-green
track-beds and ghost stations, evocatively captured by Bob on film.

I remember being deeply impressed by the film – further evidence of Bob's various talents. I turned to Bob as the film ended; "Have you never thought about going into the film industry?"

"Of course."

"Oh, right. What would you have gone in for – camera, script-writing, production?"

Bob looked at me in obvious amazement, "What do you mean? I would have been a director, of course."

He went into Parliament instead, and by the same token he should have wanted to become leader of his party, if not Prime Minister – certainly many of his Keighley admirers thought he was destined for the front bench and there's no doubt he was far more able than many of those who have stood at the despatch box for either Government or Opposition. If he secretly cherished the ambition to become a front-bencher it was a secret he never shared with me.

However, Bob was, briefly, a junior Minister in the Callaghan Government at the Department of Industry, which could have been a stepping stone to greater things, but he eventually resigned from the job, giving as his reason the fact that the Labour Cabinet had decided to withdraw Government support for the K.M.E. Workers' Co-operative on Merseyside. Of course it was sad to allow a co-operative experiment to collapse, but in comparison with the havoc wreaked by Mrs Thatcher on great swathes of British industry and the destruction of millions of jobs in manufacturing, was Bob right to relinquish his toe-hold on the ladder of advancement?

Perhaps the other reason for his resignation from that early ministerial post was that Bob was unhappy having to toe the party line as a Minister, and much preferred the freedom of the back benches from which he could, and did, speak on any issue at any time.

This must account, in part, for the fact that Bob remained on the back benches for the rest of his twenty years as a Member of Parliament: he enjoyed the role which he and his alter ego, Dennis Skinner, had carved out for themselves as men of principle who relentlessly exposed the back-sliders in their own party with the same rigour and scathing sarcasm which they directed at the Tories.

And then suddenly, shockingly, Bob was gone, and thousands recognised what they knew all along: he was a huge and unique character who could never be replaced.

'The photographer photographed' by Ann Cryer for the *Keighley News*. Bob Cryer,
Jim Harrison, for many years photographer for the *Keighley News*, and the
Keighley Centenary Gala Queen and her attendants, Victoria Park, 1976.

When the news of his death was broadcast, a great funeral meeting
was organised at St George's Hall, Bradford, to which all were invited.
I immediately recalled the lesson which Bob drew from our ill-attended
meeting in a Silsden school hall in 1975: "Better to organise a meeting
in a really small venue. Then if twenty-five people turn up it looks
crowded, rather than book a big hall, where twenty-five people look like
a disaster." I wondered whether his family, who organised the St George's
Hall meeting, remembered Bob's dictum. It would be desperately sad if
that huge concert hall, seating more than 1,600, were to be half-empty.

I need hardly have worried. The hall was packed. Bob would have been
gratified. And he would have loved to have joined the speakers; for as
well as friends and relatives there were left-wing MPs and luminaries
like Arthur Scargill, Bernie Grant, Max Madden and Dennis Skinner –
the kind of line-up Bob would relish.

As we all streamed out of St George's Hall at the end of the proceedings,
I turned to find myself touching elbows with Alf Rogers, a one-time

Keighley postman who had been a Keighley Councillor like Bob in the early 1970s, and who had delivered a crucial supporting vote from the Postal Workers' Union at the selection meeting when Bob was chosen as Keighley's parliamentary candidate, by the closest of margins. Alf had often had his disagreements with Bob, who in Alf's view was often too 'left-wing' and uncompromising for Alf's liking. But there was Alf, weeping freely, like me, scarcely able to speak, both of us grieving at our loss. And there were countless others there who I knew frequently disagreed with Bob's views and yet had come to signal their respect. Doubtless there were numerous others who wanted to be there but could not come because the meeting took place on a working day.

Other back-bench MPs have died suddenly, and though their deaths were a personal tragedy for their families, their passing did not prompt the spontaneous and widespread grief that Bob's did. Perhaps it was because his enthusiasm, dedication and integrity in his political life were extraordinary in a day and age when most of us have come to regard politicians in general either with distaste, indifference or cynical contempt.

This was one of Bob's particular achievements. He restored many people's faith in a system which, for all its faults, he loved with a passion – Parliament, and party politics.

---

## 2

## MARTIN LEATHLEY

*of Silsden, Councillor for Keighley North Ward*

I first met Bob Cryer in 1971 when I enlisted at Keighley College as a mature student. Bob taught us British Constitution and managed to make a potentially rather dry subject very enjoyable. He entertained us with a seemingly inexhaustible fund of anecdotes, imitations and observations based on his wide political knowledge – and we passed the exam too!

Although I had already been a member of the Labour Party for ten years I had become disillusioned and inactive as I had been very disappointed with the Labour Government of the 1960s.

Bob's views were a breath of fresh air and reminded me of why I had joined Labour in the first place. So when I found out that he was trying

Keighley's Centenary Gala, 1976. Left to right: Edna and Dennis Healey,
Stanley Bell, Bob, Ann and Jane Cryer.

for the vacant parliamentary seat at Keighley I decided to become active
again and help him.

When the Selection Conference took place Bob squeaked in on the final
ballot – with the help of the Silsden delegation – by 45 votes to 42, so I
felt my re-entry to political activity had been worth while.

Over the next decade I had a great opportunity to see how the job of
MP should be done. Bob was a marvel of energy, enthusiasm and
accountability. His fame soon spread and his surgeries overflowed with
people from other constituencies which had less assiduous MPs. He was
always an inspiration to campaign with and I particularly remember
campaigning with him for a 'No' vote in the 1975 EC Referendum. We
won the argument but lost the vote. On many other occasions his campaigns were more successful and he certainly put Keighley on the political
map.

I had hoped to join him on the green benches at Westminster after the
1983 Election. Instead we crawled back to a member's house after a
drubbing in Shipley only to be greeted by the news from the TV that
Bob had lost in Keighley. Tears flowed and the gloom was complete.

However, in best phoenix-like tradition, Bob rose from the ashes, via the
European Parliament, to become Member of Parliament for Bradford

South. Help was at hand again with sticky problems and I was able to get his help for retail workers under threat from Sunday trading.

Sylvia and I always looked for Bob on the front bench, below the gangway, when Parliament was on TV. Unlike many of his fellows, Bob was always there. It will take a big person to fill his place.

---

## 3

## FRANK BRAMMAH

*Keighley worker*

In the seventies I worked at a rubber processing plant in Keighley. Saying the bosses were Victorian would be a kindness, the eight hour day was still a long way off in their way of thinking. Still, it was work, I was twenty, and I needed the brass so it was head down, arse up, mouth shut and get on with it.

One day the foreman came seeking me. Since I was the most recently employed serf, coupled with our mutual hatred, it was I who got the worst jobs. He told me someone was coming to view two railway carriages that stood in the yard. They were full of rubbish, pieces of tyre, hessian sacking, and great sacks of carbon black, a compound that had the consistency of thick damp soot discolouring everything it touched. I was to clear out the carriages and be quick about it. Off I went seething with the sniggers of my workmates ringing in my ears. I wasn't exactly whistling Dixie.

Within minutes I resembled Al Jolson on a bad day. Hearing the manager's voice I re-doubled my efforts and in doing so burst a sack of carbon black. Choking, I staggered to the door to see the manager approaching with a tall visitor. I didn't know whether to laugh, cry, or break into a verse from Old Man River. The manager gave me a glare that would have stopped a truck and I knew I was in it up to my neck, then something happened that I'll never forget. The tall bespectacled visitor held out his hand and said, "Hello, my name's Bob Cryer, how are you?" The manager became all condescending and began to waffle "Er this is er, er what's your name lad?" I spat out a mouthful of midnight coloured dust which sounded like 'Frank' and the big bloke said "Well thanks for clearing these carriages out for me, Frank". I was his man from that moment on.

Presentation of a special 'ticket' to Bob Cryer when he 'opened' the refurbished British Railways Station at Keighley, 1978. The photo includes Conservative councillor Bill Proom, BR Regional Manager and Keighley station staff.

The best way I can describe Bob is through my own experiences of him. In late 1980, to escape impending unemployment, I took off to Germany to do a stint of Aufweiderzehn Pet. Not a very bright move as I was laid off over there and had to return to Thatcher's dole queue where I was instantly suspended from benefit for being out of work without good reason. In desperation I got in touch with Bob who took up my case with the dole office. As a result of his efforts I was given my dues with back pay, Bob Cryer one – System nil.

Witnessing the appalling waste created by deliberate mass unemployment I took part in a demonstration in Bradford highlighting the issue. At the demo I was handed a leaflet about a forthcoming March for Jobs to London. Interested, I got in touch with the organisers, and on May Day 1981 I left Yorkshire with 200 others on the long walk to London – it was to be an education.

A month later, fitter, leaner, and having met some the kindest folk from all over these islands of ours, we arrived in London. County Hall to be precise, where we were given board and lodgings courtesy of Ken

Livingstone's GLC. We slept on camp beds put aside for politicians who would have kipped on them in the event of a nuclear war, a point which upset the Tories. Just imagine the poor buggers having to sleep through a post-Apocalypse scenario on a bed once occupied by an unemployed northerner – perish the thought. I was laid on my bed when one of the Leeds marchers came in telling us that Bob Cryer wanted to see the lads from Keighley, all two of us.

We passed through into the Houses of Parliament, bribing the security guards with sticks of People's March for Jobs rock of all things. A beaming Bob met us in a gallery full of statues and introduced us to Dennis Skinner, MP, who, contrary to his media image, didn't look like much of a beast to us, but then we were not the enemy were we? When Bob had finished his stint in a debate he took us on a tour of both Houses which caused some raised eyebrows among the patrician classes. I was suited to bits, getting up their noses for once really made my day. He left us in a bar for a while with some of the Labour MPs of the day who made us feel – well, tired and emotional I think they call it down there. We took leave of Bob on Westminster Bridge returning to County Hall to get our heads down. In my mind's eye I can still see him waving to us as we wove our way back over the Thames.

Back in Keighley at a Labour movement function I was presented with the book *Unemployed Struggles 1919 to 1936* written by Wall Hanington. Inside the dust cover were three signatures, one of which was Bob's, and underneath he'd simply written 'Organise'! We did just that, and the Keighley branch of the Unemployed Workers Union was formed. Bob came along and helped us on more than one occasion. He was a man who actually gave a damn.

I'm of the opinion that his giving a damn cost him the town. I don't pretend to understand the machinations of those who scheme and plot on the boundary commission but nailing an up-and-coming radical MP must have looked good on their CVs. I'll never forget the night we heard that Bob had lost Keighley to the Tories. I was working shifts in a mill and my mother phoned to tell me the bad news. My face must have registered my feelings as the overlooker asked me what was wrong. I said, "Bob Cryer has lost Keighley to Gary Waller." He replied, "That's bad news mate, Bob was a good man for the town." To cap it all, the overlooker was a Tory voter. As everyone is well aware it was the addition of 15,000 Tories into the Keighley area that cost Bob the seat and cost the town the best MP it had ever had.

Through the dark years of the eighties I would occasionally fire off a letter to Bob, who was now a Euro MP in Sheffield, more to let him know that I was still on the planet than anything else, but at times for advice that was always forthcoming. Nothing was too much trouble and in 1985 I was fortunate enough to see myself in print. My brother Allan and I had a book published and when our editor asked us whom we wanted to do the book launch we asked for Bob – who else? Needless to say he did us proud and slated a system that held down the latent talents of the working class. A year later my fiancée and I planned to marry whilst on holiday in Cyprus and we needed some documentation for the authorities in Nicosia. Guess who provided it for us? I know many people who were helped by Bob. One chap had gone AWOL from the French Foreign Legion in Djibouti, managed to get to Kenya, where he became stranded. He told me that Bob had got him home safe and sound. The last I heard of the deserter was that he couldn't cope with civilian life and had gone back to France for round two. Ah well, that's what a spell on the dole in Haworth can drive you to.

Bob's commitment to peace was an inspiration to me. As many of my generation will testify, war was never far from the front pages. The long collective British memory of WW2 and subsequent colonial involvements usually glorified the organised violence that is by its very definition the Armed Forces. I had been brought up to believe that my country could do no wrong, indeed, had never done any wrong. It came as shock after shock to discover what had been carried out down the years in the name of the British people. Not once, however, had the working class of Britain started a conflict, nor for that matter had the working class of any other nation, yet the price paid by that same class was massive beyond figures. Peace was all that mattered; harmony and co-operation between peoples, cultures, and nations. All these were the hallmarks of Bob's creed. Through these inspirations I began to understand, and with that understanding came a thirst for knowledge to discover the truth. The truth about so called nuclear deterrents, the truth about the billions wasted on defence. Where that money could have been better spent, in hospitals, in schools, in industry, on the very people who were under threat of annihilation because various warmongers wanted that extra piece of land to secure their national boundaries or some such other lame excuse. It became equally important to me to get this information out to as many people as I could. This platform was provided by John Liddle who was the editor of the *Keighley News*: he gave me a weekly column to sound off my opinions, and I did. It was good while it lasted. It was part of Bob's legacy without a doubt.

The *Satanic Verses* affair showed clearly what a principled man Bob Cryer was. He stood foursquare against the Fatwa issued by the Mullahs in Iran.

Ann, Bob, Jane and John at the 1979 General Election victory, Victoria Hall,
Keighley.
(*Telegraph & Argus*)

In the volatile world that is Islamic fundamentalism passions are easily
aroused. As an MP for Bradford South with its Muslim voters, Bob
was more aware than most of where his stance could have taken him. It
was an act of courage that typified the man and it paid off, as he was
returned to Parliament by those same people of Bradford South. They
knew Bob, they knew that he would always fight their corner right
down the line.

In 1991 the Government announced the pit closure programme. The
reality was different, and now we all know it was a privatisation
programme by stealth. Lie after lie poured from the mouths of Ministers
about how no one wanted coal anymore. A rally was organised in
Keighley against pit closures. It was to be the first of many nationwide.
As I drove down into Keighley I pondered on what a battering the working class of this country had taken. At the rally I was pleased to see Bob
and Ann. Bob spoke with passion and zeal against the Government's
policy that laid waste entire communities, as did Arthur Scargill, various
trades unionists and some of the local clergy. The moral high ground was

On mike at an outdoor meeting, October 1981.
(*Keighley News*)

clearly visible and it showed just how far the Government had lowered itself. At the end of the rally I queued patiently with other Keighley people who wanted to speak with Bob and Ann. I remember the smile, the handshake, and the question from him, "Are you still writing?" "No," I replied. "Well you should be," was his answer.

I had just arrived home from work one day when the phone rang. My wife Alison answered, it was my mother-in-law calling. She had called to pass on the terrible news of Bob's death. Stunned, I phoned the *Keighley News* to ask if they were covering the tragedy and also if I could write a piece for Bob. I was told by an equally shocked and subdued reporter that it would be OK. I went to our attic to begin typing what was to prove the hardest piece I've ever done. I sat there and wept. I wept for Bob's family, I wept for this country, I wept for a diminished humanity, and I wept for me. I had lost a teacher, a friend, and somehow lost something stable in what has been an unstable life.

Now and again Bob springs to mind. As I look down from the high hills where my home is, I can see the Keighley and Worth Valley trains puffing smoke up the line. "Bob's train" my wife and I call it. The other week I came across the words of Jesus, "In as much as you have helped one of these my brothers, you have done it to me, and for me." It didn't matter to Bob whether you were a Foreign Legion deserter or a desperate pensioner, you needed help and you got it. He helped people. When I read Louis Fischer's biography of the great Mahatma Gandhi I find so many parallels between the two men: pacifism, a belief in the dignity of all people, love for their fellow man, and above all a common commitment to a better world. To me, at least, Bob Cryer was Yorkshire's Gandhi, and I miss him.

Many people, both great and good paid homage to him. Many words were spoken with conviction about our common loss, yet for me the statement that said it all came from my wife's Grandma. She said softly, "The world cannot afford to lose men such as Bob." She is right!

---

*Extract from a letter to Ann Cryer from The Rt Hon Lord Ingrow (former Conservative councillor and Lord Mayor of Keighley, President of the National Union of Conservative and Unionist Associations 1982–83, and Lord Lieutenant, West Yorkshire 1985–92)*

Though our politics differed and we crossed swords many times, we had many things in common. He was a true professional, a difficult candidate to beat, and I saw for myself how deservedly popular he was.

The last time we met was while I was still Lord Lieutenant and he was very quick to come and have a word with me. He will be sadly missed in Bradford and Keighley, and certainly the Commons will be a poorer place without him. He gave colour to often very drab proceedings.

---

## 4

## MAIDEN SPEECH

*Debate on the Queen's Address to Parliament, 12 March, 1974, 8.12 p.m.*

Mr Bob Cryer (Keighley): I am pleased to be here and to be able to make this speech representing Keighley in Yorkshire. It is a constituency of 55,000 people, many of whom are engineers who were foremost in the struggle against the Industrial Relations Act. Such people will be pleased by the Gracious Speech, which outlines so many fruitful and positive plans. My constituency also contains rural and semi-rural areas. It includes Haworth, the famous home of the Brontës, the second most important literary shrine in the country. The people of Keighley will be pleased that the Gracious Speech contains such a far-reaching programme of social change.

I pick out in particular the emphasis on comprehensive education. In Keighley we are fortunate, because unlike the majority of local authorities we have a comprehensive system of education in existence. The curtailment of expenditure by the last Government meant that the reorganisation of that comprehensive education, to bring it into line with the plans of the new Bradford Metropolitan District Authority – an authority brought into existence by the last Government – was placed in jeopardy.

I hope that the Labour Government, in formulating their financial plans, will bear in mind the urgent need for further expenditure on education so that areas such as my constituency can once more begin the essentially important task of rebuilding. Two schools in my constituency certainly date from the last century and are greatly overcrowded. One has recently been overshadowed by a large new factory. Children are being educated in circumstances which are far from ideal. This school was due to be replaced first of all in 1973 and then again in 1974. I hope that this rebuilding will be carried out by a Labour Government willing to put into effect plans which the previous administration seemed so reluctant to implement.

Comprehensive education in Keighley, although in existence, is seriously short of money, and we look forward to a lengthy period under a Labour Government when, hopefully, the defects of the last Government will be remedied. We hope that the two schools I have mentioned, Hartington and Swire Smith, will be replaced. The comprehensive education mentioned in the Gracious Speech should be a genuinely comprehensive system, unlike the bipartite system of education which in the majority of local authorities is carried on in separate schools. Many comprehensive schools are comprehensive in name only. Once inside the schools children are streamed rigorously and might just as well be in separate schools. We want a system where streaming is avoided or gradually eroded so that children are given an opportunity of being educated with their peers and not separated as though they were entering separate schools.

Comprehensive education needs to be comprehensive not only for the pupils but for the staff. Hopefully the Government will ensure that there is a degree of democratic participation by staff and pupils inside the schools. We cannot talk about democracy within the education system, we cannot expect teachers to instil an understanding and appreciation of democracy, when they have no democratic right of participation in the administration of what can be large units.

Ann, Bob and Alan Rye at a CND demonstration at Molesworth, March 1985.

I hope that the Government will ensure that there is an element of democratic participation in education and industry. I often think that, because of a rigid demarcation between management and men, the people of this country are not given sufficient opportunity, within the framework of society, to be able to participate in decision making, and to bring their varied and considerable talents to bear.

In industry and education there is a need to enable people to participate much more in management decisions. We spend far more of our time at work than in any other activity yet so often thousands of millions of people are denied any sense of opportunity or of creative sharing in their work. There are 350,000 people employed in education and it is to hoped that there will be greater involvement.

The Gracious Speech also mentions the protection of the environment and the need to reappraise major development projects. I hope that this will include much of our motorway programme, because the Gracious Speech also refers to the energy situation which has necessitated the Government taking a critical and sharp look at the energy shortage in the immediate past and future.

It is time that the Government seriously examined all the motorway projects, especially the Aire Valley motorway which, if it is ever constructed, will run through my constituency for 13.2 miles at a cost in excess of £40 million. One wonders whether that sort of expenditure can be justified at a time when the country is in serious economic difficulties.

The prospect of the motorway has already blighted the homes of many people. At least two schools along the route will have to be completely replaced and a third school will be overshadowed by a 40 ft embankment which will act as a noise barrier against the motorway. In a situation of economic curtailment one wonders whether the expenditure of £40 million is justified, especially when it means the construction of two new schools and the possible curtailment of a third.

How valuable is a motorway programme when at least until the early 1980s we shall have limited energy resources? We know that our energy resources are finite, and we cannot squander energy as we once did. We no longer have an oil glut in the world and we shall have to allocate our total energy resources with great care.

I am glad that one of the first steps of the Labour Government in solving the mining dispute and getting the miners back to work has been undertaken so speedily. First, we have to get the country back to work and, secondly, we have to embark on a programme of solving the energy crisis. The Labour Government are committed to improving the energy position. I suggest that the reappraisal of major projects should include motorway projects which are not proved to be of value to any particular community.

It is with great pleasure that I give my unqualified support to the Gracious Speech and the programme it outlines. A great step forward is the proposal to repeal the Industrial Relations Act. The Act was bitterly opposed by the trade union and Labour movement. We argued at the time that it would produce only industrial strife and that one could not solve delicately balanced industrial relationships by legalistic action. It was a hopeless illusion of the then Government to force the legislation through Parliament and to believe when they did so that it would in any way solve our industrial relations difficulties.

The Act's failure is surely indicated by the figures that show that during the period of the previous Government there were three times as many strikes as there were between 1964 and 1970 when there was a Labour Government. During 1972 alone, as many days were lost in strikes as were lost during the whole of the period between 1964 and 1970. Statistically the Industrial Relations Act has been a calamity, and it is pleasing that a Labour Government will carry out the promise to repeal it.

There is to be a new conciliation and arbitration service. It has been suggested that a conciliation and arbitration service already exists. If so, it has not been used much. The independence of the new conciliation and arbitration service is important, to show that it is not a Government body and that both sides of industry can appeal to it in the knowledge that it is independent and does not seek as an arm of the Government to impose a solution. That causes suspicion in many industrial disputes. The setting up of this service is an earnest of the Government's serious intention to avoid the confrontation that for the past three-and-a-half years has bedevilled British industry. The only solution to any industrial dispute is by agreement between the two sides round a table, and the conciliation and arbitration service will surely help in this.

It is hoped to introduce an Industrial Democracy Act. That promise is contained in the manifesto, and I am sure that Opposition Members will support an opportunity for working people to participate to a much greater degree than ever before in the general direction and management of industry. I hope that that will be an item in the future programme.

I am pleased to note that the pledge to renegotiate the Common Market terms is being fulfilled. That is an essential plank of the Labour Government's programme. At last the British people will have the opportunity to make a decision on this vital issue. The Government have made clear their intention to place this matter before the people either through a consultative referendum or in a General Election. The Common Market was foisted on the British people without adequate consultation and in spite of promises that we would never go in without the full-hearted consent of the British people. That consent was never given, and it is pleasing to note that the Labour Government will renegotiate the terms and present the renegotiated terms to the British people.

I have great pleasure in supporting the whole of the Gracious Speech in the knowledge that the Labour Government are honouring the promises made during the election.

*(Parliamentary Debates, Commons Official Report, 5th Series, vol. 873, cols. 158–62)*

© Parliamentary Copyright

# CHAPTER 6

# THE ODD COUPLE: BOB AS A MINISTER

## LIZ MELLON

*Private Secretary and Head of the Private Office for Bob Cryer when he was Parliamentary Under Secretary of State at the Department of Industry*

Bob Cryer was a man of principle, with values which he held passionately and unswervingly. In his role as a junior Minister in the Department of Industry, he imported an intensity which often sat uncomfortably alongside the pragmatism of office. My contribution to the story of Bob's life is intended to illustrate the man through frank anecdotes about his time in office.

I was a civil servant in the 1970s. I joined the civil service in 1973, on a 'high flier' programme direct from University. My official title was 'Administrative Trainee', because this was in the days before the managerialist reforms currently being introduced into the civil service. Civil servants intended for high office therefore learned about public administration, or policy formation. 'Management' was broadly regarded as keeping the files in order and not something in which administrators had to take much interest. As part of the preparation for promotion, Administrative Trainees were given positions of responsibility at a young age and running a Minister's office was one such position. I took over as Bob's Private Secretary in October 1977, when I was 26, and was with him for just over a year before he resigned. I was his second Private Secretary.

It might be helpful first to describe a little the life in a Minister's office. Being a Private Secretary to a Minister is, I am convinced, as stressful as being a Minister, but the main point is that it is a stressful existence. There is no training or induction for either job. The culture of the civil service in the 1970s (and, in many parts, it is just the same today) was 'sink or swim'. The general assumption was that if you were bright enough, you would be able to handle anything. Being 'bright' was only one potential qualification for a Minister: being politically astute, an effective networker or a good orator were just as good qualifications. The hours were long and the duties incredibly diverse. Looking back in my diary for this period, I was often in the office before 8 a.m. and left about twelve hours later. On days when Bob was speaking in the House of Commons, I would go from the office to the officials' box and listen to him and then go and check *Hansard* to make sure that his views had been recorded accurately. On those occasions, I would arrive home at one or two in the morning. Bob lived in London during the week and his days were just as long, except that he had to work weekends as well, which I did only rarely. I was, however, expected always to be on duty and available for work at a moment's notice.

Bob was a junior Minister in the Department of Industry, with special responsibility for small firms and co-operatives. However, his duties were by no means limited to activities directly related to small firms. In a typical week, picked at random from the diary, he heard representations from Blackpool, which had been refused Development Area status; attended the Inner Cities Partnership (with the Department of the Environment) in Manchester; appeared on Tyne Tees television in South Shields; attended meetings, some with MPs and some with Ministers from other Departments; and attended Parliament every day. Every weekend he travelled home to his constituency, where he was a committed and energetic MP, who always held a Saturday 'surgery' to listen to constituents' needs. This is the weekend work referred to above. The rule was that a 'Chinese wall' should be constructed between those activities which Bob undertook as a Minister, to which the resources of his Private Office were dedicated, and those activities which Bob undertook as an MP, for which there was no official support.

I ran a team of three in the Private Office. Our job was to take requests from civil servants and from other Department of Industry Ministers for Bob to represent the Department of Industry at events ranging from company openings to Ministerial meetings; to co-ordinate travel and civil service briefings for these events; to ensure that Bob was briefed on Departmental policy matters and also that his input to policy was registered with either Ministers or civil servants. This involved a lot of paperwork, which every evening filled the Ministerial red box with matters which had not been dealt with during the day. As Private Secretary, both I and my deputy, Iain, were supposed to be versed in all aspects of Government policy. This entailed reading every piece of paper which went into the box and also reading every newspaper, every day. I had to take decisions daily on what should be presented to Bob for Ministerial approval and what, of a more mundane and less political nature, could be left for officials (as civil servants were called) to deal with directly. Bob had a quick intelligence and a suspicious mind, so he tended to deal with more, rather than less, himself.

Bob attended the House of Commons religiously, because he felt that a representative of the people should be able to represent them at all times,

Portrait taken by the Department of Industry Press Officer on Bob's appointment
as Parliamentary Under Secretary of State, 1976.

on all subjects. For a Government Minister, parliamentary affairs anyway
took precedence. For example, in one particular week in February 1978,
all visits and meetings had to be cancelled, because Bob had to be present
in the House of Commons for two votes and he had also accepted
responsibility for the Committee stage of a Bill. During the Committee
stage of legislation, a Bill is considered clause by clause, with voting on

amendments, in an all-party committee. Readjusting the diary on these occasions was a full-time job in itself.

The job of a Private Secretary to a Minister was a 'macho' one at the best of times. Civil servants much more senior than I would ring the office, or present papers for decisions. My job was to present civil service advice in the best possible light, often on the basis of a quick oral briefing. Where Bob disagreed, I had to present his arguments back to the civil servants in clear but diplomatic terms. Apart from policy issues, factories needed opening, committees needed attending and meetings needed convening. The job of a Private Secretary is to understand her Minister well in order to act as an effective go-between, so that the Minister is not drowned with activity which is not central to the purpose of Government, but so that Government business gets done. Working for Bob was harder than the usual Private Secretary job from the outset. While he had many of the qualifications, as set out above, for a Ministerial post, one of his major qualifications for office was that he was difficult for Government Ministers to handle as a backbencher. He had been drafted into Government because, he felt, the Ministerial duty of collective responsibility could then be used to stifle him. He, however, was determined not to be stifled, but to use the opportunity to fight the system from the inside. My instructions were simple: do not let this man resign. As history shows, I failed to meet the major objective of my job. In those days, objective setting was not so sophisticated, so that often you were judged against objectives which were outside your control!

Bob was appointed in September 1976. The Ministerial team he joined had Eric Varley as Secretary of State, Gerald Kaufman as Minister with Lesley Huckfield as the Parliamentary Under-Secretary reporting to him and Alan Williams as the other Minister to whom Bob reported. He was a member of the Tribune Group and joined the Government at a time when the left wing of the Labour Party was unhappy about reductions in public expenditure. There was some criticism of him for having joined the Government. He therefore had two clear agendas. The first was to ensure that he continued to represent his strong left-wing views through the decisions he took in office. He did not want to be accused of 'going native'. So, for example, towards the end of February 1978, the Secretary of State could not attend a lunch with the Chairman of Finance for Industry Limited and the Governor of the Bank of England. Bob agreed to stand in for Eric Varley, but with the greatest reluctance. Not only was it a lunch (potential accusations of corruption), but it also involved spending time with capitalists. Another of Bob's strong views, not dissimilar to some other Ministers, was that the civil service would run the country if it could. His second agenda was, therefore, to make sure that he could never be accused of letting the civil service run him. Until he learned to trust my judgement, he insisted on reading every piece of paper which came into the office and putting his personal stamp on every piece of paper which went out. Even after we had established a good working relationship, I was wary of letting anything but the most routine of communications escape his notice.

If Bob felt beleaguered, surrounded as he was by civil servants he did not trust and occasionally identified with Government policies which he opposed, he did not show it. One of my strongest recollections of him was his calmness in the face of adversity. He always, at least on the surface, appeared to find the world wryly amusing and had a wicked and teasing sense of humour. Most of his strong, adverse views were expressed on paper, sometimes to his detriment and sometimes to mine. The surface, however, was unflappable. There was one occasion which is burned into my memory. Bob had agreed to travel to Exeter to present a prestigious award to a company executive who had been unable to travel to Buckingham Palace to receive it. I was accompanying him on this trip but, having been out of the office, was acting as much under instruction as he was. We duly caught the 07:30 inter-city express train from Paddington and settled down for the three-hour journey to Exeter. About an hour later, Bob inquired if he might see the OBE, as he had never seen one and was curious to know what it looked like. I stared back at him, horror-struck. Had the office not packed it into his case? Apparently not. Bob seemed quite relaxed, saying that it would be interesting to see what happened when we arrived. I was mortified: I could not let my Minister appear in front of all the Press which would be assembled and simply shake hands instead of presenting the award! Frantically, I contacted the conductor on the train and explained the situation, persuading him to make an unscheduled stop at a local station en route so that I could leap from the train and phone ahead. Luckily, the telephone on the deserted, rural platform worked and I telephoned to warn the Department of Industry Regional Office of the impending disaster, asking them to liaise with the Private Office to try and sort out the problem in the two hours' journey time remaining. We eventually arrived at Exeter, to be met by the Director of the Regional Office (a civil servant). He looked at me pityingly. "Do you think we would trust an OBE to the Private Office? It's been safe with us all the time. The Minister only touches it for the moment when it's handed over!" An intense mixture of relief and humiliation swept over me. Bob merely looked mildly amused and repeated his request to see the OBE.

Bob's curiosity about most things demonstrated his zest for life and for learning. It was typical of him to want to see the OBE. I saw more of

Bob Cryer MP, Industry Minister, with the Mayor of Hull, 1977.
(*Donald Innes*)

the inside of UK factories in the short time I spent with him in Private Office than I had seen before or have seen since. He took his role as Minister with special responsibility for small firms very seriously and we visited everything from arts and crafts co-operative workshops in London to actuator manufacturers in Yorkshire. I learned a lot about the manufacturing underbelly of the UK, wearing hard hats and walking carefully between the yellow lines in oil-drenched, deafening, dusty surroundings as Bob toured and looked and peered and asked question after question. He really wanted to understand and to know. A female Private Secretary was unusual: women in business at all in the 1970s were unusual. Firms received a Minister who did not want to be wined and dined, but did want to understand their manufacturing process, accompanied by a young woman who clearly had a proper job, albeit one which was difficult to understand. The odd couple.

One of Bob's strongest values was that of the family. His family was central to his life, but also something he kept very private and separate from his life as a Minister, but not as an MP. I rarely saw Ann, his wife, unless she visited London to assist him with constituency business. I remember one night in March 1978, when Ann and Bob and I stayed overnight at the Great Northern Hotel in King's Cross, after an adjournment debate in the House of Commons which ended at about 1 a.m. We stayed at the hotel because we had to catch the 07:50 to Liverpool for the second Inner Cities Partnership meeting on Friday 10 March. In the morning, Bob and I left for the Liverpool engagement and Ann set off home for Keighley. It would have been unthinkable for her to travel with us. It was an official engagement and Bob would never have used public funds so that his wife could accompany him, or risk being accused of that by having her accompany him but paying for her himself. On another occasion, I travelled to Scarborough one Saturday in April 1978, because Bob was speaking at the Vehicle Builders and Repairers Association annual conference. As it was the weekend, he allowed himself the luxury of letting his family accompany him, having driven himself across from Keighley, his home and constituency. He could have been driven by an official car, had he so chosen. After he had addressed the conference, he drove me with his family around Scarborough, pointing out the sights. They then all accompanied me to the station and waved goodbye as the train pulled out. I was very touched, but to them it was the most natural thing in the world, to extend family support and warmth to a visitor.

My relationship with Bob was extremely professional: polite, respectful and slightly distant. One reason for this was that Bob was very aware of the possibility of scandal. The House of Commons was, and no doubt still is, a hotbed of rumour and surmise. Even if one of the many affairs between MPs, researchers, secretaries and so on did not hit the Press, they certainly hit the grapevine inside the House. There was one occasion when yet another late night in the House, checking *Hansard* until 12.30 a.m., meant that I decided to book us into a hotel at Heathrow, as we had to catch the 7.50 a.m. flight to Newcastle the next day for an Inner Cities Partnership meeting. We bumped into a Newcastle MP doing the same thing and Bob was very concerned in case he thought there was anything going on between the two of us. Being young and naïve, I found it hard to relate to his concern.

Having said that our relationship was professionally distant, Bob was nonetheless a concerned and caring individual. I have never been so ill as I was when I worked in Private Office. The constant travel, long hours and late nights, combined with treading the difficult tightrope between ensuring that Bob represented the Department at various official functions while not compromising his strong value base, was extremely stressful. Bob was fairly isolated from other Ministers within the Department, which meant that I was also, as we did not have a great deal of business to discuss between Ministerial offices and we were all far too busy for idle chit-chat. I was therefore constantly in and out of the doctor's surgery for minor ailments which could not be left (I ignored coughs and colds, which became a semi-permanent fixture), in and out of the dentist for tooth abscesses and the hospital outpatients' department for minor, operable local infections. On one such occasion, I formally told Bob that I would have to leave early to get to my local hospital and he sat me down, listened carefully to my story (which I shall spare the reader!) and then advised me to go to Westminster Hospital as it was much nearer. It sounds a small gesture, but it made a great deal of difference to the poor, run-down Private Secretary I was at that moment.

Bob resigned once before his official resignation, but Alan Williams interceded and therefore Bob did not go through with it. There was the possibility of resignation several times, because of the circumstances in which he had been appointed and Bob's strong values. The outgoing Private Secretary, Dennis, had told me that my job was to stop Bob making a fool of himself. As I hope the description of Private Office life makes clear, the civil service takes a protective attitude towards its Ministers. They were accompanied on all official visits, so that if they needed information about a question they could not answer, it could be sought; if they made a statement which went beyond Government policy it could be rephrased or re-interpreted; if they started a meeting it could be recorded; and their informal views could be noted and used to brief officials about the likely acceptability of, or need for, policy proposals. On a practical, rather than a policy, level, it also meant that the Minister did not have to concern him or herself with travel arrangements, or even, rather like the Queen, with carrying money.

Bob did not respond well to this nannying. As far as official visits were concerned, this was good news. He was always accompanied, but sometimes this could be by someone very junior from the office, which was not at all common practice. They loved the responsibility, Bob loved the freedom and both he and I appreciated the democratic and egalitarian feel it gave to the office. The borderline on written work was much harder to judge and one of these occasions in particular gave me sleepless nights, because I was afraid it would lead Bob to resign. By February 1978, Bob was feeling very frustrated with his isolation in the office. There were no Ministerial meetings on policy, so Ministerial life was hectic, but not particularly fulfilling. Then I 'let' Bob send two internal memos to Eric Varley, criticising the situation and the Permanent Secretary's role in the situation. Bob received a reply telling him not to be so petulant and childish. Such a strong and direct exchange between Ministerial colleagues was one of the things the civil service was supposed to mediate. I felt that I had failed by allowing Bob to expose himself in this way, but had felt helpless to find a more appropriate route for his frustration. I have always felt the failure mine. Now, much later, it strikes me that the failure was also systemic. Where was the civil service support system for such a volatile situation, so that decisions did not rest at a junior and inexperienced level? It is possible that Eric Varley's Private Secretary has also been feeling bad all these years! It was also completely understandable that Bob should lose patience. One of my first tasks on joining his office had been to ask Eric Varley's office when the promised Ministerial meetings would start. He had been waiting for action for four months to my knowledge and probably longer.

Bob was very angry at the tone of the Secretary of State's reply, but I tried to convince him that to respond in kind would only lead to further deterioration in the relationship and not to what he wanted, more involvement in policy formation. Alan Williams stepped in as unofficial peacemaker. Bob was looking for an apology from Eric Varley. He did not get one, but he did achieve the institution of fortnightly Ministerial meetings, to take place immediately after Cabinet so that the Department of Industry team could be kept up to date, and an agreement to review the distribution of Ministerial responsibilities. The knife edge had been safely navigated once more.

While Bob was stung by Eric Varley's initial response to his requests, his own phrasing could be very sharp. Bob mostly expressed his negative views in writing. In 1991 I was talking to the Chief Executive of one of the Government's new Executive Agencies, for whom I was carrying out some consultancy. He quoted to me, verbatim, the words Bob had scribbled on one of his policy submissions way back in 1978 and which I had passed back direct, without mediation. He had clearly been wounded by Bob's views, but Bob had to feel that he was free to make direct comments without my interference.

Bob was teetotal. His famous calm in the face of adversity was only shattered twice with me and one of those was over alcohol. Most Private Offices kept a drinks' cabinet, to offer drinks to visitors, and a Friday night drink for exhausted staff in celebration of another week's successful work was something of a tradition. Our office followed Bob's principles and was therefore alcohol-free. However, I did submit a drinks' order for Christmas 1977 and put a copy in with Bob's papers for him to see. I was roundly instructed, in no uncertain terms, in writing, to send it all back. He only expressed disapproval to my face once, which was the second occasion on which his calm was penetrated. We were on the train going up to Birmingham and there was a power failure at Watford, so we sat outside the station in the train for one and a half hours before returning instead to London. While chatting to pass the time, Bob talked about the local council elections taking place in Yorkshire. I lived in

The Junior Minister at the Department of Industry astride a Triumph Bonneville
at the Meridan Motorcycle Workers' Co-operative, with the workers.
(*Birmingham Evening Mail*)

London, on a different election timetable to the rest of the country and so
had completely forgotten that these local elections were happening. Bob
was dumbfounded. "Where have you been all these years?" he asked,
quite unable to comprehend that something so central to his political
existence could be so peripheral to someone else.

Bob's commitment to the role he had accepted and to his constituents was
unquestionable. No drinking, no womanising, hard work, family values
and dedication to achieving a different society by complete adherence to
Socialist values were what he epitomised. However, lest he sound too
much of a saint, Bob did allow the pragmatics of politics to affect his
decisions on occasion. For example, where possible, on Fridays, he liked
to undertake Ministerial visits in Yorkshire. This meant that he was closer
to home at the end of the week and also that he could shore up popularity
in and around his marginal constituency. Visiting Bradford College on a
Friday in November 1977 was one such example. I remember too another

occasion, when the 'Chinese wall' between his Ministerial and his Member of Parliament duties was transgressed and I worked until 10 p.m. trying to delay the proposed deportation of a Pakistani who claimed to have a house in Bob's constituency.

Private Office life swung from the routine to the unusual, from many representations from different UK geographic regions about Government policy on assistance to industry, to being interviewed with Harold Lever about the budget proposals intended to help small firms. Seemingly small decisions could gain unexpected national importance, while difficult situations could melt away overnight. There was much uncertainty and little structure, even the structure that the diary offered could be swept aside at a stroke. That I was stressed showed in my stream of minor ailments, but at the same time, I was strangely energetic. My social life during this period did not fade, but grew. It was as if I was living on a higher plane, at a generally more frenetic pace.

As all the world knows, Bob did eventually resign, on a point of principle. I kept in touch with Bob and his family over the years and still catch myself looking for him on the Opposition front bench, next to Dennis Skinner. He had a magnetic personality which transcended time and distance. I am very glad that I experienced Private Office with a conviction politician of high moral standing. I never had to contravene my principles and am pleased to be able to look back and say that, whatever mistakes we made, whatever successes we had, we did honestly, openly and with good heart.

---

*Extract from a letter to Ann Cryer from Roger Sands, Principal Clerk, Registry of Members' Interests*

Mr Cryer's great quality – one which, sadly, is becoming increasingly rare – was the ability to combine the possession and expression of strongly held and radical political views with an appreciation of the importance of institutions, rules and procedures. He understood and respected the role of impartial officials; and this quality, together with his natural friendliness, lack of pomposity and quick understanding, made it a great pleasure to have dealings with him, however 'difficult' he might need to be in pursuit of his opinions.

His assiduity as a Chairman and member of Committees (including the Members' Interests Committee of which I am the Clerk) and in attendance in the Chamber was unrivalled in recent experience; and his contributions, however off-the-cuff, were always articulate and to the point. He will be greatly missed in the House, not least by officials.

*Extracts from a letter to Ann Cryer from Alan Rye of Keighley*

Bob crammed so much into 59 years. And he enjoyed life.

Of course (no doubt like Bob himself) I would have liked to have seen him as a Minister or Secretary of State in a (progressive!) Labour Government. But it would have to have been a Government which did not require him to compromise on his dearest-held principles. So the chances are (as Bob well knew) he would never have held high office with the Labour Party being what it is now.

But that doesn't mean Bob hadn't an important influence over progressive legislation while he was an MP. I know lots of people in Keighley and Bradford South will be saying (rightly) that Bob was a dedicated constituency MP. But he was also a legislator. I remember when Bob used to come to Steeton in the 70s and rave on about the minutiae of, for instance, the Health & Safety at Work Act or the Employment Protection Act. I know that as well as speaking in the debates on these Bills (and countless others) Bob must have helped to obtain vital amendments to either the Bills or – just as importantly – to the 'small print' of the Acts, by scrutinising the consequent Statutory Instruments.

Since I started working as a solicitor I have actually had to *read* the Statutes, and sometimes the Statutory Instruments, to assist in my efforts to obtain compensation for workers who have been injured at work or who have been unfairly dismissed. And the progressive legislation I rely on is legislation which I know Bob helped to promote and shape – because of his passionate wish to improve the lot of ordinary people, and because he had a fine eye for detail. Someone once remarked that he didn't think people should aim to get elected to Council just to end up being another social worker. Well, in fact, *part* of the job is just that, and Bob did it: but he also achieved a great deal more behind the scenes (as well as on the floor of the House) to push *change*.

On a much more personal note: Bob gave an awful lot to Tom and Hannah when they were kids. Hannah phoned us after hearing the news, and she said how Bob and all of you were important figures in her childhood. That was so true, remembering all our visits . . . not to mention all our bonfire nights when (as Sheila recalls) Bob would sometimes use copies of *Hansard* or draft Statutory Instruments to get the fire going – Guy Fawkes would have approved!

# CHAPTER 7

# OUT OF WESTMINSTER

## 1

## CEDRIC BINNS

*Former Keighley Labour Party Secretary*

At 10.30 a.m. on a bright Saturday morning on 16 June 1984 a procession of about 70 people left the Town Hall Square in Keighley to march the short distance along North Street then down the pedestrianised Low Street to the town's market square. The march, organised by Keighley Labour Party, was to end in a rally where speeches would be made and a collection taken on behalf of striking miners and their families.

At the head of this march was Bob who until a year (and a gerrymander) earlier had been our MP. He had just won the Euro seat of Sheffield, Chesterfield and North East Derbyshire and was taking time out in his home constituency to do what he was to repeat many times: lead a rally to gather support for workers in dispute. We had discovered that one of the Bradford by-laws allowed a collection to be taken in a public place where a rally was taking place. This enabled us to rattle buckets and collect from members of the public right under the noses of the police and they were powerless to stop it. That day we raised over £250 in just over an hour. Equally important was the fact that the Tory/Liberal coalition who ruled Bradford Council at that time and who had blocked street collection permits and house to house collections in the district, were powerless to stop it.

Bob was central to this effort; he spoke for over forty minutes and whilst he was speaking Keighley shoppers dipped their hands into purses and pockets and contributed to our collection. They also took time out to stand and listen to the person who had been described as the best MP Keighley ever had, and the sight of a crowd helped pull even more people in.

We were to repeat, on a monthly basis, these rallies in Keighley and without fail Bob would turn up and put the case on behalf of the miners. He rarely spoke for less than forty minutes, even when we were collecting in mid-January in temperatures that didn't climb above freezing point.

Bob and I quickly realised that there was only a limited amount that we could do in Keighley. We had already opened the Labour Rooms every night to collect for the miners and with the monthly rallies in the market square we had to seek some other source of funds and support for the mineworkers.

I don't know who had the daft idea, but I know when it happened almost to the minute. It was about 1 p.m. on that Saturday when I rang Bob up to tell him that the total in the buckets had topped £256 and was he OK to do another in late July or early August. Why didn't we repeat the exercise in Ilkley? The more we talked about it the better the idea seemed to become; it would give Ilkley Labour Party Branch a real focus and presence on the streets and it would get right up the Tories' noses. So we agreed a date in September and I, as Constituency Party secretary, started to organise it.

It couldn't have gone better! A number of speakers had already had their five minutes' worth and the coins were nicely rattling in the buckets as Bob and Ann arrived. Mark Best, a young school student member of the Young Socialists, was reading his prepared speech when suddenly, out of the passing stream of shoppers, burst one of Ilkley's most right-wing Tory councillors. She was incidentally also a governor at the school where the speaker was a student. She tried to wrest the microphone from the hands of the student and a bit of a struggle ensued. Fortunately a photographer from the *Whafe Valley Times* was there to record the incident. Bob took up the challenge when it came to his speech and the crowd on The Grove grew. Clearly local Tories didn't like it: one was heard to ask the police sergeant "Can these people do this?" His reply, doleful almost to the point of tears, was "Yes ma'am, I'm afraid they can." Bob's speech and the events of the morning gave Labour supporters in Ilkley a real lift. We collected over £125 that morning. This was good enough to encourage us to go back for a second time where we raised nearly £100.

Shortly after the November rally Bob rang me and told me that a representative from the Hickleton Main pit had been in touch with him about getting some help in meeting the needs of the Christmas period. They had not, unlike most other mining communities, sought a 'twinning' arrangement, but had until that point relied upon the Miners' Solidarity Fund. This fund had been set up by a number of MEPs and MPs at the start of the dispute to prevent the sequestrator getting hold of cash collected for miners' families. It had provided lots of help but as connections between pits, women's groups and supporters had been established more of the money collected had gone directly to particular areas. Hickleton were thus facing an even bleaker future. Thanks to this phone call Keighley Constituency Labour Party were able to provide them with some cash, toys and other provisions at short notice. That a pit in the Derne Valley, miles away from Keighley and not in Bob's

Campaigning for nurses in Keighley Town Hall Square, 1980.
(*Tom Rye*)

Euro Constituency had contacted him, says something about the regard in which he was held during this dispute.

Without Bob's support Keighley Labour Party would have found it difficult to raise the £1,500 that we collected for the miners at such rallies.

Although other Labour representatives were asked to speak, excuses of lateness, fog and coffee morning engagements prevailed, and Bob inevitably carried the load when we were let down in this fashion.

The lessons that we had learned in Keighley were quickly transported to Bradford. The late Pat Wall, who was then president of the Bradford Trades Council, helped to ensure that the reservations about repeating this method of collection did not prevent similar successful rallies and collections in the city centre.

The miners' strike had no sooner finished than Keighley CLP were faced with another long and bitter industrial dispute affecting many members of the electorate. The owner of Silentnight, with factories at Barnoldswick and Sutton, reneged on an agreement and drove workers to a showdown. They were forced into a strike in an attempt to protect jobs and wages. The dispute lasted nineteen months before FTAT (Furniture, Timber & Allied Trades) called off the strike, by which time most workers had been driven to seek other work.

Bob and Keighley Labour Party were in the forefront of the support as many of the Sutton workers lived in the constituency. Not only did we organise more support rallies with Bob as the main speaker but Bob did a terrific amount of work with Michael Hindley, the MEP for the East Lancashire Euro constituency covering Barnoldswick, to aid the strikers. I recall the boost that was given to the Sutton strikers when Bob and his son John arrived on the picket line for the first time. It is not easy to explain exactly what having a Labour MEP on your picket line meant unless you were there to see it. I remember the £1,500 that Bob and Mike collected for the hardship fund in just one week at the European Parliament and the way that that was valued by the strikers. Also the campaigning that Bob did with those co-operative societies who had not boycotted Silentnight beds. It was Bob who gave the North Yorkshire Police a dressing-down over their heavy-handed policing of what was essentially a well conducted and trouble-free picket and this resulted in better and less confrontational policing.

The strikers came within an inch of winning that dispute. The Silentnight group's profits were slashed from £71m to less than £2m. If only all co-operatives had taken the advice to stop selling scab beds, this blow to the trade union movement might have been averted.

It was therefore fitting that one of Bob's last major appearances in Keighley was in 1993 when on 9 January he, Ann and Arthur Scargill led another march, this time from the Railway Station to the Town Hall Square, to raise the question of Heseltine's closure of the vast majority of the British deep coalmines. I was setting up the PA system in the Town Hall Square when I noticed that people were starting to shelter from the wind in the lee of the buildings across the street from the square. I went over to talk to some of them. They weren't just there to hear Arthur speak: they were also there to hear Bob. We packed Town Hall Square with the biggest gathering since the end of the war. The case for coal was clearly put, and as ever buckets were rattled to collect for the campaign funds. This time we raised nearly £600.

It is easy in Keighley to find lots of working people who had long and fond memories of Bob. From those who constantly avow that he was the best MP we ever had, to the chap who, in the 1987 General Election stopped me on Hainworth Wood Road in the middle of the Woodhouse Estate and said "I've just been and voted for your chap Cryer..." By that time Bob was candidate for Bradford South and Alan Rye, Bob's former research assistant, was our candidate!

There were also other times when I, as Constituency Labour Party secretary found Bob's support vital in the day-to-day running of the party. I particularly remember with some gratitude his support when the Co-op party had tabled a motion of no confidence in me and the other officers. In doing this they knew that the person who would have to move this resolution at the General Management Committee would be my mother. I made a point of asking Bob to be at the meeting. He duly obliged and, in the way that only he could, tore the resolution and its supporting arguments to shreds. The motion was defeated by a margin of 10:1.

The years following the loss of the Keighley seat in 1983 as a result of the gerrymandered boundary changes were hard. If we couldn't have relied on Bob's help and support, often when other elected representatives had found excuses not to, those times would have been a great deal worse.

---

## 2

## LES HERD

*Former President of the National Union of Dyers,*
*Bleachers and Textile Workers*

I first met Bob when he was standing for the Darwen Constituency in Lancashire for Labour. He made contact with me during the Denby dispute in Baildon. Bob was a very good cricketer and played for the Denby's Mill team at the Tong Park Cricket Club. During the dispute, which lasted from 1963 to 1965, he disassociated himself completely from them – though before leaving, a changing room comment to one of the Directors

With Les Herd, Shipley Market Square, 1974.
(*Telegraph & Argus*)

who played at the Club was: "Come the Revolution, Directors like you will swing from the 'Y' of 'Denby' ".

Typically, he gave very good support to the Denby workers, writing articles for *Tribune* and other newspapers asking for financial and moral support.

Bob also gave support to Trade Councils and Labour candidates during election campaigns, later taking the platform as a Member of Parliament. I remember one occasion when he addressed the people of Shipley standing on the back of a wagon in Market Square. He spoke there frequently in support of the miners during their dispute, and on other occasions arguing on behalf of the Campaign for Nuclear Disarmament. He never refused an invitation to meetings of the Textile Union in Shipley. As Member of Parliament for Keighley he visited the Airedale Dyeing Company on a few occasions, and especially during the election when Gerry Sargent, the District Officer, accompanied him.

Speaking at a textiles support group meeting with Keith Vaz MP, and a woman delegate, Brighton Labour Party Conference fringe meeting, October 1991.

3

# PETER BOOTH

*National Secretary, Transport and General Workers Union Textile Group*

Bob was a stalwart supporter of textile workers in West Yorkshire, and in particular the Bradford wool textile industry and its workforce. During the national wool textile dispute in 1986 he gave tremendous support to the wool textile workers, both in the local Press, in the European Parliament, and later when re-elected in the House of Commons. This was a bitter dispute with the wool textile bosses and Bob declared himself in support of the workers in the very early stages of the dispute and argued the need for a fair wage increase in that year's negotiations. This was the first dispute in the wool industry for over fifty years, and the support of Bob and other local MPs played no small part in giving encouragement to workers who were taking on a very well organised body of employers.

Bob also made a point of speaking in all the textile debates, particularly when the renewal of the Multi-Fibre Arrangement was at issue. He also provided support for the Union's lobbying team during a lobby of Parliament in October 1990, helping delegates to meet with MPs, providing facilities for meetings as well as access to the House of Commons cafeteria. He also assisted with a meeting and afternoon reception during that lobby of Parliament.

Needless to say, Bob spoke extensively in that, and other, debates on this important issue to the industry. In his opening remarks in one of the debates he said how proud he was to represent Bradford, the centre of the wool and textile industry, particularly as he was brought up in Saltaire which, in its heyday, was once the biggest integrated textile mill in Europe, employing 4,000 people.

He also drew attention to the fact that this mill now stood idle, a reflection of the decline of the industry which he witnessed throughout his lifetime. Because of the importance of regulations in the textile industry, Bob consistently argued for the renewal of the Multi-Fibre Arrangements and he was central to the Union's lobbying activities in the House of Commons.

Bob was a member of the 9/601 Branch of the Transport & General Workers' Union, a fact of which the Branch Committee was particularly proud. It was not uncommon to attend a meeting of that Branch and see Bob sitting there as a Branch member, making his points along with those of other Branch members on issues relating to Bradford and the textile industry. Bob was well known to all within the broad Labour movement in West Yorkshire as an MP who would always, where possible, attend and address meetings of Union Branches and Trade Councils as well as local Labour Party meetings.

In addition to the meetings he addressed organised by the Shipley Trades Council, he was also well known to members of the Bradford Trades Council, Keighley Trades Council, and the Otley and Aireborough Trades Council. Speaking on many of the important issues of the day to the Labour movement, he influenced many within the movement during that period on matters central to the advancement of socialism and to the strengthening of working class organisations throughout West Yorkshire.

To those of us who knew Bob, through both the NUDB&TW and the Textile Trades Group of the TGWU, he will always be remembered as a hard-working MP, a Labour activist, and a friend.

# CHAPTER 8

# EUROPE: BOB CRYER, MEP

## 1

## JEAN CROMAR

*Secretary and personal assistant to Bob Cryer,*
*MEP for Sheffield, Chesterfield and North East Derbyshire*

I first met Bob in August 1984 when he interviewed me for the position
of his secretary/personal assistant although I had previously heard him
speak a couple of times in Sheffield. I was excited, though somewhat
apprehensive, when he offered me the job. Bob envisaged the job as not
only providing support to himself but also to the wider Labour movement
and that philosophy was put into effect throughout his period as Euro MP.

### SELECTION

Bob was selected for Sheffield, Chesterfield and North East Derbyshire
Constituency on Monday 9 January 1984. There were two main
candidates, the other being Roger Barton, the favourite of the Sheffield
Establishment for the nomination.

Bob stood on an anti-market ticket. As a member of the Labour Common
Market Safeguards Committee he supported its view that membership had
been extremely damaging and that we could not solve our problems as long
as we continued to endure the burden of membership. It considered that
membership had done enormous damage to our country, with the loss of
hundreds of thousands of jobs in British industry, prompting the huge
flood of manufactured imports, imposing an unfair burden on the British
taxpayer, unnecessarily pushing up food costs, disrupting our trading
relations around the world and depriving us of control over our own trade,
industrial, agricultural, monetary and regional policies.

His election address endorsed the position reflected in the 1983 Labour
Party Election Manifesto and reiterated in the 1984 Labour Manifesto
for the EEC Elections:

> The next Labour Government, committed to radical, socialist policies for
> reviving the British economy, is bound to find continued membership a
> most serious obstacle to the fulfilment of those policies. In particular the
> rules of the Treaty of Rome are bound to conflict with our strategy for

Bob with Peter and Jean Cromar on the deck of a ferry at Hull on the way to Strasbourg, September 1986.

economic growth and full employment, our proposals on industrial policy and for increasing trade, and our need to restore exchange controls and to regulate direct overseas investment. Moreover, by preventing us from buying food from the best sources of world supply, they would run counter to our plans to control prices and inflation.

For all these reasons British withdrawal from the Community is the right policy for Britain – to be completed well within the lifetime of the Parliament. That is our commitment. But we are also committed to bring about withdrawal in an amicable and orderly way, so that we do not prejudice employment or the prospect of increased political and economic co-operation with the whole of Europe.

Bob felt one of the reasons he was selected was because the constituency party believed that he would not change his mind after he was elected.

## THE CAMPAIGN

During the campaign public meetings were held throughout the constituency including one organised by the Young Socialists in Attercliffe; a meeting in Heeley at which the Chair of the Labour Party, Eric Heffer, spoke; an Asian meeting at the Mandela Building organised by Central Constituency; and a meeting at Tupton Village Hall, Chesterfield. Despite these efforts it was not easy to generate public interest in the election.

At the meeting of the Euro Constituency on 3 June 1984, Bob reported that there had been a lack of publicity for any of the statements that he had so far made in the campaign and he hoped that greater interest would be taken in the campaign by the local media in the remaining days of the campaign.

Bob was elected Euro MP for the Sheffield, Chesterfield and North East Derbyshire Constituency on 14 June 1994 and at the first meeting of the Euro Constituency after his election, Bob thanked colleagues for the excellent work undertaken by the Party despite the lack of interest from the wider Labour movement and the generally lacklustre campaign that had been fought across the country. He was pleased though that he had the opportunity through visits to working men's clubs and other institutions to meet many of the electorate during the course of the election. He believed the result showed a clear shift to Labour and locally had shown the success of the campaign waged by the Party. He paid particular tribute to the agent, Jim Mason, and to Chris Prescott for carrying a large part of the burden of the campaign.

## FINANCE AND THE EUROPEAN CONSTITUENCY PARTY

The Sheffield European CLP had no funds when the 1984 Euro Election took place. The money provided by the EEC for election purposes was mostly spent nationally and only a small grant of £200 plus subsidised election addresses were provided by the Labour Party to constituencies. Consequently a large sum of money had to be found in a short period of time, which put a great strain on the finances of all eight CLPs.

The election campaign had cost over £8,000. Each of the eight constituencies making up the Euro Constituency had been asked for £600 for election funds but only £3,000 had been collected in July. As a result of our inability to raise the amount required, an interest-free loan of £2,000 was made to the constituency by Bob. This loan was not repaid until July 1985. The view of the Euro CLP was that it would be far better to have sufficient funds in hand to be able to fight the next election adequately without having to call on CLPs for a large sum of money at short notice, or having to request the candidate to provide a loan to pay outstanding bills.

The constituency recognised that if it had to rely on a loan from a potential candidate this could set an unhealthy precedent in view of the party's broader commitment to selection of the best candidate irrespective of their individual financial circumstances. It agreed therefore that it would be wise to build up the organisation's funds over the next five years in preparation for the 1989 Euro Election. It was agreed

Ann and Bob in the grounds of the European Assembly Buildings at Strasbourg, making a film of his work for his European Constituency Party.

that the annual affiliation fee for CLPs should be £100 per annum from 1 January 1985.

Following Bob's election as MP for Bradford South, his extra salary – a result of being both a Euro MP and a UK MP – was split equally between Sheffield Euro Constituency and Bradford South Constituency. The Sheffield share was paid directly to the Euro CLP and meant that the financial call on CLPs was less at the 1989 Euro Election.

The financial strategy was successfully achieved. There was £11,600 in the account for the 1989 Election.

Bob did not seek re-election to the European Assembly in 1989 as he had been re-elected to Parliament for Bradford South in the 1987 General Election. The Euro Constituency held its selection conference on 6 December 1987 and Roger Barton was selected.

## THE OFFICE AND THE LABOUR MOVEMENT

My first task was to organise an office. Bob was very keen for the office to be not only accessible but also visible. He favoured a shop front, but it was not possible to find one suitable. A temporary office was set up in Sheffield Town Hall for the first few months before a permanent office was established on the Third Floor, 48/62 Pinstone Street, Sheffield. Bob had this rewired, decorated and carpeted following alterations which were carried out by Sheffield City Council, who provided this accommodation. The facilities of the office, including typing, duplicating and photo-copying, were available to the wider Labour movement. Not only was this location central for the movement, it was also very handy for Bob and Ann to indulge their passion for traditional high tea at Tuckwoods on Surrey Street.

In addition, the Sheffield District Labour Party provided a great deal of useful information and research work to assist Bob's work in the Assembly, and were paid a suitable sum of money to compensate the amount of time which the secretary of the District Labour Party had to spend on this work. The amount paid was £3,200 in the first year, rising to £5,000 per annum in later years. Following a request from the officers of the Sheffield District Labour Party, Bob employed Roger Barton directly as research worker from the beginning of 1989 and therefore there was no contribution to Sheffield District Labour Party for research in that year.

All members of the British Labour Group were allocated a sum of money each year known as 'Euro Days Money' which was available to constituency parties and other sympathetic organisations in the Labour movement, for promoting socialism. All publicity material, advertisements, leaflets, etc., had to contain a reference to sponsorship by the British Labour Group of the EEC Assembly. The sort of activities covered included hire of premises, publicity material, typesetting and printing costs, hire of the Labour Party bus and campaigning efforts, but the proposed expenditure had to be submitted to the office beforehand for approval by the treasurer of the British Labour Group. All proposals had to be detailed and payment was only made on original invoices.

The money was useful for activities of a campaigning nature and was provided by the Socialist Group of the European Assembly. Bob tried to ensure that there was a reasonable distribution throughout the whole of the constituency. The total sum allocated was £6,750 and was used to support a wide range of activities. Among the many projects sponsored perhaps the most visible and significant was a grant of £1,150 towards the purchase and running costs of the Hillsborough bus, which was used for campaign work in the Labour movement. Many organisations gained support from Bob's imaginative use of this money to develop their campaigns on a broad range of issues including action against unemployment, international solidarity, support of those involved in long running and bitter industrial disputes, cultural events and the peace movement.

Bob also made a payment of £3,200 to the Euro Constituency for research services during 1988. In addition, following my election to Sheffield City Council in 1987, Bob's support was not only in terms of time off for Council duties but also he continued to pay my full salary so that my attendance allowances were donated to the Euro Constituency.

In 1989 £4,000 Information Money was made available but was subject to a European Court decision which expressly excluded any expenditure on election purposes. The money was used in Sheffield, Chesterfield and North East Derbyshire through advertising in *The Star* newspaper. It had to be spent before the end of January. The advertisements highlighted the need for better childcare in Britain and the fact that most of the other countries in the Common Market spent more on under-5 provision than Britain while women also received more child and maternity benefits, plus longer maternity leave in other Common Market countries.

As I mentioned earlier, Bob wanted the office facilities, including my time, to be available to the wider Labour movement. A large number of organisations made use of these facilities. These included five of the constituency parties, over 20 Labour Party branches, several Trade Union organisations, Labour CND, Miners' Support Groups, Menwith Peach Camp, Campaign Group, LCC-Tribune Group and Sheffield Campaign Against Racism.

## THE EUROPEAN ECONOMIC COMMUNITY

Bob had strong opinions on the institutions and language of the EEC. He objected to the word 'Europe' being used when it referred to the Common Market, when there were 40 countries in Europe but only 10 in the Common Market. (Spain and Portugal entered later.) Bob did not agree with the word 'Parliament', preferring to use the word 'Assembly' because it only passed an opinion, whereas he argued that a Parliament is a legislative body that has real impact on people's lives.

When Bob was elected as European MP in 1984 Britain paid £3,081 million into the EEC budget. Along with his colleagues in the British Labour Group (BLG) he began to articulate some hard hitting criticisms. The principal objections were:

- UK fourth-poorest member of EC but made second-biggest contribution to budget.
- UK and West Germany were the only net contributors to the budget.
- Two-thirds of EEC budget spent on agriculture while only one-eighth spent directly on Europe's 13 million unemployed people.
- The UK gets less back – in 1982 we received only £791m or 11% of CAP payments.

Despite these objections, and the particular focus on the inequities surrounding the operation of the Common Agricultural Policy (CAP) in 1985, a new budget was passed with an increased amount for CAP at 72% of the total budget.

The British Labour Group produced a discussion paper in October 1986, setting out its views, which Bob supported. They considered the main problems facing the EEC and citizens of the member states were:

- Massive unemployment, then at least 15 million.
- The number of people living in poverty, well over 30 million.
- The CAP, which had led to artificially high food prices, huge surpluses and the destruction of millions of tons of food. This had led to an inequitable distribution of contributions to the European Community's Budget and to problematical relations with the Third World and with other countries outside the European Communities due to the inadequacy of its help for developing countries.

The paper pointed out that the Treaty of Rome, on which all Community decisions were founded, is based on two contradictory beliefs: on the one hand, that the creation of a large free market and the removal of all barriers to competition will automatically solve the problems of industry and raise the standard of life of industrial workers, and, on the other hand, that agriculture can only flourish within a highly subsidised and

Bob Cryer MEP for Sheffield and North Derbyshire (fourth from right) on a visit
to Stocksbridge Steel with Norman West, MEP (second from left) and Jean
Cromar (third from left), 1986.
(*Jean Cromar*)

protectionist system. This confusion of principles had produced the worst
of both worlds: rising unemployment in industry and the waste of
resources in agriculture. The Treaty, therefore, placed enormous obstacles
in the way of any government which sought to plan the use of resources
to deal with the problems of the new technological age and which was
determined to bring down unemployment and to end waste.

The document further argued that the CAP had raised food prices to
a level far higher than they need be and to the severe detriment of
consumers, especially pensioners, the unemployed and the low paid. It
had encouraged – at enormous cost – the creation of huge mountains
of unsaleable food and huge lakes of unsaleable wine. It had contributed
to the undermining of Third-World agriculture – thereby, albeit unwit-
tingly, adding to the problems of famine which it then sought to resolve
by the dumping of EC surpluses. By demonstrating these outcomes of
the existing policy framework they gave a clear indication that the time
for change in agricultural policy had long since arrived. What was needed
was a policy that gave preference to the needs of consumers, the family
farm and the countryside user rather than to the demands of big farmers,
agribusiness and large food conglomerates.

The paper supported the re-structuring of the European Budget with a far larger proportion going to the regional and social funds, to development and food aid for the developing countries, for increased spending on the environment, public health and consumer protection, and for energy and technological research. This would necessitate a massive and progressive reduction in spending on the CAP. All of this would be necessary because the existing spending on non-agricultural policy had only a marginal effect on the economic problems of the European Communities.

In addition the paper opposed the proposals for a so-called European Union which was designed to transfer more and more economic and social decisions from the national parliaments to European institutions acting on a majority vote. There was a fundamental belief in each country having the right to carry out policies it believes to be in the best interests of its people. Any increase in the powers of the European Parliament was opposed and there was a call for the restoration to national parliaments of the right to make final decisions on any proposed EC legislation. In particular it opposed Britain joining the European Monetary System (EMS) as this would reduce the ability of a future Labour Government to control exchange rates and the value of the pound.

Bob was very pleased with this discussion paper as he was a committed anti-marketeer and continued to campaign for Britain's withdrawal from the EEC whilst playing as full and vigorous a part as possible on behalf of working people as long as we remained a member of the EEC. He believed membership had damaged the country. A common market based on private enterprise and capitalism was bound to be constantly at odds with the principles of socialism.

He was, therefore, very disappointed when, after six months' waiting to hear the views of the National Executive Committee (NEC) on the document, the British Labour Group received a telegram advising them that it would be best not to distribute the paper at that time.

In 1989 Bob was concerned about the watering down of Labour Party policy over the Common Market. Labour's policy, which was contained in the document 'Campaigning for a Fairer Britain' passed by the Labour Party Conference, made it clear the Labour retained the right of withdrawal. He argued that Labour must retain the right of withdrawal and express a clear reservation on this in the manifesto being drawn up by the EEC socialist parties.

In his House of Commons days Bob was constantly plaguing Ministers with a barrage of questions and he was no different in the European Parliament; ever present at Question Time prying and prodding and generally trying to make life as uncomfortable as possible for the Commission and Council. He found debates in Strasbourg extremely flabby – a succession of set pieces rather than an interchange of ideas.

## FOOD SURPLUSES AND FAMINE

One of the reasons for Bob's opposition to the Common Market was the Common Agricultural Policy which sucked up three-quarters of the budget. The bias in favour of agriculture discriminated heavily against Britain. He said it had been demonstrated, time after time, that reform of the CAP was impossible because of too many vested interests in maintaining the status quo. Reform was an illusion with representative after representative from France, Ireland and West Germany pontificating about how vital the CAP was to their farmers.

Bob considered the CAP to be obscene, propping up bulging grain and meat warehouses, ever expanding butter mountains and wine lakes when there was famine in many parts of the world.

The stockpiles of food at the end of 1884 were:

|  | *1,000 tonnes* |
|---|---|
| Butter | 1,042 |
| Skimmed milk | 896 |
| Beef | 500 |
| Hard wheat | 782 |
| Ordinary wheat | 3,730 |
| Barley | 1,160 |
| Rye | 320 |

A reply to one of Bob's questions revealed the cost simply of storing some of the various food mountains in 1984 was:

| Skimmed milk and butter | £895 million |
|---|---|
| Beef and veal | £490 million |
| Cereals | £186 million |

The total cost for all food storage was £1,631 million and the actual value of the food was over £5,000 million.

There was also a tobacco mountain which cost £17 million to store in 1984 whilst farmers in Italy were being paid £3,310 per ton to produce it.

Bob was angry about the bulging wheat warehouses of the Common Market compared to the pitiful supplies of food to Ethiopia and other countries of Central Africa.

One major cause of concern in 1984 was the famine in Ethiopia which evoked an enormous humanitarian response from people all over the country. Anger at the obscenity of bulging EEC grain warehouses compared to the famine in Ethiopia was widely felt. Bob received over fifty letters on the issue and two petitions were sent to the Assembly President as part of the wave of concern and protests. Well before the general expression of concern, Bob wrote to the Commissioner for Agriculture asking him to make arrangements for the food transfer. The letter was transferred to the Commissioner for Development at the beginning of September but a reply was not received until 22 November. Some money was allocated for EEC food aid, about £15 million, compared to £200 million which the Commission had allocated to increasing the butter mountain in July.

The Sheffield Euro Constituency were also angry about the massive stockpiles of food whilst there was famine elsewhere and passed the following resolution:

> This Constituency deplores the spending of thousands of millions of pounds on storing 'mountains' of food and in destroying surpluses, while vast numbers of people are starving to death in North Africa and the Third World and further moves that this food be used for relief of starvation in famine areas, irrespective of the politics of the Governments of the countries involved.

The British Labour Group also put a resolution to the European Assembly expressing distress at the human suffering whilst there were massive stockpiles of food in Europe, asking for food to be released and sent to the famine areas.

Some of this surplus food was distributed in Britain but there were several complaints about the chaotic nature of the food distribution, principally butter, which was made in Sheffield. This was not to criticise the charities which undertook distribution but the Tory Government for placing the burden on them in the first place. For instance Age Concern had said it cost them £175,000 to administer the distribution of food and they were not prepared to take part in any such scheme again unless they were compensated. Bob said it emphasised the Tories' detestation of local authorities who are well organised to distribute foodstuffs to the most deprived but who were ignored. The distribution failed to make any significant reduction in the food piles.

The EEC set up a committee of 12 to inquire into food surpluses. All but one had financial interests in farming. The British Labour Group set up its own committee of inquiry into the food stocks and produced a campaigning handbook, *No to the Food Mountains*.

## COAL AND STEEL

A lot of families in the Sheffield Euro Constituency area were affected by the Miners' Strike which had been ongoing for some months when Bob was elected, and were suffering hardship. A resolution of support was narrowly defeated in the Assembly. Bob was furious about this because if all the members of the Socialist Group had troubled to turn up it would have been won.

Nevertheless, members of the British Labour Party who work in the EEC donated £150 to the Sheffield Toy Mountain, which was organised by the Sheffield Centre Against Unemployment.

The British Labour Group worked very hard to get an inquiry set up into the strike and particularly the policing aspects. They got the necessary number of signatures for such an inquiry but the right wing sabotaged it. When three names were submitted for carrying out the inquiry they were all defeated in the vote at the plenary session. Hence, although there was an inquiry properly constituted, the Assembly would not vote for it to operate. Bob felt that this was an indication of the fruitless nature of the claim that somehow if we wait long enough the EEC could all be changed to a socialist venture.

Sheffield was a steel town and had been badly affected by closures – 20,000 job losses between 1979 and 1984 – and Bob believed the UK had been made to shoulder an unfair share of the burden. Italy, for example, increased its capacity.

Applications for redundancy pay whereby the European Coal and Steel Community, precursor of the Common Market, made up the wages of redundant steel workers for a period of time to the level of steel earnings made in 1980, still had to be decided in 1984, when Bob became the Euro MP. He was very angry about the slowness of the cumbersome bureaucracy instituted by the EEC. The issue was complicated by the fact that the scheme only applied to firms paying the levy and consequently firms which provided services or goods to the steel industry, even though of vital importance, did not necessarily qualify.

The announcement by British Steel that Tinsley Park works was to close was another massive blow to the manufacturing base in Sheffield. Bob was angry that Common Market policies, backed by the Tory Government, had eroded the once powerful base of the Steel City of the United Kingdom. The latest closure, for example, involved the loss of a modern plant, Tinsley Park, built in 1963, so it was not just a question of cutting back on obsolete equipment and re-investing.

Bob proposed the following resolution at the British Labour Group:

> The British Labour group expresses deep concern at the announcement by British Steel that Tinsley Park Works is to close with the loss of 800 jobs, urges British Steel to reconsider this decision and urges the Commission to provide financial support if necessary to maintain this modern and efficient plant, especially in view of the fact that the United Kingdom steel industry has already lost double the number of jobs compared to the steel industries of other Member states.

The resolution was passed unanimously and copies sent to British Steel and to the Commissioner in charge of Industry, Mr Narjes. Bob also placed a resolution down on the Agenda of the Assembly for consideration by the appropriate committee.

But, in 1985, the Commission had in mind yet further cutbacks in the EEC steel industry and by the end of 1985 they proposed that financial support for the steel industry throughout the Common Market would be ended. Nonetheless, Bob felt that the Commission should be confronted with the consequences of their damaging policies of cutting back on capacity and continued to press the case for the retention of Tinsley Park works.

At the same time, the EEC agreed to send home 350 officials on £20,000 per year until they reached retirement age, to allow room for 350 Spanish and Portuguese officials. Bob was very critical of this and opposed it.

The explanation Bob gave for his vote is as follows:

> My comrade put down a resolution, as I put down several resolutions, to relate these payments to steel workers and the payments that steel workers get. The steel workers in Sheffield and elsewhere won't find it very amusing to hear that comfortably-off, well-paid people find it funny that there should be a suggestion that Commission officials should go home for a few years to allow other people from Spain and Portugal to come in on their redundancy terms. The Conservatives feel that the redundancy terms are so modest, indeed they do!
>
> In Sheffield the 500 workers facing the dole queue at Sheffield Forge Masters and the 100 workers facing the dole queue at Sheffield Tinsley Park, a 20-year-old factory, will ask the question: "Since I have been put on the dole by a combination of Commission policies and Tory Government policies, why can't I have the same terms and conditions as they dole out for Commission officials?" And I say this, that if Commission officials were made to retire on the same terms and conditions that they give to steel workers, they would not be so damned keen to get home and retire early. So I am going to oppose this wretched instance of double standards which is very typical of the whole rotten Common Market.

Many people in ISERBS courses, paid for from the Common Market Steel Levy for redundant steelworkers, experienced difficulties due to delay in payments and Bob was able to take this up by means of questions to the Department of Trade and Industry. This was a continuing thorny issue. These delays give the lie to the claim by the EEC that they were concerned about the social consequences of steel closures brought about as a result of decisions on the steel industry made between the Common Market and Thatcher's Government. Bob believed that the payments were deliberately delayed in order to use them as a lever in negotiations with the UK Government.

It was not until July 1988 that Bob was able to report that the ISERBS payments to the redundant steel workers had now been made – fifteen months after the workers were made redundant.

Bob was also, eventually, successful in obtaining redundancy terms under the Treaty of Paris for several workers who were not employed by Tinsley Park works but who were directly involved in production.

He received representations in 1984 over the increasing price of scrap and the damage that this had been doing to the steel industry which depended, particularly in the Sheffield area, on the supply of reasonably priced scrap as a raw material. It was also claimed that scrap merchants were deliberately creating artificial shortages in order to increase prices. Whatever the validity of these claims, Bob made presentations to Commissioner Narjes and the Commission submitted a scheme to the Council of Ministers in which the European Federation of Scrap Merchants guaranteed scrap supplies to the industry and all orders were copied to the Commission in order to ensure that there was scrutiny over the system.

## THE SINGLE MARKET

In 1985 Jacques Delors, the President of the Commission, announced that the internal market, with the removal of all barriers, would be completed by 1992. Bob was never a supporter of this. He did not go along with the idea that the removal of internal barriers was a solution to the, by then, fourteen million people on the dole.

He was concerned about the control over the movement of animals and was worried that the United Kingdom would cease to be rabies free. Also, without any scrutiny of animals at customs barriers there could be no guarantees regarding the standard of treatment, and animals in transit would suffer even more than they already did.

Then there was the problem of drug abuse. With the removal of customs barriers it would mean that there would be no limit to the complete freedom of movement of hard and soft drugs and the potential for more young people to be caught up in the drug world.

Bob quoted a report from the Society of Civil and Public Servants in which they made specific reference to the massive increase in drug smuggling. The indications were that between 1979 and 1985 the smuggling of drugs had increased as follows: heroin, 680%; cocaine, 210%; cannabis, 25%. The results of successful drug smuggling were illustrated by the 335% increase in heroin addiction over the same period. He believed the removal of controls would allow a much greater interest in drug smuggling and an increase in heroin addiction.

He was also worried about the increase in lorry weights and the effect on safety and the environment. An undertaking was made by the Secretary of State for Transport in the House of Commons that the United Kingdom weight of 38 tonnes would be kept. Removal of barriers would mean that lorries of up to 44 tonnes would be thundering along the United Kingdom's roads.


## PEACE

Bob was very committed to the peace movement and was horrified by the attack on Libya. He was therefore delighted when the British Labour Group passed a resolution after the use of United Kingdom bases by American planes for the bombing of Libya. They condemned the "outrageous act of aggression committed by the armed forces of the USA against Libya and the callous and needless loss of life and injury inflicted on innocent Libyan citizens".

In addition the Assembly reacted against the bombing raid and a resolution was adopted stating that the Assembly was "deeply incensed" at the air attacks on Tripoli, Benghazi and Libyan military installations. "The raids," said the resolution, "were a flagrant violation of international law and the deaths caused were to be deplored." At the same time the resolution condemned all forms of international terrorism but felt that the American method was the wrong way to combat it.

Bob was a member of the EEC Peace Group which organised the demonstration when Reagan spoke in the Assembly. The Group was later successful in promoting a resolution in favour of the United Nations nuclear Non-Proliferation Treaty. The Group also organised meetings on the theme 'Is Western Europe to become a Military Superpower?' Bob attached great importance to this Group since it was the only section of the Assembly devoted to promoting nuclear disarmament and peace. The British Labour Group formed the largest part of the Peace Group.

## THE CONSTITUENCY AND THE EUROPEAN ECONOMIC COMMUNITY

A lot of inquiries to the Office were about getting grants from the EEC which Bob felt had an undeserved reputation for providing money for all sorts of projects. Rarely were 100% grants approved. Under the Social Fund only 50% was allowed at that time. Consequently, other additional sources had to be found, usually the local authority. Bob was very happy to try to obtain grants. He saw it as being some of our money being returned.

During his time in Europe Bob had meetings with representatives of Sheffield City Council, Chesterfield and North East Derbyshire District Council on local authority applications to the EEC and potential EEC assistance. He organised several delegations from Sheffield to Brussels in order to meet Commission representatives over the Lower Don Valley Scheme and the Technology campus. He also organised a visit of the Transport Committee in 1985 to South Yorkshire to see the, then, excellent transport system.

Applications were always vastly oversubscribed. The Fund consisted of only 4% of the EEC budget. In 1985/86 the application of the existing rules was tightened because other member states complained about the United Kingdom being so successful in the past. New technology had to be an aspect of training schemes though this was not previously the case. The Government strongly denied the claim that they had tried to influence the Commission to support MSC schemes rather than local authority applications. Bob did not believe this to be the case.

Bob spoke at a large number of meetings in the constituency. A lot of these meetings reflected his interests in the peace movement and transport. These included debates at Sheffield University on the issue of the arms trade with the third world and on Radio Sheffield on unilateral nuclear disarmament; an International Socialist Teachers' Conference in Sheffield on peace and education; many local CND groups; a conference promoting the Midland Main Line; East Midlands Airport Committee on airport development. He also spoke at Chesterfield and Dronfield May Day rallies and held meetings with the Tinsley Park Shop Stewards, Stocksbridge Joint Shop Stewards' Committee, Shardlow's Retired Workers' Club, the Coalfield Communities Campaign, a pensioners' group at Eckington and numerous other local groups. In addition Bob made many visits to local firms. These included Tyzack's in Sheffield to see the apprentice training scheme and Stocksbridge Steel.

In September 1986 Bob asked me to go to Strasbourg to see the Assembly in action and since we went by car he offered to take Peter, my husband, along as well for the marginal additional cost. The trip was very interesting since Bob arranged for us to attend meetings of the British Labour Group as well as the sessions of the Assembly when the report on Declining Industrial Regions was tabled. His offer to us to put any gift and souvenir shipping directly into the boot of his car was one which brought a smile to his face on our return to Sheffield where he complained at the sluggish performance of his car on the return journey. On opening the boot he discovered that our passion for continental beers had found expression in the purchase of about 30 bottles of Alsace lager which added considerably to the weight and explained the car's seeming lethargy. He never did look at us in quite the same way again!

---

## 2

## MICHAEL McGOWAN
*MEP (Leeds) 1984–*

I first met Ann and Bob Cryer at the Thornton's in Manningham more than 30 years ago. It was the annual New Year's Eve party of the Bradford Left at the home of Jean and Peter Thornton and I had been taken along by Dorothy and Joe Greenald.

It was an occasion of Bradford politics and humour, a night away from base for the friends of Bradford Left Club, where support for CND was taken for granted and everyone present know that the Woodcraft Folk were not apprentice carpenters.

I listened with some awe to a confidence, directness, and vitality that never waned over the years I got to know Bob Cryer during campaigns in the peace movement, my work at the Co-op and later in the European Parliament.

Bob was batting on his home wicket, holding forth with his ironic sense of humour on everything from world politics to Yorkshire cricket which he liked to talk about, knew about and even played.

From that first meeting and right through his stint in the European Parliament, Bob always had a good tale to tell. I recall his account of

Michael McGowan (left) and Alice McMahon MP, planting a tree in memory of
Bob Cryer at Menwith Hill, 1995.

the selection conference for Bradford South when a woman delegate asked him who ironed his shirts. Always with a ready answer, Bob said that Ann ironed his shirts but he pressed his trousers. When the next budding candidate, a well known Bradford councillor, appeared, he was also asked who ironed his shirts, he replied: "I arn't quite sure, I just get 'em out the wardrobe".

Although I never met Bob's father, I know he was secretary of the Co-op Party in Shipley and that Bob had that privileged background where the Co-op influence played a part. When I worked for the Co-op in Leeds, I invited Bob to speak at many of our conferences and he never failed to raise the temperature.

I did meet Bob's mother when I spoke at a meeting in Shipley Labour Party and have a vivid recollection of the powerful presence of a dignified and erect elderly woman.

Bob was vintage CND, instinctively against the Bomb, a familiar figure at Menwith Hill. Always the superb propagandist, he relished the march, the demo and the political platform. His message was always clear, simple and uncomplicated. He was the master of the art of street and mass politics, now regrettably out of fashion.

After he lost his Keighley seat in the House of Commons, Bob became the Member of the European Parliament for Sheffield where he was active in the all-party Peace Group and most at home amongst Green and Communist members.

Bob did not hit it off with his old anti-Market ally, Barbara Castle, who was leader of the British Labour Members and was annoyed that Bob insisted on calling the European Parliament the European Assembly.

He obviously missed the atmosphere of the House of Commons with its more confrontational style of debating and never really came to terms with the European Parliament where seeking agreement and consensus is an essential feature of the work.

When not with Ann, Bob was often a loner. He was highly disciplined, liked to know the score, was a man of routine, and did not like to eat too late.

Bob was always good company, a wonderful story teller, and a merciless leg puller. Any event, a meeting or a journey, was more interesting and felt more important because Bob Cryer was there.

There are so many over the years who fought elections and campaigns and then, with pride, said it all: "I worked for Bob Cryer".

## CHAPTER 9

# "CAN I SHAKE YOUR HAND, MAN, FOR HAVING SUCH A SMASHING CAR?"

### ALAN PETFORD
*Nephew of Bob Cryer*

Bob's enthusiasm for cars began early and lasted a lifetime. Glimpses have come down to us of a little boy fascinated by all forms of transport, the proud possessor of an early and impressive 'Tri-ang' steam roller, iron shod and boilered in tubular cardboard, which rolled over many miles of domestic carpet. There still survives a rather solid wooden lorry with radiator detail carefully drawn on by its seven or eight year-old owner and inscribed 'Leland'. There was a clockwork caterpillar tractor of American manufacture and a vaguely remembered 'Schuko' car of some sophistication. Truly the child was father of the man.

An eclectic collection of cigarette cards, donated by heavy-smoking relatives, provided a conspectus of the contemporary car scene and under-scored the bewildering variety of motor manufacturers in immediate pre and post-war Britain. There were trips in an uncle's elegant Daimler; but no car at home, for although Bob's father had owned an Austin he rather provokingly refused to drive it.

Bob has written about how, at the age of eighteen, he acquired his first car:

> In January 1953, behind the Gaumont cinema, Saltaire, near Bradford, a large black saloon lay gently rusting. Snow covered the long bonnet, filling the gaps between the separate wings and stood six inches deep on the running boards and roof. It had one headlight, the other side had only a stem rather like a toothless socket.

Prophetically the car was an Armstrong Siddeley; a 1934 twenty horse power, long chassis seven seater landaulette to be precise. Sporting the distinctive pointed Armstrong radiator grille, a coach-built body and equipped with the Wilson pre-selector box, YG 6984 epitomised the dignified saloons with which Armstrong Siddeley had made their mark with the upper middle classes in pre-war England. By the early fifties these cars, with their dated styling, modest performance and heavy fuel con-sumption were to be had at genuinely bargain prices. To those able to do their own repairs they offered a cheap way into motoring, and so began Bob's lifetime of owner maintenance. Before the year was out, the thirsty

Bob's first car, an Armstrong-Siddeley 20 h.p., long chassis seven seater Landaulette. "It had one headlight, the other side had only a stem rather like a toothless socket."

twenty horse power landaulette had been replaced by a more economical twelve horse power model which in turn gave way to a 1937 Fourteen Saloon.

Running cars like this as a university student of limited means was only possible with the most stringent economies. The cars were bought cheaply, usually had significant faults and demanded constant running repairs. Necessity is a good teacher and it was through necessity that Bob acquired his impressive knowledge of car mechanics. Private hire work, notably weddings for which large pre-war saloons were well adapted, secured space at a local garage in Shipley. Here Bob undertook increasingly ambitious engineering tasks on his cars. Decoking became a common-place, engine rebuilds were enthusiastically embarked on and suspension overhauls completed; only major bodywork repairs were avoided In later years for Bob the householder, first in Oakworth and latterly in Shipley, a large garage was a priority, and one speedily put to good use. He was never one to run up large garage bills while confining his attention to chrome polish and Turtle Wax. Weeks before his death he had overhauled and refitted the cylinder head on his 346 saloon and was in the process of renovating the rather unusual rear heating system on his Star Sapphire.

By 1961 some fifteen Armstrong Siddeley cars had passed through Bob's hands, and, although he had briefly owned the products of other companies, his attachment to the marque was confirmed. Armstrong Siddeley ownership, begun almost by chance, had become a conviction. As he explained,

> We do not own Armstrong Siddeleys because they have some sort of prestige cum snob value which will make Mrs Jones smart with envy. We run them because they are frequently beautiful cars, because care has gone into their making, because craftsmen have put their skill and expertise into them, because they are smooth, dignified and timeless and because they possess that elusive and so much missed quality of charm.

To these appealing characteristics Armstrongs were soon to add that of obsolescence. In 1958 Armstrong Siddeley Motors had merged with the Bristol Aeroplane Company to form Bristol Siddeley Ltd. Almost immediately the new company obtained profitable aero work with the Ministry of Defence, car sales of the single model then in production, the Star Sapphire, remained disappointingly modest and in the summer of 1960 it was announced that car production would cease. Armstrong Siddeley owners like Bob were faced with a dilemma. Hitherto they had been running cars, albeit often of pre-war vintage, but the products of a company still in business and still interested in providing a service for its erstwhile products. Henceforth, with Armstrong's retreat from the

A 1933 17 h.p. saloon which Bob bought in the late 1950s, photographed outside
15 Albert Road, Saltaire.

car market, Siddeley owners could only contemplate a bleak future of
dwindling spare parts supply, declining company interest and the ultimate
extinction of the breed. Subsequently Bob was scathing about Bristol
Siddeley's decision to concentrate on the aircraft side of the business.
Writing in the *House Magazine* of November 1993, he drew attention to
the manipulation of the Ministry of Defence contracts:

> In the four years 1959 to 1963 these contracts were worth nearly £17 million,
> yielding profits of over £7 million. Following a Select Committee of Public
> Accounts examination in session 1966–67 and a Committee of Inquiry in
> 1968, Bristol Siddeley repaid £4 million. It was a sorry tale of easy pickings
> and soft options.... It was a telling example of how defence expenditure, far
> from stimulating manufacturing industry, actually weakened it, Armstrong
> Siddeley cars, born out of peace, perished on the altar of the Cold War.

Almost as soon as Armstrongs announced that car production would
cease, Bob wrote a letter to *The Autocar* suggesting the formation of an
Armstrong Siddeley Owners' Club. The inaugural meeting was held in
October 1960 at the Arden Hotel, Birmingham, attended by a mere
fourteen enthusiasts. Predictably Bob emerged as secretary and *de facto*
editor of the bulletin, offices to which he soon added that of acting
treasurer.

Bob's 1952 Armstrong Siddeley 'Hurricane' in the process of restoration at his Oakworth home in the early 1980s. When purchased in 1981 the engine "gave barely enough power to clamber aboard the transporter".

As one turns the pages of those first Armstrong Siddeley Owners' Club bulletins it is possible to recapture the now vanished world of early sixties motoring, a world where:

> A 14 h.p. saloon of 1938 in nearly immaculate condition has just been rescued from the breaker's hammer near Shipley. After being kept aside for the consideration of several offers it was eventually sold for £20.

It was a world where the Ten Year Test was not yet too exacting, witness one member's report of a journey in his 1948 Lancaster saloon,

> I met a headwind plus a bumpy road with a loose door catch on the near side front; as you know these doors are hinged at the rear so I have a three door Lancaster at the moment.

This was a situation which Bob as secretary and editor urged fellow members to remedy:

> Mr Cox is keen to have a more normal four door saloon, so if any member has a front nearside door he will be pleased to know.

The early membership lists reveal what a concentration of enthusiastic Armstrong Siddeley owners there was in the environs of Shipley, a testimony to the secretary's vigorous proselytising. These were the members bidden to meet on

> December 20th. at the Rosse Hotel, Bradford Road, Shipley (by Saltaire Roundabout) 8.00 p.m. for a pleasant chat about the marque.

Arranging meetings like this and producing the bulletin, now entitled *Sphinx*, were not Bob's only activities. He organised the production of a rather stylish club radiator badge and, in September 1961, masterminded the first club rally. This was duly reported in *Sphinx*,

> The rally was in fact a fairly stiff Treasure Hunt with a time limit . . . The route proved too difficult for all save police driver Joe Ogden . . . much to the surprise of the Secretary who had negotiated it on a previous occasion, a fact which he stressed with some heat.

And well he might, for of course Bob's Armstrong was his only car, and as such, in daily use. Interestingly, even as early as 1961, some owners of elderly Armstrongs were only bringing them out in fine weather for short trips and clearly found the forty-mile course planned for them by their enthusiastic Club Secretary rather too much. Bob's cars were always for use and he poked gentle fun at the Lagonda fraternity for fair weather motoring in a report of their monthly meeting near Tadcaster at the Olde Sunne Inn at Colton,

> . . . I duly rolled up. Not unnaturally I expected to see a row of shiny Lagondas lightening the gloom outside only to discover a selection of modern tin-ware and a distinguished looking Lea-Francis. Two Lagondas did venture forth later but I am led to understand that Lagonda owners regard them as unsuitable for winter, bringing them out only on gentle summer days. Did Lagonda advertise their product as 'The Summer Car' I wonder?

'Modern tin-ware' was something the Secretary inveighed against in the columns of *Sphinx*, on one occasion observing of the then recently introduced Mini:

> Those dreadful little cars no doubt go very quickly and seem to be driven by brash youths with a tremendous urge to fulfil the death wish, but aesthetically the 7 and the Mini-Minor offend me deeply. I have taken, therefore, a modicum of comfort from the fact that Armstrong Siddeley have ceased production and have not sold out to the all enveloping B.M.C. whose hungry maw would have stamped these tin boxes with a Riley badge, then a Wolseley illuminated sign and then, horror, a Sphinx and pointed tin front.

In addition to penning much of the 'News and Views' column of *Sphinx* Bob wrote articles on individual models and the general history of Siddeley Motors. In a contribution entitled 'The Splendid Fourteen' he admitted:

"In a world of mediocre side-valve engines the 14 was a refreshingly straight-forward o.h.v. of some 1666 ccs." EUM 744 was one of several examples of 'The Fourteen' that Bob owned.

If these motor cars were to be judged solely by performance we should have to be rather harsh, but they had other qualities which gave them a charm not possessed by faster but inevitably noisier breeds.

He had owned several examples of this model and clearly rather liked it, notwithstanding its propensity to develop a serious crack in the engine block:

This, alas, was the main fault on an otherwise pleasant machine... There are many explanations which vary from a severe frost in 1940 to a more simple explanation of a weak block.

Nevertheless he concluded, with all the optimism of affection:

In a world of mediocre side valve engines the 14 was a refreshingly straight-forward o.h.v. of some 1666 ccs.

Combining his interests in cars and the cinema Bob contributed an entertaining series of articles to *Sphinx* under the title of 'Armstrongs on the Screen'. The following excerpt gives the flavour of these pieces.

Recently... I.T.V. re-screened an edition of The Invisible Man series in which the villain shot an accomplice from the comfortable front seat of an Armstrong Siddeley Typhoon. Intending cut-throats might care to note that although the get away will be commendably smooth this model is not

noted for the briskness of its acceleration and the Law will welcome the somewhat lethargic departure.

Inevitably other interests made heavy demands on Bob's time; the publication of *Sphinx* was frequently delayed. On one occasion,

a damaged duplicator and Local Council elections are to blame for this.

he explained. Increasingly it was his growing involvement in the Keighley
and Worth Valley Railway Preservation Society that occasioned delay.
Apologising to members for the tardy production of *Sphinx* and at the
same time exhorting them to support the cause of railway preservation
he wrote:

I always like to think that we Siddeley owners seek the smoothness and silence
in internal combustion which steam always gives.

Obviously something had to give and the June 1964 issue of *Sphinx* was the
last which Bob edited. For a while the future of the club was in doubt but
fortunately others took over. The club was revived and after 1972 became
the principal source of Armstrong Siddeley spares when it purchased the
remaining stock of motor car parts from Bristol Siddeley Ltd.

When Bob bought his 346 Sapphire saloon in 1964 it was simply a large,
well engineered but unfashionable product of defunct manufacture
which had been brought by depreciation within the means of a technical
college lecturer. Ten years on it was a 'classic car'. The Ten Year Test
and subsequent M.O.T. regulations had done their work; British roads
had been cleared of the fascinating range of ageing, if frequently hazar-
dous, machinery that had formerly graced them. By the 1970s, cars
much over ten years old were becoming a rarity, and it was out of this rarity that the classic car movement was born. Restoration and preservation
of old cars, rather than running them on a shoe-string, now became the
order of the day. Bob still used the Sapphire on a regular basis, although
the demands of politics dictated that it was supplemented by more modern
products. These in themselves were an interesting bunch. There was a Hill-
man Imp, manifestly unsuitable for someone of Bob's physical stature,
but chosen on the grounds of fuel economy, engineering ingenuity and
perhaps out of a predilection for lost causes. Then there was a Wartburg,
unbelievably recommended by a neighbour who assured Bob,

I like a car that really performs – and the Wartburg certainly does that.

Ownership proved this encomium an exaggeration and not even its East
European origin could persuade Bob to retain its services for very long.
These experiments in modern car ownership were followed by a buying
policy designed to support the ailing British car industry and subsequent
purchases were all of B.M.C. and later British Leyland manufacture.

The wedding of Jane Cryer to David Kilduff, at Canterbury, December 1990. Patrick Kilduff (left), Bob Cryer (right) and his Armstrong Siddeley Sapphire wedding car (TPW 370).

Meanwhile in 1981 Bob had bought a 1952 Armstrong Siddeley Hurricane specifically for restoration.

> It stood forlornly in the short drive, the rear wings only a gesture, fungus growing healthily on the rear seat and the hood tatty and split. Originally black, the paint had weathered to a dull grey, but the tyres were good and the owner assured me that it ran.

While body renovation was handed over to professionals all the mechanical restoration, with the exception of line-boring the white metal bearings, was done at home. The project took three and a half years and produced a very presentable car which Bob used in the 1990 Norwich Union Classic Car Rally. He took considerable pride not only in the restoration of this car but also in running it. Writing in *Sphinx* about its appeal he said,

> On summer days with the hood down the car is a real pleasure, acceleration and road holding are good and the engine is pleasantly smooth when the hydraulic tappets behave themselves.

Bob had always been rather disparaging about the last model produced by Armstrong Siddeley, the Star Sapphire. Writing in the very first bulletin of the Armstrong Siddeley Owners Club in 1961 he commented on the evolution of the Star from the Sapphire.

> To the regret of many the 3.4 litre engine was bored out to 4 litres, the bonnet was re-shaped (this was extremely well done), two small tail fins were added, the interior was re-vamped and offered in various alarming shades. For all this nearly a thousand extra pounds were charged and it was, therefore, not surprising that no eager queue of would-be purchasers lined up outside the factory gates.

What was more, the Star was only offered with Borg-Warner automatic transmission, thus deserting Armstrong's long allegiance to their most characteristic gearbox, the Wilson pre-selector. Bob had a long-standing affection for the Wilson box and early in his ownership had substituted one for the conventional syncromesh change originally fitted to his Sapphire. Few were the excursions in that car which were not punctuated at some point by a disquisition on the merits of the Wilson pre-selector box, accompanied of course by a demonstration of its refinement. The re-styling, larger engine and automatic transmission put the Star beyond the pale for Bob for many years, until in the summer of 1992 he saw one advertised for sale in apparently pristine condition. Intrigued he went to look. Some weeks later, and at a much reduced price, he was the owner of 278 MRA, a 1959 Star Sapphire saloon, one of only 902 built before car production ceased in 1960. It was not in the pristine condition advertised but was mechanically sound and its bodywork was in much better shape than the now much patched Sapphire. In short it was an Armstrong for daily use. Bob's suspicions of the automatic transmission soon vanished and he became a firm convert, taking great delight in demonstrating the ingenious variable hold control mechanism which is unique to this model. He appreciated the power steering and disc brakes which cope so easily with the car's one and three quarter ton weight and make the Star such an easy car to drive in modern conditions. And drive it he certainly did, rapidly deciding to concentrate his efforts on making this most usable of cars the mainstay of his Armstrong Siddeley collection. A programme of running repairs and gradual improvement was planned to return the car to its original condition. To this end the remains of a Star Sapphire (actually the fifth made) which was rusting in a Dewsbury garage yard was purchased and Bob spent many contented hours at weekends stripping this car down to the bare body shell, bringing home boot-loads of spares from each successful visit.

Maintaining three ageing cars is no easy matter and in his search for spare parts Bob became a habitué of Huddersfield auto jumbles. One sees him

TPW 370 at Bob's home in Shipley.

now, a tall figure, working systematically down the rows of stalls, hunting diligently through boxes of grubby and superannuated car spares in the hope of supplementing his collection of obsolete and unobtainable hexagonal drive sockets, emerging triumphant with the missing 'King Dick' spanner for the Star Sapphire tool kit. Bargain hunting was generally punctuated by a retreat to the George Hotel for lunch, over which he would peruse some recently purchased and arcane piece of motoring literature. Then back to the fray. To the uninitiated this might seem to be a retreat from politics. Not so; he always took his politics with him. On more than one occasion he lectured a recalcitrant stallholder on the errors of privatisation in the coal industry and his pleasure in finding a Russian Oil Products petrol can of 1930s vintage had its political dimension.

The hunt for spare parts frequently took Bob further afield; indeed the further the better, for that allowed a longer journey in one of his Armstrongs. Journeys with Bob were always memorable. Invariably they included a close analysis of the performance of the vehicle in which we were travelling and a potted history of any piece of older machinery that we might happen to pass. But there was more to them than this, much more. One remembers the happy cry of recognition on sighting former Co-operative Society premises, the knowledgeable stream of

LOX 21 restored and ready to take part in the 1990 Norwich Union
Classic Car Rally.

comment called forth by the appearance of a cinema, disused or otherwise, and the running commentary on any defunct railway lines we might meet with. And, increasingly, there was architecture.

Over the years Bob came to value the building inheritance of his native West Riding more and more highly. One of his most often expressed regrets was that he had not done more to protest against the destruction, in the process of post-war rebuilding, of Bradford's Victorian city centre. One of his more entertaining architectural preservation schemes was the rehabilitation of the disused Upper Independent Chapel, Heckmondwike as a museum of motoring lost causes. Soon journeys in search of motor spares became an opportunity to explore the buildings of a different town. Morley is a case in point. Here, one Bank Holiday, a disappointing auto jumble was compensated by an afternoon examining the architectural glories of that much-neglected town. The late classical town hall of 1895 drew forth Bob's enthusiastic praise and provoked harsh comment on the 1974 local government reforms which have done so much to emasculate local democracy in England. And then there were chapels, at least four of them, splendid in their beleaguered glory. For a committed atheist Bob had remarkably catholic sympathies where ecclesiastical buildings were concerned. It surprised many when he spoke warmly in support of the 1994 Pastoral Amendment Measure which gave the Redundant Churches Fund a new name and new financial basis.

> Whatever our views on religion, the fact remains that many churches are a focal and important part of the town or landscape. They are objects of beauty, which were established with great affection both by the patrons who provided the money, and by those who built them. We should not ignore that; whenever possible, we should try to treasure and preserve such churches.

As he motored about England in his Armstrong Siddeleys, increasingly alive to townscape and countryside alike, Bob enjoyed the camaraderie which comes with running an old car. He welcomed those who came to admire his cars, those who wandered over to reminisce, and those who were simply curious. Let us leave him filling up his Hurricane with petrol and chatting genially to a young motor cyclist who had come over to look at the car and whose parting comment was:

> Can I shake your hand, man, for having such a smashing car?

---

*Extract from a letter to Ann Cryer from Peter Wall of Ilkley*

I remember Bob so well from my early days at Cox's [garage]. He was always such fun and we always had a lot of mutual leg-pulling. When one of our mechanics had an accident whilst testing your car, I had the unenviable task of ringing Bob to tell him the bad news. I will remember his reaction as long as I live – "Is anybody hurt?" "No, fortunately," I replied. "Well, no doubt you will lend me a car and repair mine as soon as you can. And don't worry about it." That was typical of a very great man – not many people would have reacted like that.

His climb up the political ladder was an example to us all. His 'style' and his honest beliefs were obviously admired by all sides of The House and he will be missed by countless friends and associates.

# CHAPTER 10

# A PASSIONATE POLITICIAN

## FOR JOHNNY
by John Pudney

Do not despair
For Johnny-head-in-air;
He sleeps as sound
As Johnny underground.

Fetch out no shroud
For Johnny-in-the-cloud;
And keep your tears
For him in after years.

Better by far
For Johnny-the-bright-star,
To keep your head,
And see his children fed.

Bob was extremely fond of Anthony Asquith's 1945 film *The Way To The Stars* in which Michael Redgrave (in a voiceover to Rosamund John reading the poem) reads 'For Johnny'. It was printed in the funeral meeting programme, and Tony Benn read it as part of his graveside oration.

---

## 1

## MAX MADDEN, MP

Bob Cryer was my political ally for more than two decades. His belief in democratic socialism never faltered; in any political debate you could always be confident on which side Bob would be.

Above all Bob was a Yorkshireman. His political principles and his courage to dissent were rooted in Bradford's radical history. (He was also a very useful all-round cricketer who even found an afternoon when a Government Minister to play for the House of Commons team.)

A teacher, Bob took great pride in the educational services pioneered in Bradford. Bob was a passionate politician: he campaigned against the

130

With Barry Seal, MEP for West Yorkshire, and Max Madden MP, for Bradford West, at Bradford City Hall, December 1989.
(*Telegraph & Argus*)

obscenity of nuclear weapons with the same intensity he campaigned for health and safety laws to protect those at work. Yet he was without equal when it came to a knowledge of films and the British film industry.

Although he was admired (and feared) by Ministers for his mastery of parliamentary procedures, Bob was also a very practical man. He respected craftsmanship and worried about Britain's demise as a manufacturing country: he despised how Thatcherism put greater value on those who made money than skilled people who made things.

Bob was a skilled engineer. I remember visiting a Bradford engineering company with him. He asked penetrating questions throughout and finished having an animated discussion with the manager about pistons.

He serviced his own cars including the classic cars he cherished; he was the principal architect in the rescue of the Worth Valley Railway; and he was a vigilant defender of the textile and clothing industries.

Bob and I entered Parliament in 1974. We quickly became close political allies. We both understood the virtues and sins of the Government, first under Wilson and then under Callaghan.

We voted for (and against) that Government more often than many of our Parliamentary colleagues. Bob amazed us when he accepted an invitation from Jim Callaghan to join the Government (most other left-wingers having resigned or been sacked).

Bob was responsible for small businesses. Although he mastered his brief quickly, he soon became frustrated and his resignation from the Government became inevitable.

Many saw his defeat as the MP for Keighley at the 1979 General Election as being equally inevitable. But Bob, always a popular and hardworking MP, beat off the Tory challenge retaining Keighley by a narrow majority. His defeat in the 1983 General Election was largely due to unfavourable boundary changes.

Bob again surprised colleagues by becoming an MEP. As a leading critic of the Common Market, friend and foe speculated about Bob's motives. However much he afterwards laughed off the EEC as "the best job creation scheme ever devised", Tory Ministers lost no chance to taunt Bob about his time in Brussels when he returned to the House of Commons after the 1987 General Election (as the MP for Bradford South).

His selection for Bradford South was controversial. Bob had never been "a favourite son" of the Bradford Labour establishment. There was a determined bid to keep Bob off the shortlist for Bradford South which backfired. Bob won support from people outraged at how he was treated.

The 1987 General Election remains a joyful memory. Pat Wall, denied election as the Labour MP for Bradford North in 1983 as a result of the Labour vote being split, joined Bob and myself in lively election meetings.

We were all elected (Bob's majority being smaller than any had expected) and carried the election campaign into the House of Commons. We all used every parliamentary opportunity to raise the issues of concern in Bradford – poverty, unemployment, the economy and peace – in a national context.

Bob and I had disagreements, too. The fiercest was over the book *Satanic Verses*. Bob, a humanist, never understood the depth of offence the slurs in the book caused many Muslims in Bradford and elsewhere.

While we both condemned the death threat to Rushdie – and called for the outdated blasphemy laws to be abolished – Bob never supported my argument for a new law against incitement to religious hatred.

Bob argued that the right to free speech could not be fettered and those offended by views they did not like should be big enough to shrug off their anger.

It was a tragedy that Pat Wall's parliamentary contribution was cut short by his early death; and a few years later for Bob to be killed on the M1.

Bob would not have been happy – or silent – in Tony Blair's New Labour.

He would have been angry at the readiness to jettison the principles and values which brought him into the Labour Party in the pursuit of office and power.

His anger would have been heightened by the unwillingness or inability of the New Labour leadership to spell out what they want to do with the power they seek.

If Bob were alive I have no doubt his voice – inside and outside the House of Commons – would have been raised on behalf of those he always represented and never forgot. The men and women who by hand and by brain create the wealth of our country and who deserve a fair share of that wealth for themselves and their families!

---

## 2

## JOHN CRYER
*Journalist and Son*

When television cameras started to roll in the House of Commons in 1989, the intention was that the Tory, Ian Gow (a favourite of Mrs Thatcher) should be the first MP before an expectant public. Mr Gow's moment of history did not materialise, however, as Bob Cryer got in first by opening a debate on the sessional orders. As Tam Dalyell wrote in his obituary of Bob five years later, "Had it been almost any other member, he or she would have been muttered out of the Chamber by colleagues who thought that the member speaking was simply concerned with publicity. Cryer was heard in silence and got away with it because he had done the same thing many times before, especially late at night when the Press gallery was sparsely populated and before the days when cameras were present."

It is worth recalling the Bradford South MP's words in full:

> I understand that, as with other sessional orders, this one on the Metropolitan Police is debatable. It is the right of honourable members to exercise that function in the debates of the house, whether there are television cameras

Bob as a delegate from the Shipley Co-op Party addressing the Annual
Conference, Easter 1962.

here or not. I am concerned. I fully support the notion that honourable
members should have access to the house, and agree that any obstructions to
such access should be removed, but I can recall not very long ago when some
members of the citizenry – students – wanted to come to the house and express
a point of view. It is important the house considers extending these rights to the
citizens and tax-payers who pay for this institution, so that they may have access
to this place, and we may know that when they come to make representations,
the police will help them as well, and not cause an obstruction, which is what
occurred with the students' demonstration.

He was thus able to speak to a Chamber less than pleased by his appearance and remain within the rules of order on a very narrow issue. This, as

Wedding Day at Blackburn, 3 August 1963.

the clerks of the House will confirm, is a rare skill. But then Bob Cryer was a rare parliamentarian: assiduous, highly capable, one of the very few Labour MPs able to really worry the Tory whips and their front bench. As Conservative whip Greg Knight said at a memorial meeting for Bob: "He gave me more headaches than any other backbench MP. Night after night, he forced us to keep 100 MPs in the house in case there was a late-night vote. He was one of only a handful of MPs who could talk for an hour, an hour and a half, on a very narrow motion and remain within the rules of order."

What lay at the root of his parliamentary abilities? Undoubtedly, it was a commitment to radical Socialist principles, for which he would have been prepared to go to the scaffold. He realised, perhaps even before he entered Parliament, that it is an insidiously seductive institution. It can also be a highly intimidating one.

Bob came from an industrial, working-class family. In February 1974, when he first entered Parliament, he saw that the Tory benches were full

Speaking to the Labour Party Conference, Scarborough,
as parliamentary candidate for Darwen, October 1963.
(*Mirrorpic*)

of public school and Oxbridge men who saw holding a place in Parliament as their inalienable right and viewed the working-class ranks opposite with loathing and sometimes fear. A rare glimpse of the patrician Tory's real contempt for the Labour Party came in the mid-seventies. One evening, following a narrow Government victory in an important vote, a group of about 30 Labour MPs, Bob among them, decided to sing the Red Flag in the Chamber of the Commons. Michael Heseltine, during a customary rush of blood, picked up the mace and started swinging it around his head while hurling abuse at the Labour Members of Parliament. A former Minister in the Attlee Government said shortly after he left office: "I have not forgotten the tension of rising to answer questions or conduct a debate under the cold, implacable eyes of that row of well-tailored tycoons, who hated the Labour Government with a passion and fear which made them dedicated men in their determination to get it out of office and to limit the damage it could do to the world which they saw as theirs by right."

Bob would have agreed with that. He saw one of the first challenges to a working-class MP as psychological: overcoming the feeling of alienation in an institution built for the ruling class. He saw that the enemy would first try to break and intimidate a fiery young left-winger; if that failed, they would try to draw him into their cosy world – how many have followed that path!

There were also dangers from one's own side. When Labour enters government there are always a few firebrands who make a name for themselves on the backbenches early in a Parliament. An emissary from the Prime Minister will often visit an MP with a message along the lines of: "We recognise your abilities. Keep your mouth shut and there'll be a job for you." Often, these MPs do keep their mouths shut and, with nothing much to do, turn into bar flies. Indeed, Bob's predecessor as Labour MP for Keighley, Johnny Binns, had become a noted habitué of the bars of the Palace of Westminster. His attendance in the chamber and in the constituency was rather less dedicated.

Bob was determined to avoid all such minefields. From the beginning, his full-blooded socialism infected all his speeches and comments. He never wavered from his principles, from his ideals, or his commitment to the people of Keighley and Bradford. He mastered the House of Commons very rapidly and used it to considerable effect; he avoided the watering holes and never tried to foist stories on the journalists. They searched him out, not the other way around. He stuck to issues and pursued his objectives steadfastly. And with Dennis Skinner he formed one of the most effective and colourful double-acts in modern parliamentary history.

Bob Cryer, Labour Party Parliamentary Candidate for Darwen, opening a Labour Party Bazaar with fiancée Ann Place, June 1963.

Behind Barbara Castle as Parliamentary Candidate for the Darwen, Lancs, constituency in the 1964 General Election.
(*Lancashire Evening Telegraph*)

However, Keighley was not the scene of his first attempt to enter Parliament. In 1964, he had stood in Darwen, a small east Lancashire cotton town which had, perversely, consistently elected a Tory MP with a healthy majority. The incumbent in 1964 was one Charles Fletcher-Cooke, an unremarkable man who had, nevertheless, resigned his job as a junior minister shortly before the election. A young man had been found in possession of a car owned by the Darwen MP, an odd circumstance for which there seemed no ready explanation. So amid rumours of homosexual liaisons, the unfortunate Fletcher-Cooke returned to the back benches.

While Bob would never have dreamed of exploiting such a situation, it certainly occurred to him that the voters of Darwen would take a decidedly dim view of such goings-on. Coupled with the expected extravagant swing to Labour, he was feeling pretty confident. His agent was a bright young barrister called Jim Lowe who happened also to be a friend of Bob's. Unfortunately, Jim Lowe liked to take risks, a tendency demonstrated by the fact that he drank and drove. This had led to earlier scrapes – on one occasion he awoke at the wheel to find a tree growing out of the bonnet in front of him. It was only a matter of time before a real tragedy came along. Driving home after a customary fluid evening, he hit a wall and was thrown from the car, dying from head injuries. As well as being a personal blow to Bob, Lowe's job as agent passed to a pompous figure by the name of Alderman Austen Kaye. Warning bells began to ring for the candidate when he noticed that this pillar of respectable society referred to local cotton bosses as, say, 'Mr Peter' or 'Mr Alec'.

Whether these events had anything to do with Fletcher-Cooke's triumph at the polls is doubtful. The expected slaughter of the Tories failed to materialise: Harold Wilson won, but only by the narrowest of margins. Bob did not set about finding more promising pastures. Other events dominated his life for the remainder of the sixties. I was born in 1964, my sister in 1965 and there was the Keighley and Worth Valley Railway, cricket and Armstrong Siddeleys to take up much of his time. This changed in 1971 with his election to Keighley Borough Council. The town then had a Tory MP, Joan Hall, Johnny Binns having been defeated in 1970. But it was a seat which usually went to the winning party and with the miners' victory in 1972 the Heath Government looked vulnerable.

Bob won the Keighley nomination by a single vote over Binns, who then joined Dick Taverne's social democrats and stood as a candidate under their colours at the February 1974 Election. Binns' opportunistic action was expected to make Keighley a difficult seat to win for Labour and probably explains the narrow margin of victory (878 votes). The two elections of 1974 brought in a wave of young and vigorously left-wing MPs, emboldened by the miners' humiliation of the Tory Government. As Dennis Skinner recalls, "In the middle of the campaign public opinion started to shift decisively towards the miners and toward Labour. Many Labour MPs felt more radical because the miners had helped them win."

On his first day in Parliament, Bob sat next to Dennis Skinner on the front bench below the gangway, as near as they could get to the enemy. He had met Skinner at the Labour Party conference 12 years before when they were both raising points of order and making life difficult for the conference platform. In 1994, they were still doing the same thing to the Tories in the House of Commons.

Bob was the first MP of the 1974 intake to make his maiden speech. The MP for Bolsover remembers: "On the first day back after the General Election, the House of Commons used to pack up at around 7 p.m. but there was nothing procedurally to stop anyone speaking. So Bob made his first speech and he made a first-class one. Anyone watching him that day would have seen he was someone of great ability and someone who would need watching because he made it clear he was a socialist right from the start."

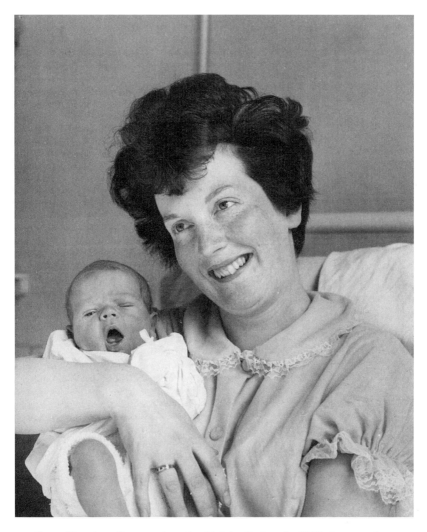

Councillor Ann Cryer and week-old John Robert in 1964. A press photo
due to 'Mr Robert Cryer' being the prospective parliamentary
Labour candidate for Darwen.

He soon became one of the most vociferous critics of Ted Heath's detested
Industrial Relations Act. He also regularly pressed for a new wealth tax
and was ready to attack Kissinger's murderous policy in Vietnam in
suitably passionate tones. He also sat on the committee which saw
through Labour's new Health and Safety at Work Act; health and safety
was one of his most enduring campaigns and he was one of the first MPs to
point to the dangers of asbestos.

Bob had been a member of CND since the fifties and in the seventies the cold war had been given fresh impetus by Nixon and Brezhnev. Bob established a reputation as one of the cold war's most vociferous critics. He was especially incensed that US installations and weapons of mass destruction had been allowed on to British soil without any debate in Parliament. Indeed, his last adjournment debate, shortly before his death in April 1994, concerned the Menwith Hill spy station in north Yorkshire. Menwith Hill is a gigantic 'big ear', one of only two bases in the Western world with such listening power, the other being the Pine Gap base in Australia. The debate was with the then Defence Minister, Jeremy Hanley. His reply to Bob's speech descended into a vituperative personal attack which failed to answer most of the questions raised. However, it is worth quoting some of Bob's rather more objective contribution as a flavour of his persistent questions and criticisms over many years.

> Its [the base's] establishment has been accompanied by lies, evasion and deceit and a persistent refusal on the part of ministers to provide proper information to elected representatives in this so-called mother of Parliaments. Indeed, the Minister for the Armed Forces has refused to allow Labour MPs around the base ...

> There is no glory or wonderful purpose involved in Menwith Hill. That is all the more true now that the cold war is over. Ministers justified the Menwith Hill base saying it was part of the cold war, but we understand that has finished. What is their justification now? ...

> There are two large US firms within the military-industrial complex: Loral Space Systems Incorporated, formerly a part of Ford, and Lockheed Aerospace. They sell much of the spy equipment and they are both involved in arms sales to third world countries. Menwith Hill gains information that would be useful to them. Lockheed and Boeing, for instance, oppose the success of Airbus Industrie, which has sold many aeroplanes around the world. Can the minister guarantee that information about commercial matters relating to Airbus Industrie and the sales of the Airbus 300, for example, has never been picked up by Menwith Hill and has never been passed on to part of the US military-industrial complex? ...

> What is the first priority of Menwith Hill? Will the minister publish the agreement that allows Menwith Hill to be operated at the base near Harrogate? Why should not the people of the United Kingdom know about these matters?

Another issue which Bob frequently dominated was the outside business interests of MPs. He pursued the moonlighters – principally Tories – assiduously and it was only at the time of his death in 1994 that the national media were beginning to focus on the issue of 'sleaze'. By that time he had been campaigning against MPs lining their pockets with

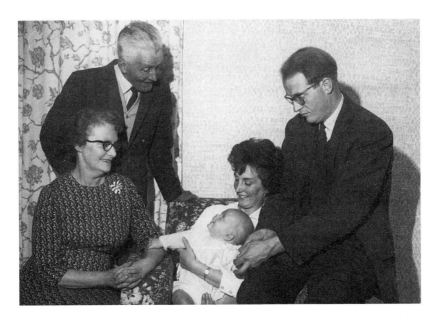

Five-and-a-half month old John Cryer with Granny and Grandpa Place,
and parents Ann and Bob, in Darwen. Photo taken for the
October 1964 General Election.

commercial interests for 20 years. In 1975, he led the campaign to set up
the Register of Members' Interests, after which he said: "The next step is
full-time MPs, just as other workpeople are full-time and cannot have a
dozen lucrative directorships occupying the time between, or during,
shifts."

Shortly before his death, he wrote an article in *Tribune* in which he
attacked professional lobbyists:

> Among the thousands of ordinary lobbyists...are people without a cause
> except that they wish to make money. They are the professional lobbyists
> who are paid to make their way to Parliament. Some pay fees to Members
> of Parliament who, in turn, book private dining rooms for their clients.
> There, the corporate rich can dine well, subsequently telling their friends in
> the corporate hierarchy how well the fare at the Palace of Westminster
> compares to other lush pastures denied to those problem people whom
> Peter Lilley MP speaks so much about: single mothers and other recipients
> of welfare benefits...Tories have elevated greed to a principle of faith.
> Labour MPs do not, and should not, follow suit.

As the 1974–79 Labour Government lurched toward monetarism and
the charms of the International Monetary Fund, spending cuts in health

and education were imposed. In 1976, Bob voted against these and met a howling storm of protest from right-wing members of his own party in Keighley. His opposition probably went down rather well, however, with the voters in the town, for the Government which had been swept into office on a tide of radicalism was now deeply unpopular.

However, Bob then surprised both the right and left of the party. Harold Wilson resigned unexpectedly as Prime Minister and Jim Callaghan, the Foreign Secretary, defeated the Secretary of State for Employment, Michael Foot, in the battle for the leadership. Callaghan decided that he wanted a left-winger in the Government. At that time, there were three rising stars of the left in Parliament: Dennis Skinner, Neil Kinnock and the MP for Keighley. The Prime Minister decided on Bob and he became the Under-Secretary of State at the Department of Industry. There were stories around the lobby that Kinnock had been first choice and had turned down the job; the source of the stories was certainly not inside the Government and they were probably untrue.

Undoubtedly, many of Bob's supporters on the left felt he might be deserting his principles. In fact the promotion almost certainly damaged his career and almost certainly he knew it. The Government was unpopular in the country and hated by its own rank and file. The left was in the ascendancy in many areas and a badge of credibility was often hostility toward the Callaghan administration. For Bob Cryer to join the Government at that time meant suicide as far as getting on to the all-important National Executive was concerned.

Why did he do it? He discussed it with like-minded friends such as Tony Benn, Dennis Skinner and Alan Rye, who later succeeded him as the Labour candidate in Keighley. They tended to confirm his view that as a Labour MP he was surely there to keep a Labour Government in office and how could he attack the decision-makers if he refused to become one of them?

"It's a problem everyone faces," says Tony Benn. "Do you just abandon the battle or do you go in and argue your case and if you're beaten you're beaten, but at least the case has been put."

Sadly, Bob's two years in Government were largely a string of battles with senior civil servants who were, by every instinct, antagonistic toward the Labour Party. His Secretary of State, Eric Varley – Tony Benn had been moved from the post to the Department of Energy in 1975 – was also a born enemy for whom Bob had minimal respect. Before his move to energy, Benn had set up two workers' co-operatives with Government cash – Triumph Motorcycles in Meriden and KME, which made various household goods, in Kirkby on Merseyside. The threats to the

Speaking at a Sheffield CND meeting, 1978. Left to right, Richard Caborn,
Fenner Brockway, Bob Cryer, Joan Maynard and Martin Flannery.

co-operatives led to some of Bob's bitterest battles and eventually his
resignation. On one occasion, he discovered that senior civil servants
were plotting to sell Triumph to Kawasaki.

In 1978, Callaghan asked Bob to announce the closure of KME. He
refused and was forced to resign – one of the very few occasions since
1945 that a minister has resigned on a matter of principle. He was actually
delighted to return to the backbenches and really saw himself as a
backbencher. He was a born rebel and could hardly look at a pillar of
authority without knocking it down. Even so, his contemporaries believed
that he was a highly effective Minister. This was certainly the case in his
performances at the dispatch box. During a pretty difficult period, he
was one of the few Ministers who really tore into the opposition with relish
and always from an avowedly socialist perspective.

Tony Benn comments: "Jim [Callaghan] actually had a high opinion of
Bob and like Wilson he recognised the need for having a balanced team
of left and right. I'm very glad he was in Government because, although
it's very difficult to remain in a Government with which you don't
altogether sympathise, you do learn a hell of a lot from the experience,
and he made very good use of his time as a Minister."

Bob Cryer, Max Madden and Pat Wall at a morning press call during the 1987
General Election campaign.
(*Telegraph & Argus*)

Without doubt Bob did make use of the lessons of Government and it
probably made him a more formidable opponent. However, the new sense
of freedom was clear in one of his first comments after resigning:
"Ministers are turned into daleks by the Whitehall machine. You either
keep you mouth shut and toe the Government line or resign. There is a
doctrine called collective responsibility which means if you are a Minister
you must accept the Government line."

His resignation played an instrumental part in keeping Keighley a Labour
seat at the 1979 Election, which he won by 78 votes. It was one of the most
remarkable results of that General Election. Keighley had previously gone
with the winning party at election after election; now, with a considerable
swing to the Tories, he held on.

The early 1980s were marked by increasing demands on Bob to address
anti-nuclear meetings all over the country. Naturally, his interests in other
areas – MPs' outside interests, industry, health and safety, anti-racism –
continued. In 1980, he introduced a Bill to outlaw telephone bugging after
the Home Secretary, Willie Whitelaw, refused to say whether Bob's own
telephoned had been bugged. The following year he backed Tony Benn
for the deputy leadership of the party against Denis Healey. Bob was a

gifted organiser and in the 1970s, for instance, had set up the Labour Co-ordinating Committee. This became a powerful pro-Benn organisation and, indeed, exists to this day although it is now a cab-rank for the party's more inept wannabees.

Following Benn's defeat, he came up with the idea of forming the Campaign Group of Labour MPs. He was its first convenor and in 1982 it started with 19 MPs – today it has more than 30. However, he knew that his time in Parliament was drawing to a close. The Boundary Commission planned to bring the solidly Tory town of Ilkley into the Keighley constituency. With minimal opposition from the Regional Labour Party, the plan went through.

By the 1983 election, Bob was becoming a figure of national prominence. CND was a vast and growing organisation and he was one of its leading lights. In such a strong position, Bob could have moved to a safe seat; indeed, he was approached by a number of Constituency Labour Parties. But he refused to leave Keighley, knowing that he was facing unemployment. A trade union leader who was active in the Bradford area at the time once told me: "Really, he committed political suicide, didn't he?"

The winning margin for the Tories was only 2,500 but the defeat was the biggest political blow of his life. It was, however, inevitable that he would bounce back. He was nominated for Bradford South for the 1987 election. Like Keighley, Bradford South has been traditionally dominated by textiles and the industry still plays a strong role albeit a diminished one. Bob had been born in the constituency and raised a few miles away in Saltaire. His records on industry, anti-racism, peace and health and safety and his high reputation for constituency work went down very well both with the local party and the voters. Bob was defending a majority of only 100 but Labour was expecting to do well – there was even talk of a Labour Government in the run-up to polling day.

The right-wing Press attacked him with more vigour and imagination than previously. Bob issued a writ against the Tory Party chairman, Norman Tebbit, for describing him in a newspaper advertisement as a fund-raiser for *Militant*. The *Daily Express* was forced to apologise and to pay a donation to War on Want for accusing him of inviting IRA terrorists into the House of Commons in 1985. This would have been a remarkable achievement as he had not been an MP in 1985. With a minuscule national swing to Labour, he increased the Labour majority by only 200.

Back in Parliament, he rapidly discovered that he had to build his reputation all over again. This he undoubtedly achieved. He also found the Parliamentary Labour Party, under a leadership increasingly paranoid

Doing a television interview in the garden, Shipley, 1988.

about the left, a good deal less congenial. He also found the Labour leader, Neil Kinnock, alarmingly ineffective against Margaret Thatcher and
the Tory front bench. As Dennis Skinner recalls, "We used to say when
Kinnock was on his feet, 'When is he going to cock it up?' and Bob would
say, 'Well, he's been speaking for ten minutes and he's not blown it yet.'"
Nevertheless, Bob soon returned to his old role of being one of the most
effective enemies the Tories faced. Again, Skinner says: "Everyone knew
that whenever Bob Cryer got on his feet he would upset the Tories, sometimes make our own front bench quiver and that he would never betray his
own people in Bradford and Keighley. When the Tories saw him around
the chamber at 10 p.m. they immediately felt there was danger."

Immediately after the 1987 Election, he returned to the two committees on
which he had served before – Members' Interests and Statutory Instruments. He had served on the latter from 1974 to 1979 as vice-chairman
and from 1979 as chairman. He returned to the chair in 1987 and remained
in that position until his death.

Two years after re-entering Parliament, Bob ran into a storm of con-
troversy over Salman Rushdie's *Satanic Verses*. The fundamentalist
element in Bradford's powerful Muslim community swung into action
against Rushdie. The leader of the Muslim Parliament, Khaled Siddiqui,
is even credited with persuading the Iranian regime towards issuing the

fatwa against Rushdie. Some leading Muslim organisations, notably the Bradford Council of Mosques, pressed for the extension of the Blasphemy Laws to cover Islam. Eventually, there was a public book-burning in Bradford's city centre which led to a riot.

Bob could have gone along with the chorus demanding an extension to the Blasphemy Laws and could just have kept a low profile. But in typically disputatious style, he not only attacked the stance of the fundamentalists and poured scorn on their campaign for turning Rushdie's book from a failure to a sales triumph, he even introduced a Bill to abolish the Blasphemy Laws altogether. In introducing his Bill in March 1990, he gave a glimpse of the tolerant view of society which he cherished in recalling the Bradford of the 1960s: "It was possible on a Sunday evening on Broadway to hear the secularists speaking yards away from an advocate of the Catholic Truth Society. I knew and admired both speakers. That spirit of tolerance and exchange of ideas must be preserved, and my Bill will help to do that." He naturally went on to attack the threats to Rushdie's life:

> A faith can and, indeed, does, persuade and urge followers not to see a film or read a book, but, for example, groups within the Muslim faith cannot impose censorship on the rest of the nation through the withdrawal of *Satanic Verses*.... Our general tolerance is seriously scarred by the fact that Salman Rushdie cannot argue his views in a spirit of tolerance.... The placing of all faiths on an equal basis would be a demonstration of our determination that the mutual exchange and discussion of various ideas should take place free from imposition and threats.

One would imagine that such a confrontational approach would have imperilled his slender 300-odd majority in Bradford South. Yet by the 1992 General Election he was established as a fearless and extraordinarily committed constituency MP. His majority rose to 4,500, with a far bigger swing than Labour received either nationally or regionally.

Although the loss of the election nationally was a major disappointment, he was pleased to see the accession of John Smith to the leadership of the Labour Party. Although they disagreed on some fundamental issues, Smith's approach was always far more open and pluralistic than his predecessor's. A key area where John Smith and Bob disagreed was Europe. The latter had always been opposed to membership of the Common Market. When he re-entered Parliament, it was after serving three years as an MEP. This merely made him an ever more ferocious opponent of the now renamed European Union. He would often say of the European Assembly in Strasbourg: "If it blew away tomorrow, no one would notice." His comprehensive and lucid attacks on membership

Campaigning with ambulance workers in Bradford.

of the EU make today's much-vaunted Eurosceptics in the Tory ranks look inconsequential. This had nothing to do with nationalism; he saw that the Single European Act and the Maastricht Treaty had nothing to do with peaceful co-operation and everything to do with creating a businessman's and a banker's Europe. He often warned John Smith that his support for the ERM would neutralise Labour at some point in the future and undoubtedly Smith's principled pro-ERM position left the party hamstrung when the Tories crashed out of the mechanism in September 1992.

In the same year, warning shots were fired in the Government's early moves in two of its most notorious sell-offs: coal and rail. Bob joined the miners' rally in Hyde Park in October of that year and never lost an opportunity to attack Michael Heseltine, who was determined to crush the battered mining communities.

As a former steam locomotive driver, the attempt to flog off Britain's railways appalled him. In 1993 he reported to the Bradford South party: "One of the major areas of potential disaster pursued by the Government during last year was the Bill to privatise British Rail. As many as 14,000 separate contracts could be involved between the track authority and various franchises. There are layers of administration covering the system,

Filming a television interview in 'The Office' at home, 1991.

all to be paid for by long-suffering passengers. Facilities such as through-ticketing will disappear. The Transport Minister was actually unaware of this when I questioned him in the Commons." He was one of Parliament's great authorities on transport; he would now be in the thick of the battle to keep a rail network run for public service and not for private greed.

At a memorial meeting some months after his death, former Tory MP Alan Clarke gave a highly lucid appreciation of Bob's powers from the point of view of the Tory benches: "Often single-handedly, Bob was taking on and proselytising values which ought, but very seldom are, to be in the minds of all people elected to the House of Commons. Very often he was fighting, alone, for people outside and away from Parliament who think, in their innocence, that is how all Members of Parliament behave. With his departure, the Commons is very much poorer and may not ever recover, and it is my belief, although it is none of my business, that the Labour Party is also very much poorer." A number of speakers at the meeting, including Dennis Skinner and Gina Cook, the manageress of the House of Commons cafeteria, recalled that Bob's mastery of parliamentary rules and custom was not utilised for self-glorification. Indeed, he often sustained debates until after 10.30 p.m. because after that time the catering staff were entitled to free taxis home.

As Don Dixon MP said, Bob was a rare parliamentarian in that he was a genuine socialist "who did so much for others but so little for himself".

*Extract from the 'Special Report From The Joint Committee On Statutory Instrument 1986–1996'*

"Mr Bob Cryer, MP

The Committee wishes to record the sad loss of its Chairman, Bob Cryer, who died in a car accident on 12 April 1994. Mr Cryer was a member of the Committee for thirteen years, from 1974 to 1976, from 1979 to 1983 and from 1987 to 1994, and was its Chairman for eleven of these years from 1979 to 1983 and from 1987 to 1994. His good-humoured, careful and down-to-earth approach to the Committee's work is still very much missed."

*Extracts from a letter to Ann Cryer from Liz Simblet of the Oswestry Labour Party*

What can I say? I have never before wept for the loss of a political figure, but Bob is irreplaceable. Ken Livingstone, Dennis Skinner and Tony Benn encapsulated, on Radio 4, all the Socialist morality which Bob embodied. He was possibly our only inspiration to those on the left, as all became darker.

I would like to express our real gratitude that, over the years, he troubled to come to speak in places like Oswestry, where his audience would be small, but where his presence was *so* appreciated.

Having a husband whose life was public property cannot have been easy. The last time I saw you both was having to provide hurried sandwiches after an awful journey north, but you were obviously such devoted partners.

I shall always treasure the fact that he wrote personal letters in reply to political ones.

We greatly admired the fact that he did not desert Yorkshire, even when the boundary changes of 1983 ensured defeat, at least temporarily. It was a symptom of both principle and his love of his home area.

# CHAPTER 11

# BOB AND THE MOVIES

## JIM GREENHALF
*Journalist, Telegraph & Argus*

Part One: 1934–58
*Sons of the Desert* to *The Vikings*

Among the 55 reel-to-reel British and Hollywood movies in Bob Cryer's private collection are three by Laurel and Hardy: *Sons of the Desert*, *Way Out West*, and *Blockheads*. His favourite was the first, *Sons of the Desert*, made the year he was born. A black and white photograph of thin Stan and fat Ollie on the living-room wall of Bob's comfortable Shipley home conceals a slot for a movie projector in the kitchen next door. Away from politics, from late night sittings in the House of Commons, he loved nothing better after his favourite Saturday tea of fish and chips than to draw the curtains, pull down the movie screen, and convert the living-room into a cosy cinema where he could invent classic double-bills such as *The Third Man* and *Brief Encounter*, relish the vim and vigour of *Singin' in the Rain* (Ann's love of musicals rubbed off on Bob), or if grandson Conor was round, delight the tiny boy and himself by showing examples of America's most original contribution to 20th Century visual culture – cartoons. The beauty of this arrangement was that Bob didn't have to pay to get in or queue, which he absolutely loathed and refused to do. Moreover, he was the only one who knew how to work the projector.

"Leeds is rather more civilised than Bradford, but to my mind – and remember, I am a Bradfordian – far more dismal and less interesting. It has not the authentic, queer, carved-out-of-the-Pennines look of Bradford and some of the other towns." The chubby novelist and playwright J. B. Priestley made this comparison in his book of travels, *English Journey*, which he undertook in 1933. The bustling city into which Bob was born the following year was a place of dirt and grandeur. Its murky skyline was punctured by hundreds of mill and factory chimneys and its steep and cobbled thoroughfares packed with markets, offices, cafes, trams, cinemas and freight yards. From the age of two Bob lived between the two greatest loves of his life: the railway and the cinema (politics was his vocation). In later life he did not lament that he had never been Prime Minister, no, his greatest regret was that he had never directed a major motion picture.

The Saltaire Picture House, as it was grandly called before becoming yet another Gaumont, stood at the summit of Albert Road. One of more than 40 cinemas in Bradford it advertised itself as: "The Cinema with the Golden Dome. Designed in Renaissance Style. The Most Magnificent and Comfortable Picture House in the Country." Bob's mother and father loved going to the pictures, and from an early age he followed in their footsteps. "We used to go to Saltaire cinema on a Saturday morning. It was a riot! I still remember the cowboy films with Tex Ritter and Johnny Mack Brown. We would all join in the fights," recalls Raymond Hoare, a wartime evacuee from London whose grandparents lived in Saltaire. One of the projectionists from 1939 to 1942 was Jack Scwires. Now 82 and living in Shipley, Jack says the Picture House was one of five Rank cinemas in Bradford and pioneered Sunday screenings (the Sabbath was all cabbage water and Bible-bashing in those days). For some reason the Picture House attracted a lot of Polish soldiers during the war. Jack, whose late wife Rose used to live in Albert Road, was on friendly terms with Bob's father. "He was an enthusiast for steam wagons, alternative road vehicles, locomotives, and films. He loved to talk about films. When the Worth Valley Railway opened he used to say, 'Oh you'll have to go along to see our Bobby'." Cinema prices ranged from 1/6d (7.5p) to 3/9d (18p); children got in for half price. Unlike today, customers could watch a programme through two or three times, and a programme consisted of two feature films, a newsreel, cartoons, and what were known as coming attractions. Bob used to meet his girlfriends outside the Picture House. Among his schoolboy notebooks I found the following little note:

> Going out with Betty – Saltaire Picture House, outside 5.30, August 18th.
> Three long and trying weeks ahead. Hope I keep my chin up – or forget.
> Seen her since then – will probably receive a postcard from her sometime.
> So it's alright now.

Inside the plush darkness of the 1,500-seat auditorium he would lose himself for hours, emotionalising his otherwise systematic mind with evocative images. Bob was lucky in his neighbours. Next door to Number 15 lived the Buccleuch family, the father of which managed a big cinema in Bradford (Jack Scwires thinks it may have been the long-since demolished Ritz in Broadway). The two families evidently got on because Mr Buccleuch gave them complementary tickets for *Gone With the Wind*.

At the bottom of Albert Road, terminating it in fact, was the railway laid down by the Midland Railway Company and opened in 1846. The

Garry Warren, Bernard Cribbins, Sally Thomsett and Jenny Agutter
at Oakworth during the filming of *The Railway Children*, 1970.
(*Production still by Associated British Productions Ltd.*)

opening of this line, perhaps more than anything, persuaded Titus Salt to remove his worsted textile business from central Bradford and relocate on a green-field site between the railway and the Leeds–Liverpool canal. Salts Mill opened in 1853; Bob once worked there. From his corner house, among the posher in Titus Salt's model village, the young Bob could hear express trains roaring through from London to Scotland, and to the west coast via Carnforth – the station where David Lean spent two weeks shooting exteriors for his 1945 classic, *Brief Encounter*. The acrid smell of smoke and cinders hung in the air of Bob's childhood, and did as much as those moving pictures at the top of the hill to furnish the mental rails along which his imagination could glide excitedly but securely.

The 50th anniversary of VE Day inspired thousands of articles many of which proved both informative and educational. Among them was a piece by Bevis Hillier for the *Daily Telegraph* in which he sketched the explosion of creativity in the arts during and after the war.

At the end of the war, cinema attendance was at an all-time record level. And, as film historian George Perry has pointed out, the new Labour Government

155

elected with a landslide majority in mid-1945, "now consisted of men and women to whom the cinema had been a major entertainment, the first government of ordinary picture-goers in British history".

It was a golden time for the British film industry. David Lean, who made *Brief Encounter* in 1945, directed the first great post-war film, an adaptation of Dickens's *Great Expectations* (1946). Michael Powell and Emeric Pressburger gave us the surreal masterpiece *The Red Shoes*, in which the beautiful Moira Shearer, now Mrs Ludovic Kennedy, danced herself to death. The Boulting Brothers issued two fine films in 1948, *Brighton Rock* and *The Guinea Pig*, with Richard Attenborough, in, respectively, hard-boiled and soft-boiled parts. And the Forties were also the decade of the Ealing comedies.

Hillier could also have mentioned Carol Reed's *The Third Man* (1949), Laurence Olivier's *Henry V* (1945), as well as those fine wartime movies, *The Life and Death of Colonel Blimp* (1943), *In Which We Serve* (1942), and a film Bob much admired, *The Way to the Stars* (1945) directed by Anthony Asquith. This is the film in which John Mills recites John Pudney's poignant and bitter poem 'Johnny-Head-In-Air', also recited by Tony Benn at Bob's graveside on 22 April 1994.

The end of the war also meant more elbow room for Bob, for his sister Joan went off to Manchester University and he was able to move out of the workroom where his mother did her marvellous sewing and into Joan's back bedroom. Picture him at the age of 11 in that upper back room dreaming of the movies he would one day direct and the runs he would pile up for Yorkshire. The tall, thin ginger-haired boy had an old head on his shoulders, however: he knew that without preparation nothing worthwhile can be achieved. This is revealed in a two-page essay called Amateur Movies, which Ann thinks Bob wrote when he was 12 or 13. Referring to a home movie he had made, Bob wrote:

> The finished film not too bad for a beginner like myself, but lacks continuity. This is due to 'shooting' film without any prefixed plan or script.

For his projected movie *The Bar and the Bottle*, the mogul of Foetus Films, Montage Films, and Spiro-Eagle Film Unit, wrote out a shooting script containing 66 shots, a property list and a cast of unlikely characters – Irma Beerbarrel, Ivor Flatnose, plus several 'country yokels'.

A grubby blue school exercise book, 'Important Notice' written in ink on the cover, contains a few pages of an untitled film which he intended to shoot in and around Saltaire. To himself he assigned the tasks of script-writer, cameraman and sound effects assistant. Bob's leading lady was Margaret Hall, whom Joan thinks went out with her brother for quite a while until she moved abroad with her family. Other books list gramophone records Bob thought suitable as soundtracks for the movies he was able to complete and show to friends. These books show a systematic, meticulous mind, perhaps even a slightly hierarchic one. He knew his own worth, was sure of himself. In April and May 1948, for example, the 13-year-old Bob wrote to D. Walter Distribution Co, Lant Street, London SE1, and to Wallace Heaton Ltd, Berkeley Square, London W1, inquiring about the cost of purchasing 16 mm cine-projectors, way above the weekly pocket money he grubbed from his grocery round. He signed himself Mr G. R. Croft in his letter to Wallace Heaton Ltd, showing a tongue-in-cheek appreciation of subterfuge beyond his years. Or was he just batting cautiously in case his father found out?

Kirk Douglas, one of my favourite Hollywood stars, happens to have closed more Bradford cinemas than any other silver screen legend. Three of his films were playing at the very last picture show at three cinemas between 1957 and 1958. Appropriately in the circumstances, Stanley Kramer's *Champion*, Richard Fleischer's *The Vikings* and Vincente Minnelli's biopic of Vincent Van Gogh, *Lust for Life*, all conclude with Douglas's death. *Lust for Life* was the last movie to light up the screen of Saltaire's Gaumont. The "Most Magnificent Picture House in the Country" closed on 19 October 1957; the building was later demolished. A petrol station now stands on the site.

Bob, who was away at Hull University at the time, would have been shocked but perhaps not surprised; he knew that television was taking away customers from cinema box-offices. Like all radical politicians, however, he hated the idea of change in his personal life. The Picture House was not merely one of 42 cinemas in Bradford: it was a landmark, a mile-stone on his road from childhood to manhood. So too was Kirk Douglas. One of the first films which Ann and Bob went to see during their courting days in 1961 was *The Vikings*. Ann still remembers Mario Nascimbene's score. Who could forget it? As the flames consume Kirk Douglas's body and the funeral ship slips into the darkness of the fjord, the theme music swells to an inspiring climax, and my heart breaks.

Part Two: 1959–70

*Look Back in Anger* to *The Railway Children*

Four days after the closure of the Saltaire Gaumont, Bob sat down at his typewriter and hammered out a stiff letter to the editor of the *Hull Daily Mail*. The 22-year-old student had taken exception to the views of a Mr Robert Freeman concerning so-called highbrow films. Always confident of his opinions and never afraid to air them, Bob took his opponent to task in the manner of a professor correcting an uppity student.

Lionel Jeffries, back to camera, lines up the three railway children
on the platform at Oakworth Station, June 1970.
(*N. R. Knight*)

If Mr Freeman imagines that the current trends in the cinema reflect "honest
to goodness" entertainment then he is mistaken. There is an increasing
tendency towards the exploitation and glorification of brutality and an ever
greater emphasis on sex. Presumably if these films make the turnstiles click,
Mr Freeman is satisfied, whatever their effect on the audience. What, for
example, does Mr Freeman think of the misuse of the X Certificate "the X-
iest film yet" etc. This certificate was introduced so that adult films could
be made and shown, films that examine people more deeply than the superficial inanities that Mr Freeman suggests. Why should I be denied them,
and have to see so many films designed to cater to the backward adolescent,
simply because the exhibitors and producers consistently underrate audience
intelligence?

Some of this letter would not be out of place in the worried 1990s of
Michael Medved; the American movie critic was also alarmed by the
glorification of brutality and emphasis on sex. However, examples of
cinematic sex-n-violence from the early 1950s do not readily come to
mind. *Genevieve*, *The Man in the White Suit*, the *Doctor in the House* series
hardly fit the bill. I am unwilling to assume that the iconoclastic and
opinionated young Cryer was thinking of Elia Kazan's *On the Waterfront*
or Anthony Mann's *The Man from Laramie*. And yet Bob's letter speaks
to us today, for we know how much of a violent lurch Hollywood did take
towards the gory and then the ghoulish in the late 1960s, as though the
murders of the Kennedy brothers, Martin Luther King, and the inferno

of Vietnam, completely blew the train off the tracks. Bob may have understood the mood which produced such angry and violent movies as *The
Wild Bunch*, *Straw Dogs*, *The Texas Chainsaw Massacre*, *Taxi Driver*;
but I doubt if he cared for them.

What's unusual about the squib to the *Hull Daily Mail* is the certainty of
Bob's upright pessimism at a time when the British film industry was about
to enter a decade of artistic and commercial success with films such as *The
Bridge on the River Kwai* (1957), *Ice Cold in Alex* (1958), *Look Back in Anger*
(1959), *Lawrence of Arabia* (1962), *The Servant* (1963), *Alfie* (1966), *Oh
What a Lovely War* (1969). Bob ran the university's film society with fel-
low-student Alan Coulson. "The Bob I knew often arrived greasy-handed
and late for our appointments and meetings because en route he had been
repairing the Armstrong Siddeley," he recalls. In his other capacity as
President of the Students' Union, Bob motored all over the North and
into Scotland, doubtless splicing business with the pleasure of seeing films
considered too highbrow for general release.

He was still disposed to look darkly through his viewfinder in the summer of
1958 when he wrote a short article called 'The Decline of the Cinema' for
*Torch*, the student magazine. He wrote with the testy imperiousness of
the impending political firebrand, his line of attack deliberately provocative.

> It has been said that the British Cinema seeks escape into "Shakespeare, the
> Royal Navy or the Royal Air Force". *Reach for the Sky* is, perhaps, one of
> the best examples of escape into the RAF.... War is no longer real, it exists
> on the screen like some dreamy adventure story, where goodness and the
> stiff upper lip finally triumph, where men are officers, and where the ranks
> are divided into bluff Yorkshiremen and comic relief cockneys.

Where are the independent producers? he cries.

> Could *Marty* or *Bicycle Thieves* have been made in a British studio?

The way he poses the question does not invite an answer, especially in the
affirmative.

The young delight in alarming their elders with talk that is both uncompromising and apocalyptic, particularly when everyone is feeling comfy
and self-assured. While others were falling over backwards to find new
encomiums to praise Ealing Studios or Laurence Olivier (I nearly said
Lawrence of Olivier), Bob defiantly contemplated the disintegration of
the British film industry. Again, his cinematic ejaculations proved to be
premature although right on target. The British film industry thrived until
the end of the 1960s – until the Americans left town. Only Bob's eyes
were short-sighted; where films were concerned at least, he was very
long-sighted indeed. 'The Decline of the Cinema' goes on:

> Whilst the French and Italian Cinema are far from perfect, at least they do
> produce films which demonstrate a sympathy for, and an understanding of,
> people and the lives they live. For example, one has only to see the exquisite
> use of location photography in *Jour de Fête* to appreciate this.

I don't suppose many people outside student film societies and the National
Film Theatre would have been acquainted with Jacques Tati's 1949 satire
on the modern obsession with speed (velocity, not the narcotic).

Why was Bob so disenchanted with the prospect of the future in 1958?
Perhaps he thought films made in a country governed by wing-collared
Conservatives were bound to have some inherent flaw. Didn't cinema
have a sharper edge during the war and just afterwards, in Bob's words
"reflecting the people it seeks to entertain"? Those were the years of
Humphrey Jennings whose seven documentary films made between 1939
and 1945 are still acclaimed today. The late Lindsay Anderson said
Jennings was the "one real poet" of British cinema. Perhaps the poetry
drained out of the silver screen after Suez. Forget De Sica and Fellini,
Renoir and Renais, could British cinema even be compared with Hollywood in the 1950s? Films such as *All About Eve* (1950), *Sunset Boulevard*
(1950), *An American in Paris* (1951), *Ace in the Hole* (1951), *High Noon*
(1952), *Shane* (1953), and *On the Waterfront* (1954) have maturity, depth,
passion and artistry far ahead of our best. Bevis Hillier's remembered
creative explosion wasn't quite the big bang in atomic America. Perhaps
Bob's Jimmy Porter exasperation was caused by a gnawing feeling that
Britain had become second rate. The rush of energy embodied by Attlee's
post-war Welfare State Government had been spent. In its place self-
satisfaction had come in, kicked off its shoes and sat warming its feet at
the fireplace. Bob wasn't to know at the age of 22 that the Conservatives,
who had governed the land since his 17th year, would continue to do so
until he was 30. Bob was first and foremost a political animal whose
Socialist beliefs to some degree coloured his views on every other subject.
Among his papers I found an example of this. On the back of three buff
polling cards, the sort activists use to check on voter turnout at an election, are handwritten notes for a speech on the subject of the difference
between Socialist morality and the prevailing spirit of the times (there is
no clue to the date). Film producers, says Bob, are turning to sex and
sadism, blatantly exploiting the X certificate, aiming at the teenage
market. "No evidence of social responsibility", he says. That's followed
by a note about a couple of American films, including *On the Waterfront*.
This film exemplifies what happens when democracy becomes morally
corrupt and no one takes personal responsibility. Bob's uncompleted
idea seems to be this: democracy is only possible when people accept
personal responsibility for what they do. Though a Socialist, Bob doesn't

appear to have been an admirer of the collective per se; he was not a "four legs good, two legs bad" dogmatist. His admiration for French and Italian cinema during the mid-1950s may have been influenced by the rise of the Left in France and Italy. I suspect, however, that Bob saw that European cinema had been touched by the war in a way that British cinema had not, and that this experience had invigorated it, as had the aesthetic doctrines of Existentialism. There was a ferment of ideas and artistic creativity across the English Channel, frustrating both the artist and the politician in Bob. England, to his horror, had become parochial – narrow-minded, smug, backward-looking. Hence his anguish.

When Bob was made a governor of the British Film Institute one of the first things he did was to check his film creditation as technical adviser on *The Railway Children*, Lionel Jeffries' directorial debut in the early summer of 1970. Bob had already assisted the BBC in a similar capacity for its four-part serialisation of E. Nesbit's classic. Julia Smith, who later invented East-Enders, heard of this Yorkshireman who had founded the scenic Keighley & Worth Valley Railway and got in touch. Bob advised on locations and what sort of locos should be used. The serial so impressed Lionel Jeffries that he set himself to writing a script for a movie feature and Bob, once again, found himself among gaffers, grips, and movie people.

Ann and her two children, John, then six, and four-year-old Jane, had cameo parts in crowd scenes, for which they were paid a total of £20. Bob, she thinks, was paid about £100 for his work, which included walking the five miles of the railway with Jeffries and producer Bob Lynn. The money paid for the Cryer family's first holiday.

Rubbing shoulders with the principal players, as Bob old-fashionedly called them – Bernard Cribbens (Perks the porter), Dinah Sheridan (the Mother and in real life the mother of former Tory Party chairman Jeremy Hanley), Sally Thomsett (Phyllis), Jenny Agutter (Bobbie), Gary Warren (Peter), and William Mervyn (the Old Gentleman) – was a welcome change of pace for the Keighley Technical College lecturer. The man with whom he struck up a special feeling of kinship was not an actor but the cinematographer Arthur Ibbotsen, whose credits included *The Horse's Mouth*, *The League of Gentlemen*, *Tunes of Glory* and *Anne of the Thousand Days*, for which he had been nominated for an Academy Award. "Bob had such regard for people who had knowledge of the craft of cinema. I think Arthur was a Conservative, but his skill transcended politics," Ann said. Her husband didn't always see artistic eye-to-eye with Lionel Jeffries. After the shoot was over, Bob told her there were insufficient cut-aways in the can. Sure enough, two months later a second unit arrived in Haworth to complete the picture. "Bob always said the film could have been a classic in the hands of an experienced director," Ann said. Bob, formal rather than punctilious, was bound to be at odds with a man who insisted on everyone dressing for dinner. Arthur Ibbotsen, on the other hand, had been a clapper boy for *Brief Encounter* – a fact Bob proudly pointed out in his account of the filming which he wrote for the autumn issue of *Push and Pull*, the Keighley & Worth Valley Railway magazine.

In his article Bob illustrates his disappointment with the quality of the Press coverage by quoting from one popular magazine's efforts. "*Reveille* described one engine," he says with almost disbelief, "as a lovely, old, genuine huffer-puffer train, over 80 years old." Huffer-puffer! Bob's face must have been a picture. Only the article written by Merete Bates for *The Guardian* impressed him. Bates compared the filming of *The Railway Children* with Ken Loach's approach to *Kes*. Bob eagerly summarised the main thrust of the article.

> The whole production of *Kes* reflects a new and radical approach to filming, they cut out the chauffeur driven cars, and the caravans, the director Ken Loach actually arrived to work on a bus, costs were cut to a minimum and as a result the film was made for £150,000, less than half the cost of *The Railway Children*. Fresh from television Ken Loach has no time for the tradition of ostentatious and expensive luxury and is more interested in expressing ideas.

The year of *The Railway Children* brought to an end six years of Labour Government as well as signalling the end of the epoch-making Sixties, in which the British film industry swung. By the time Ted Heath replaced Harold Wilson at Downing Street, the industry was swinging like a corpse at the end of a rope. In one of Bob's 70 or so movie books I found the following passage from *British Cinema: The Lights That Failed*, by James Park:

> The revival of the 1960s petered out when American finance was withdrawn. And the creative energies triggered by the formation of Goldcrest Films and Channel Four in the early 1980s were rapidly dissipated by over-ambitious companies and over-confident directors.

Some 30 million dollars had been invested in 13 British films in the late 1960s, all of which had flopped. In the 1980s Hugh Hudson, carried away by his success with *Chariots of Fire*, spent tens of millions on *Revolution*, but not even the film's vivid battle sequences could save it from flopping at the box office. Crisis, which experienced movie people will insist is endemic in their industry, returned; for the second time in 16 or 17 years Britain's film industry disintegrated. Bob's prophecy of the mid-1950s had come to pass.

Part Three: 1971–94

*The Last Picture Show* to *Four Weddings and a Funeral*

Although Bradford is the UK's fourth or fifth largest metropolitan district, on bad days it feels like that one-horse town, dusty and dying, in Peter Bogdanovich's poignant black and white movie *The Last Picture Show*. Ill-judged urban improvements, unemployment, and latterly out-of-town shopping, have all taken their toll of central Bradford. But for the city's theatres, concert halls and cinemas (especially the IMAX screen located in the National Museum of Photography, Film and Television) the city centre would be dead. Culture is keeping Bradford's pulse beating, and cinema is playing its part, although you wouldn't think so judging by films made about Bradford, films such as *Blood and Peaches*, and *Band of Gold*, which seem to take their cue from *Rita, Sue and Bob Too*. South of Watford, Bradford is the place of Pakis and tarts; the place where brassy schoolgirls kick their knickers off quicker than a ferret goes down a hole; the place of the Yorkshire Ripper and Islamic book-burners. Before the war Bradford had a music hall stereotype as the place of flat caps and whippets. Now that has been replaced by a cinematic stereotype, more modern (or post-modern); but a stereotype all the same. Bradford has always been rough in parts, but neither the pre-war image nor the one it has now tell the whole story. There is a lot more to this city, one of the most cosmopolitan cities in the UK. In 1933, J. B. Priestley observed:

> There was, then, this odd mixture in pre-war Bradford. A dash of the Rhine and the Oder found its way into our grim runnel – "t' mucky beck." Bradford was determinedly Yorkshire and provincial, yet some of its suburbs reached as far as Frankfurt and Leipzig. It was odd enough. But it worked.

Bradford may have seen better days, but in places it retains its air of grandeur and worldliness. With its architectural mix of 19th century Italian Renaissance, dilapidated 1950s *Look Back in Anger* modernism and fuzzy side-burned 1970s Arndale car-parking-facility, Bradford's rising and falling panorama reminds me both of Prague in all its glory and the most depressing parts of East Berlin. No wonder it was thought the ideal location for filming Alan Bennett's movie about Kafka, *The Insurance Man*. Other films shot here in the past 35 years or so include *Billy Liar*, *Room at the Top*, *The Dresser*, *Yanks*, *The Railway Children*. The movie directors James Hill (*The Belstone Fox, Born Free*) and Tony Richardson (*Look Back in Anger*, *The Entertainer*, *Tom Jones*) were born here. No wonder Bob never wanted to leave the place.

Cinema and Socialism meet in Chapel Street, home of the Playhouse and Film Theatre where Bob saw many movies, just round the corner from Peckover Street where, in 1893, the Independent Labour Party was

Arthur Ibbetson, film cameraman on *The Railway Children* pretends to film Ann, Jane and John after 'proper' filming finished. Keighley & Worth Valley Railway near Ebor Lane Bridge, June 1970.
(*Photo by Bob Cryer*)

formed. The Labour Party was born in Bradford near a cinema, the cinema which Bob helped to save in 1991.

The British Film Institute was considering switching the Film Theatre's annual grant, about £36,000, to the city's new Pictureville cinema. Bob convened a meeting of Bradford's MPs (five including himself) at the House of Commons, to which he invited the head and deputy head of the BFI, Wilf Stevenson and Ian Christie. "That was the turning point," said John Waller, then chairman of the Playhouse. "The BFI realised this was something very serious. In all their dealings with Bradford in the past they had never before been confronted by five MPs. That's when the BFI decided to throw its weight behind the Bradford Film Advisory Committee, which is chaired by David Puttnam, and which includes both Pictureville and the Film Theatre. Now the BFI channels money to the committee and programming for the two venues is worked out by Bill Lawrence. Had the BFI's decision not been reversed, thanks to Bob, the grant would have stopped and Bradford Playhouse and Film Theatre would have closed."

The Playhouse showed its gratitude, honouring Bob's memory with a special screening of *Brief Encounter* and *The Third Man* on 18 February 1995. Ticket sales raised £600 which was donated to Amnesty International. In the autumn of 1993 Bob was appointed one of the BFI's 19 governors. Ann says he was thrilled and never missed a meeting. "It's a tragedy for us that he's dead," said Wilf Stevenson. "Just before he died he got a question to the Prime Minister about the BFI which drew a little more attention to us." This is what passed between Bob Cryer and John Major in the House of Commons on 24 February 1994.

> MR. CRYER: Does the Prime Minister accept that I am very proud to be a member of the unpaid board of governors of the British Film Institute? Will he comment on the lack of Government action in helping to finance and develop the British film industry which is a very important industry, not only for the cultural representation of this country but because it both creates employment here by making films and develops Britain's image abroad, which cascades down to British manufacturing industry? Will he give a guarantee that he will support the industry in the future?

> THE PRIME MINISTER: I am happy to congratulate the Hon. Gentleman on the work that he does for the British film industry. (HON. MEMBERS: What about its future?) I shall come to that, if Hon. Members will just relax. I am told that the Hon. Gentleman does an excellent job on the board of the British Film Institute and that he has been appointed to it because of his personal abilities and not because of his political affiliations, as is the case with all appointments to such public bodies, without exception. As regards the future of the British film industry, I am keen to see it thrive. One of the areas that will benefit significantly from the establishment of a lottery is the arts in general, a part of which I hope will be the British film industry. It is likely over the years that it will provide considerably more resources for the arts as a whole, and very probably the film industry as well, than even the most benevolent level of Government funding is likely to do, whatever Government we may have. I hope, therefore, that the Hon. Gentleman and his fellow members of the British Film Institute will fully support it.

Cynics might comment that the only way the BFI is likely to get lottery money is if it changes its name to the Winston Churchill Film Institute. Like many other publicly-funded bodies in recent years, the BFI has found itself strapped for cash. Not having enough to go round was the root of the problem with Bradford Playhouse and Film Theatre in 1991. Bob carried the memory of that time with him when he joined the BFI board a couple of years later. "During one of our recurring budget crises, Bob ensured that we didn't just play to the national institutions in London," said Wilf Stevenson. "As a result the budget into the regions suffered less of a cut than would have been the case." Had Bob lived longer he may have reopened his campaign to stop TV companies from splicing commercial breaks into cinema films shown on television. Bob maintained that current practice contravened broadcasting rules that advertisements should only be shown at the beginning or end of programmes. He was rebuffed by the Independent Broadcasting Authority back in 1986; but Bob was not then in a position of influence within the film industry.

Labour MP and acknowledged cinema fan Gerald Kaufman shares Bob's concern about the state of the industry and its future. The National Heritage Select Committee, which Kaufman chairs, spent eight months checking up on its health, and reported after Bob's death. On 6 April 1995, Kaufman wrote an article for the *Daily Telegraph* which provided a withering analysis of the patient's ills. Adopting his favourite technique of playing Devil's Advocate against his own line of argument, he begins by saying, in so many words, 'Crisis, what crisis?' If the British film industry is indeed on its last legs as so many claim, how come it manages to turn out such popular and profitable movies as *The Madness of King George* and *Four Weddings and a Funeral*? The latter, by the way, became the biggest British box office hit of all time before Hugh Grant's well-publicised indiscretion, I almost said cock-up, with a Los Angeles prostitute named Divine. After setting up the reader nicely, Kaufman clinically knocks him down.

> *Four Weddings and a Funeral* was funded principally by the subsidiary of a Netherlands-based multinational company; the bulk of its profits will end up in Hamburg, where it is registered for tax purposes. *The Madness of King George* was funded substantially by the Samuel Goldwyn company in Hollywood. Such British-financed films as do get made generally cannot afford to hire space in British studios, which are occupied by American-financed films...

At the British première of *The Madness of King George*, the highlight of the second Bradford Film Festival in March 1995, Alan Bennett described how the film's producers had had to scramble around for money so that certain scenes could be shot. Kaufman contends that Britain's tax system is a disincentive to film makers. He compares it unfavourably with the set up in the Irish Republic where the green welcome mat is personally laid down by arts minister Michael D. Higgins. Nothing is too much trouble across the water, whereas in Britain central Government seems to perversely pride itself on putting up as many obstructions as possible. So what's the remedy? Provide tax incentives for British companies, as well as individuals, to invest in film making, and give more power to the six film commissions (including the Yorkshire Film Commission) – "beef them up" in Kaufman's words. In June 1995, John Major's Government announced what the Press described as an 'aid package' for the British

Extras John, Jane and Ann Cryer photographed by Bob Cryer when rain stopped filming at Oakworth during presentation scene, June 1970.

Film Industry. The main component of this package was £70m to £84m of National Lottery funds spread over five years to the year 2000. At least £10m is to be used to promote new British movies (set against the £120m cost of Kevin Costner's *Waterworld*, that doesn't look much). Sir David Puttnam was underwhelmed. "It's enough to keep us hopping along for a few months," he said grudgingly. I have no doubt at all that Bob would have poured scorn on the proposal. Half-measures did not impress him. In 1972, as prospective Parliamentary candidate for Keighley, he wrote a letter to the *Telegraph & Argus*, declaring that the only sensible way of dealing with the British film industry's problems was to nationalise the main cinema circuits and the studios. Lenin regarded cinema as the most important cultural innovation of the 20th century. In his own inimitable way, so did Bob.

Unlike Gerald Kaufman, Bob never made it to Hollywood. As chairman of the Parliamentary Labour Party's Film Industry Study Group (he had insisted on the inclusion of the word 'industry'), he thought he ought to go way out west. Friend and long-standing colleague Lord Jack Dormand was roped in as a prospective travelling companion. "Bob and I were having lunch one day and he said, 'Jack, let's go to Hollywood.' I said, 'Great, next week, fix it up.' Needless to say I thought no more about it, but some time later he came to me and said, 'Hollywood, Jack, I think I've got some concessionary travel arrangements, and I've got a contact at

MGM studios.' I was stunned: he had actually meant it. He was still talking about it when I last saw him."

The 60 years of Bob's life embraced key periods of innovation and change in the motion picture industry. Colour was introduced and became the norm; Vista-Vision, Cinemascope, and other wide screens came in (he wrote about that too in Hull University's *Torch* magazine). Latterly, video has become commonplace. Bob was uneasy about video. He feared, rightly, the medium would be exploited by traffickers in brutality and sex, and by video pirates indifferent to the financial damage to the legitimate film industry.

The year of his birth, 1934, Gracie Fields starred in *Sing As We Go*, reputedly one of the few British films of the time to make reference to unemployment. Bob passionately believed that films should reflect how people really lived. Deep down, however, he just liked movies. He was a fan who started out wanting to be moved, provoked, stimulated, or royally entertained. He was not a man of small emotions. Nor was he a doctrinaire aficionado who maintained that all left-thinking people should admire *Battleship Potemkin* and nothing else. Looking through the red-covered list of his movie collection some people would be surprised by its contents. Three films by Laurel and Hardy, but none by Eisenstein; *Hello Dolly*, *Meet Me in St Louis*, *Singin' in the Rain*, *The Third Man*, *Brief Encounter*. The latter remained a favourite of his throughout his mature life.

Almost 12 months to the day of his death, on 10 April 1995, the *Daily Mail* ran a story which would have cut Bob to the quick. Carnforth station, where Trevor Howard and Celia Johnson had acted out the scenes of their hopeless passion (the noise of steam trains providing a leitmotif), was in a state of disintegrating dereliction. The later offer of the station's sale by Railtrack, hoping that a private developer would turn the station into a Brief Encounter theme park, would have desolated Bob's heart. *Brief Encounter* fulfilled his requirement that cinema reflect the lives of the people it seeks to entertain. But let the last word be Bob's.

> The film did not attract big audiences, one suspects because it portrays the fallibility of humanity at a time when people were wanting more certainty in their lives. All the elements of fine writing, acting, photography and editing combined to ensure its acceptance as a genuine classic of the British cinema.

# CHAPTER 12

# TOWARDS BRADFORD SOUTH

## 1

## MAVIS GILES

*Teacher and for many years activist in the Labour Party and CND*

It has always been very important to me who the MP is, because the job carries with it a great responsibility and the opportunity to change things. People's lives are greatly affected by what is done in Parliament and tremendous power is exercised there by a few. This makes it essential that we elect the committed rather than the corrupt. However, all kinds of people become MPs, including the good, the bad and the almost indifferent. Over the years they come and go and only a relatively small number leave their mark. These are usually what we call 'conviction' politicians. Bob Cryer was one of these.

When Bob lost his Keighley seat I felt a sense of loss and also some insecurity. But why? I had never met him, or closely followed his political career, and yet I felt that, in some sense, Parliament was diminished without him. I have always felt strongly that we all have a real duty to participate in or monitor political activity and Government actions in order to safeguard our children's futures. When my own two children were small I can remember watching them playing and laughing at some trivial thing and feeling terribly guilty because they were growing up in a world of proliferating nuclear weapons and cold war. Later I began to take an active role in CND and then the Labour Party.

I became aware of those Labour politicians who took an interest in nuclear issues. Bob seemed to me to be just about the most well informed and effective of them. He was a careful and thorough researcher and I saw him as a kind of watchdog of an industry cloaked in sinister secrecy. He was also known and respected among all the Yorkshire anti-nuclear groups. Obviously the loss of his Keighley seat reduced the effectiveness of his opposition. As an MP he could, and did, raise the profile of urgent issues in many ways.

In 1984, Tom Torney, the Bradford South MP announced his intention to resign. A number of people made it known that they would seek nomination for the seat. Now at that time I had been active in the Labour Party for a number of years, and along with my friend and Labour Party colleague Jan Walker, took a keen interest in the selection process that was due to begin. Jan wanted Bob Cryer for the seat and I wholeheartedly agreed. We both recognised the good qualities of some of the potential candidates but we felt that the person we wanted above all others in the seat was Bob and we would do our utmost to get him selected. Bob was the MEP for Sheffield and North Derbyshire at that time but wanted to get back into the House of Commons.

As the selection process got underway it became clear that the seat was to be hotly contested. Jan and I set out on a campaign to contact and work with all the people who, like us, wanted Bob as MP. We also drew up plans to canvass and persuade those members who were uncommitted to any particular candidate and even try to turn some people who were committed elsewhere. It was a gruelling but exciting few months. Bob participated in public meetings, branch meetings and selection meetings. Jan and I drew up interminable lists of names and literally, towards the end, spent every single evening on the task. What helped enormously, of course, was the quality of our candidate. He was known as hardworking, extremely competent and above all had great integrity. Bob was also left-wing. We knew we could not sell his candidature to right-wing comrades who quite understandably wanted someone of their own political persuasion. However, in the end Bob, Ann, Jan and I steadily worked through to a winning position.

As the parliamentary candidate Bob became part of a terrific election campaign and took the seat. I can't speak for Jan but I feel that helping to get Bob selected and elected was one of the most worthwhile things I have done in my life because it had a direct, beneficial effect on so many constituents and upon Parliament itself. Bob did a fine job as MP and was greatly admired and respected by constituents of all shades. He fulfilled all of my expectations.

---

## 2

## TRISH AND ANDREW WALKER

*Trish was Bob's Personal Assistant/Secretary, 1987–94*
*Andrew was an officer of Bradford South Labour Party 1987–94*

During his time as the prospective candidate for the constituency, between his selection in May 1984 and the General Election in June 1987, Bob had studiously tried to avoid any actions which could be viewed as upstaging or embarrassing Tom Torney as the sitting MP. He was very well aware

Bob and Ann Cryer (left, right) canvassing Smith Avenue with Bradford South
Labour Party members Mavis Giles, Paul Riley and Jan Walker, winter 1985.

that the Press would be looking for situations when he, on the left of the
party, could be portrayed as clashing with Tom, who was a right-winger
and party loyalist. In addition his selection as the constituency's candidate
had only been by a small majority and Bob was aware that it was not in
the interest of himself or the Constituency Labour Party for there to be
serious divisions within the local party during the election campaign
when he would be defending such a slim majority.

As the General Election grew closer Bob's profile within Bradford South
increased and by the time the election was called he was regularly seen
both within the constituency and in the local Press and television.

The campaign in Bradford South was successful and largely non-eventful
in spite of Bob being named in a national newspaper advertisement by
Tory Party Chairman, Norman Tebbit, as one of a group of dangerous
left-wingers who would hold the party to ransom if Labour won the
Election. Clearly Tebbit did not frighten the voters in Bradford South
as Bob was elected with a majority of 309. While Bradford South was still
one of Labour's most marginal seats, as Bob noted in his victory speech at
St George's Hall on Election night, he had succeeded in tripling Labour's
majority.

Once elected to Parliament again, Bob immediately set about representing
the people of Bradford South with a will and with his customary enthusiasm for issues both large and small. He never felt that anything was

too trivial for him to give time to, and would take up causes and concerns whether they affected large numbers of constituents or an individual.

By the time that the election was called Bob had already won round some of the party members who had voted for other contenders, and once elected to Parliament, most of the others fell in behind him, won over by his hard work as an MP and his principled stand on a number of issues.

Bob never attempted to influence the constituency party in its actions or decisions, although he always attended the monthly meetings of the General Committee, and was glad to visit Branch meetings whenever he was invited. Despite criticisms of some of Bob's positions, the General Committee always supported him, particularly when he took difficult stands on issues of principle. It passed resolutions supporting his position on the *Satanic Verses*, the Spring Ram development and Bob's stand against the Gulf War, when he and the few other Labour MPs, who called for an immediate end to the war and the use of economic sanctions, were held up to ridicule in the Press.

## CONSTITUENCY OFFICES

Bob began looking for a suitable constituency office even before he was elected as the MP. This was not to say that Bob took his election for granted, rather that he wanted to establish the office as quickly as possible. Within weeks of being elected, Bob advertised for a secretary who would work in the constituency office. Once recruited, Bob, Ann, and the secretary, Trish Walker, began the search for an office. Bob's plan was that, ideally, the office should be in Bradford South. The problem with this was that, since the constituency was spread out, yet did not extend into central Bradford, no one ward was easily accessible by all the other wards. Assuming that many constituents would travel to see Bob by public transport, this was an important consideration. The decision was made, therefore, to look to the city centre, which was well-served by bus routes, for a property.

One such property considered was the old Bradford Left Club at Number 6 Edmund Street, off Little Horton Lane. This building, which was complete with barn and which pre-dated the 1820s vintage of most of this street, had been donated by an elderly Bradford socialist in the early 60s for the use by individuals and organisations on the political left. Bob joined the Club in its early days just after leaving university, and always regarded the talks and discussions there as having had a major influence on his political development and thinking. He therefore very much warmed to the idea of continuing the building's tradition. However, it was in very poor condition and, after a structural survey revealed that one of the outside walls was sinking and would cost considerable amounts of money to correct, Bob and Ann decided that it would be too expensive to repair and maintain. Eventually, another property in Edmund Street became empty and after a number of protracted negotiations with the Health Authority, to whom the building had once belonged, Bob and Ann bought 22 Edmund Street. Bob was keen that the large property should be put to full use and since there were a number of spare offices after taking one for himself and one as the secretarial office, Bob found tenants in the shape of the Bradford Branch of the National Union of Teachers, and Bob Jones, who ran a socialist book shop. In later years, the attic was repaired and made into a further office and this was rented to the Yorkshire and Humberside Campaign for Nuclear Disarmament. The building was expensive to maintain and though the annual rents which came in were just enough to keep it going, any major repairs were a real drain on finances.

The constituency office was opened on May Day 1988 by Alice Mahon, MP for Halifax. An exhibition of Labour Party history and memorabilia marked the event. The office was staffed five days a week. Constituents were encouraged to visit the office and talk to Bob, when he was there, or in his absence, secretary and personal assistant, Trish. A large number of cases were taken up in this way.

The weekly advice surgeries held on a Saturday morning at various venues around the constituency were another way in which constituents were assured of being able to speak to Bob himself. He held an average of over forty advice surgeries each year, a high number compared to other, less diligent, MPs. These generated well over a thousand new cases each year and were in addition to the other cases which continued from year to year.

The offices at Edmund Street also comprised a meeting room. Bob lent this room, free of charge, to Bradford South Constituency Labour Party. The General and Executive Committees met here for most of the time between 1988 and Bob's death in 1994. Bob hired out the meeting room, at a minimal fee, to different organisations. These included a socialist climbing club, a vegetarian club, a meditation group, various trade union meetings, and a group campaigning for infertility treatment on the National Health Service. The room was popular and cheap!

Some of the main things which Bob campaigned on ran throughout the whole of his time as MP for Bradford South, while others arose briefly and were settled. It was one of Bob's strengths as an MP, both at constituency and national level, that he was always ready to follow things through to their conclusion. He never let the slow pace of local and

Alice Mahon MP, Halifax, officially opened the Bradford South Constituency Offices at 22 Edmund Street, on May Day 1989. Seen here with Bob and Secretary/Assistant, Trish Walker, with items from the exhibition inside.
(*Yorkshire Post*)

national Government put him off, he was always willing to write yet another letter demanding a response to his inquiry and many constituents were rewarded with an answer which they had been unable to achieve for themselves.

His period as MP was, from time to time, marked by disputes with Bradford Council. Bob pursued what he felt were the legitimate interests of his constituents whether the Council was Tory or Labour controlled. This led to sometimes acrimonious exchanges between him and the Labour group on the Council who felt that as a member of the same political party Bob should support them and be seen to do so.

## BRADFORD'S 'WEST END' DEVELOPMENT

A good example of this arose over the plans for Bradford's 'West End', which were first published in 1989. Bob felt that the original scheme was both grandiose and foolhardy. The idea of building a Planetarium, an Electronic Zoo, hotel and Omnimax big-screen cinema were all very well but he felt that the estimated £4 million of Council money which this would cost might be better spent directly on the residents of Bradford, on housing and education. He was also very concerned that the Council appeared to be entering into a deal on the development with a company, 3D Developments which had no record of success in this field, and which he discovered had only 97 £1 shares as capital. Bob never felt the fact that it was the Labour group making such plans should prevent him from publicly calling them into question. No doubt the leader of the Council might have preferred Bob to make his opinions and objections known in private, but Bob always felt that such private discussions, both at local and national level, were not in the public interest. It is interesting to note that the plans were quietly and gradually scaled down over the following year. Had he still been alive Bob would have not been proud of the fact that his prognosis had come true, but sad that some Labour councillors had merely seen his comments as 'interference' in Council business.

## SPRING RAM

Bob's willingness to enter into debate and possible conflict with anybody when he felt it was in the interests of constituents was seen in other events throughout his time as Member for Bradford South. He was instinctively on the side of the minority, of the small group against the large, of the challengers against the power and bureaucracy of large organisations, whether they were public or private. He supported the Woodland's Resident's Action Group against Spring Ram Group's plan to build a huge factory on the greenfield site at Woodlands, never for once believing that the company's promise to bring over a thousand jobs to the area was more than an attempt to influence public opinion and soften up the Council and other opponents of the scheme.

When, in July 1992, the Low Moor area of Bradford South was exposed to possible pollution by the huge fire at Allied Colloids, he consistently pursued the rights of residents to have a full and open inquiry by the Health and Safety Executive, and to be given information about what chemicals Colloids were producing and storing on their site. Colloids had, from the time of his election, invited him on visits to the site, visits which Bob was only too happy to make, not to sit and dine with the Directors, but to use the opportunity to question the company about its activities and policies, and to make a point on such tours of always insisting on meeting with Trade Union representatives from the site.

## THE RUSHDIE AFFAIR

Bob's willingness to stick his neck out and say what he felt was right in spite of the possible consequences was perhaps most notable over what came to be known as 'The Rushdie Affair'.

In late 1988 Salman Rushdie's novel, *Satanic Verses*, was published. It horrified Muslims by its depiction of the Prophet Mohammed and led to the announcement of a Fatwa on Rushdie by the Ayatollah Khomeini in Iran. In Bradford the book caused great upset among Muslim members of the community and led to a number of rallies in the city, at one of which the book was publicly burnt. Bob's response to this was to call for tolerance of the opinions of others, of whatever faith. He stated publicly that he was opposed to the book burning and to calls for the book to be banned and withdrawn from publication, believing that no group had the right to impose censorship on the rest of the population. He emphasised that he deplored slurs on religion but that comment and discussion was a vital part of a democratic society.

These views did not please the Muslim community in Bradford and in March 1989 the Council of Mosques called upon him to resign if he did not support their wish, and that of the Muslim community in Bradford, for *Satanic Verses* to be banned. The Council also called on Muslims not to vote for MPs and councillors who did not support their stance. With an Asian electorate of around 7000 and a majority of 309 Bob was faced with a potentially tricky decision. However, he resisted all pressure to compromise his views and continued to call for the abolition of all blasphemy laws and not for their extension to faiths other than Christianity.

Bob received the support of the Constituency Labour Party and a number of admiring comments in both the local and national Press for his stand. Bob felt convinced that the whole affair was a potential danger to race relations within the city and that to have taken any path other than the middle one, which he felt to be right, would only have increased the tensions which there were within the city.

In March 1990 Bob used the Commons Ten Minute Rule Bill to raise the issue within the House of Commons, by introducing a Blasphemy Bill which would have scrapped the offences of Blasphemous Libel and Blasphemy. Although the Bill stood no chance of becoming law Bob was still worrying away at the issue long after it had left the headlines and when, to many, it would have seemed more sensible to let the matter quietly drop. When it came to the 1992 General Election the issue did not seem to excite any interest on the doorsteps and there was no evidence that Bob lost any significant support from Asian electors in the constituency.

## WESTWOOD HOSPITAL

One issue which ran throughout Bob's time as MP began only two months after his election for Bradford South. The Bradford Health

'Official opening' of a bus shelter he campaigned for at
Low Moor, Bradford, 1992.

Authority announced plans to move patients out of Westwood Hospital at
Horton Bank Top. Westwood Hospital was home to many people with
learning difficulties who were unable to live with their families or in homes
of their own. The plan to move people out of the hospital was in line with

the Government's 'Care in the Community' programme which Bob recognised as part of the Thatcher Government's attempt to reduce welfare spending in surreptitious ways. There was some sense in the premise that people with learning difficulties, and some who were mentally ill, would be better served by living in smaller homes than in large institutions. However, the Tory plan also allowed the Health Authority to contract out the services for these new small group homes.

Bob felt that what the Health Authority was doing was essentially to 'privatise' these patients along with the services which they required. The plan, named 'Operation Springboard' by the Authority, was opposed by many of the families of patients, who felt that the benefits to be gained by their relatives in living in smaller groups would be outweighed by the loss of amenities and support which they were able to receive living on the Westwood site. Bob's other objection was a concern that one of the Health Authority's prime motivations for 'Springboard' was the opportunity to make capital by selling the Westwood site for housing development.

The patients' families and the hospital trade unions combined to form a Joint Working Party to look at the Health Authority's plans, and came up with the idea of allowing patients to remain on the site but in a small village complex with houses, hostels and some provision for sheltered workshops. They calculated that this new development could be funded through the sale of two-thirds of the site for housing provided that the revenue so raised was ploughed back into the care of the patients of Westwood and not used for other Health Authority projects.

Just as this plan was being debated locally the Government began the next phase of privatising the National Health Authority with the establishment of Hospital Trusts. Although Westwood was not in the first Bradford Trust application (which involved only the acute hospital services) the danger was that it would be in the second phase, with the consequent diminution of local accountability.

Along with members of Bradford South Constituency Labour Party, Bob and Ann Cryer spent a number of Saturdays campaigning in the constituency against the Bradford Hospital Trust's application for Trust status. As a result of this, constituents sent 560 letters to Bob expressing their concern and another nearly 600 letters were forwarded to the then Health Minister, Kenneth Clark. Figures of letters received in support of the Trust application were never revealed by the Regional Health Authority, but it was little surprise when the Secretary of State granted Trust status.

Campaigning outside Rackham's, Bradford.
(*Andrew Walker*)

In April 1991 Stephen Dorrell, the Under-Secretary for Health, requested plans for the development of the 'village' scheme at Westwood to be sent to him. This scheme was now being vociferously campaigned for by BRADCAP, the organisation of parents, relatives and friends of the patients at Westwood. In spite of the Government's apparent interest, Bob and others feared that the publication of the second Trust application in Bradford, for the Community Health services, to include Westwood Hospital, would only lead to confusion at a time when a decision about the hospital's future appeared to be nearer than at any previous time. Shortly after this, in November 1991, it was announced that the whole hospital was to close and all patients were to be moved out.

In spite of this blow to the supporters of the 'village' scheme, Bob continued to support them. He was never happy to walk away from a campaign merely because it appeared to be a lost cause. Nearly eighteen months later he was still actively fighting for the 'village', believing that it gave the patients the benefits of small group living with the advantage of remaining somewhere which many of them felt as their home, having lived there for many years. In April 1993 Bob raised the issue in the House

179

of Commons, knowing well that any mention of local issues in the House of Commons was likely to be picked up by the regional and local Press, and that such publicity both encouraged the scheme's supporters and also made the Health Trust aware that they were not able to operate away from public scrutiny.

## PROMOTION

The Conservative Government from 1979 allowed MPs to make money for themselves on a scale never seen before, accepting fees for lobbying, consultancies and directorships. This was absolute anathema to Bob who believed that MPs had one job, to represent constituents, and that to work for some other private interest lessened their effectiveness at doing that job.

However, Bob was happy to use his position to promote causes which he saw as being for the common good. His love of railways is documented elsewhere in this book, but it involved something much more than nostalgia for steam trains. It was part of a belief that public transport was a benefit to everyone, both for those unable to afford cars, and also that it was environmentally much more friendly having five hundred people on a train or fifty people on a bus than the equivalent number sitting in private cars.

## TRANSPERIENCE

Bob's interest in public transport meant that he was naturally very interested in plans to set up a transport museum in the constituency on a site at Low Moor which had been earmarked for the project and for which £800,000 was held by the West Yorkshire Residuary Body, the organisation set up to administer the funds remaining following the Tories' abolition of the West Yorkshire Metropolitan Council in April 1985.

In August 1987 he was involved in the Low Moor Transport Gala, which became an annual event on the proposed site, organised by a group of enthusiasts who were determined that the plan for the museum should not be forgotten. In February 1990 the formal plans for the museum were published and building began at what was to become Transperience in 1994, the museum finally opening in 1995, a year after Bob's death.

## DANGEROUS DOGS

One of Bob's abiding interests during his time as MP for Bradford South was the campaign to limit the freedom of dangerous dogs. Bob proposed

Campaigning in Bradford South with wife Ann, Trish, Andrew,
Hannah and Rosie Walker at Wibsey, 1992.
(*N. Ostler*)

an amendment to the Local Government Bill to allow councils to draw up
a register of dangerous dogs. This would allow councils to monitor and
keep track of a dangerous dog. Bradford Council had appointed the
country's first dog warden and Bob was very supportive of this action.
Indeed, he raised many constituents' complaints with this officer. As far
back as July 1987, soon after being elected, Bob raised the matter in the
House of Commons following a ferocious attack by rottweilers on a Bradford Headmaster who was accompanying an unwell child back home from
school. Not long after there was the terrible mauling of a small girl in
Bradford by a pit bull terrier.

## WHEEL CLAMPING

Around 1992 the wheel clamping of vehicles became an issue in Bradford
after a locally based firm began clamping vehicles on land which had
barely visible signs warning drivers of the dangers of parking. Often there
were no signs at all and drivers would think they were parking on a piece

of derelict land, because often this was all it was. The car parks were not staffed or maintained in any way. The issue became increasingly serious after a number of drivers, on summoning the clamping firm to unlock their vehicles, were on the receiving end of threatening and abusive language and behaviour from the staff.

Indeed, one woman, who was accompanying her blind father back to her car was abused by the staff. One incident was witnessed and filmed by a 'News at Ten' film crew, who had been in Bradford on another story. This incident involved a 'security guard' abusing a driver unwilling to pay the £75 'unlocking' fee. The story was run that night on the news programme. The matter was a serious one, though, and often involved women returning to their cars in the evening and having to wait around for the 'security guard' to arrive and then to have money demanded from them. Bob tried to get the practice of wheel clamping made illegal. He campaigned for the same laws which applied in Scotland, whereby wheel clamping was considered as extorting money, to apply in England and Wales.

Despite numerous letters to the Home Secretary, the police and the wheel clamping company, which Bob discovered was not registered as a legal company, he was still campaigning against wheel clamping up until his death.


## CONCLUSION

Bob was immensely proud to have been an MP, not for the glory which he could gain from such a position but for the honour of having served working people and the Labour Party and movement. His pride was increased in 1987 when he was re-elected to Parliament as the member for Bradford South, the constituency in which he had been born. When Bradford South CLP formally selected him as their candidate to fight the seat he told the nomination meeting of one of the reasons why he was a socialist. When he was a young boy he had been very ill and his mother had finally had to call the doctor to come and see him. In those pre-National Health Service days visits to or from the doctor had to be paid for, something his parents could not easily afford. To make up the balance of the costs his mother, a talented seamstress, made a dress for the doctor's wife.

For Bob, the time he served as MP for Bradford South, like so much of his political life, was part of a struggle to ensure that working people were free from such fear. His long hours spent in the House of Commons were not to gain publicity for himself but to ensure that the Tory Government's policies, aimed as they were at increasing the wealth and powers of the 'haves' at the expense of the 'have nots' in Britain, should not go by with-out being exposed to public scrutiny and challenge in Parliament.

---

## 3

## JEREMY CORBYN, MP

St George's Hall was full for the funeral meeting for Bob; it started as a reverential affair with people from all walks of life filing in and listening with hushed tones to the speeches. After a while people spoke more freely and with great passion, and it became a meeting with Bob there in the coffin.

All his life was mentioned – politics, Bradford, peace, old cars, railways, cricket, education, wit and passion. It was a wonderful and very fitting occasion and there was no contrast of all his interests – it merely empha-sised his complete life and love for his family. His burial above Bradford was very fitting. Bob with the city he loved.

As a Member of Parliament elected in the disaster of the 1983 defeat I passed Bob as he lost Keighley so I knew him as a great campaigner and socialist and founder of the Socialist Campaign Group. He became a Member of the European Parliament and we did not meet much until the 1987 Election when he won Bradford South by a few hundred votes.

In Parliament Bob was indefatigable; at any late night sitting when the Tories might be on the run but Labour members would be tiring of being there so late, Bob would move divisions and create havoc for the Government. He well understood that a handful of determined Labour MPs could keep over a hundred Tory MPs up all night.

In the House Bob was a master of procedure and knew all the tricks and how to turn them to advantage.

However, for Bob the House was not a sophisticated debating society, it was a place to speak up for people and ideas. Bob used the Chamber to great effect in exposing fraud in the European Community, defending the Settle to Carlisle Railway, supporting the women's peace camp at Menwith Hill or demonstrating how the Tories continually try to circum-vent the process of democratic scrutiny.

We live in a world beset with divisions both within our own society and between the rich and poor in the world. For most of the past fifty years there has been the spectre of the cold war haunting us. The cold war led to massive arming of the USA and with it NATO against the alleged Soviet threat.

In turn this meant a huge arming of the Soviet Union and Warsaw Pact countries and the waste of the arms race.

In total the arms race meant the Soviet Union was incapable of providing for the needs of all its people and the US exploited large areas of the globe to pay for its arms.

All of Bob's life was dedicated to peace. A lifelong member of CND he never wavered in his belief in unilateral nuclear disarmament and support for the peace movement. The strength of CND meant that the Government and its agents harassed peace groups and used the secret service to gather information. This became a threat to the civil liberties of everyone and, post cold war, the threat is still there. Menwith Hill, a US listening post is still there and listening to the whole world for signs of dissent from the global market world order.

There never was any justification for nuclear weapons or the arms race and now it is nakedly clear that the real target of the armed power of the West is to ensure its economic supremacy over the rest of the world.

The peace movements of the cold war period are just as relevant in the gruesome era of the global market as earlier.

Bob showed courage and commitment in maintaining his principles throughout his life and as one generation lays the foundations for another his work should be seen as a basis for all of us to carry on.

Unless the Labour movement wakes up to the need for real internationalism and solidarity with the poorest in the poorest parts of the world then a terrible price will be paid. The welfare state in Europe is being decimated on the altar of the falsehood that it cannot be paid for. The answer is that the richest in the West should pay more and that companies using the fear of job losses to force low taxation should be phased out.

Bob had a vision of a world based on justice, peace and democracy and always put these principles first. He represented two highly marginal constituencies and defied the accepted political wisdom that such seats are held by people who keep quiet and maintain a grey obscurity in national politics. Bob's obvious qualities and honesty shone through and, in the great tradition of radical socialism, won elections.

New Labour appears to be trying to remove the memories of the past. Refusal to study and look at history is very dangerous – the strength of socialist ideas around the world comes from an understanding of the forces that work for private gain and greed and the need for collective action. Being a representative in any capacity is never easy and mistrust can become the norm. With Bob there was never any mistrust only respect and affection.

Those who seek to ignore our movement's history and traditions are not likely to be able to achieve the goals of justice and socialism.

*Extract from a letter to Ann Cryer from Annie Larkin of Bradford South*

I just had to write to you. I lost my dear husband last July and whilst he was very ill I was having trouble with my insurance society in Leeds. They wouldn't pay me on a claim for my leaking roof. I was in a terrible dilemma and didn't know which way to turn. I'm 73 and rather old for this sort of thing. Then I thought of Bob Cryer. I wrote to him at Westminster and he promptly took up the 'cudgels' for me and straightened the insurance society out! I wrote to thank him, and he wrote back to me to *thank me* for writing to him! I shall always treasure that letter.

He was one of nature's gentlemen, Mrs Cryer, and his death will be a tragic loss, not only to you and your family, but for many others. A lot of people depended on him for his fearless courage and his fight for the underdog. He will be respected as a man who did everything in his power to help anyone who needed help.

May God bless him.

*Extract from a letter to Ann Cryer from Mr Booth of Bradford South*

I do know that Mr Cryer was not a believer in the full sense, but I am firm in my belief that there are now people blessed for his presence. . . . Mr Cryer will be missed not only by the constituents, but by the country in general. He was someone who made you feel important no matter what your circumstance.

# CHAPTER 13

# A CLEVER USE OF PARLIAMENTARY PROCEDURE

## 1

## ALICE MAHON, MP

*(Based on an interview with Rory Hegarty)*

Bob Cryer was a political giant in Yorkshire, and when I first met him, at a Regional Conference in Bridlington, I was slightly in awe of him. Yet when I spoke to him, I found him such a warm and approachable person, so very down to earth and easy to talk to, that I instantly liked him.

When I became an MP in 1987, I travelled down on the train with Bob for my first day in Parliament. I was obviously a bit nervous, but he put me completely at ease, giving sound advice about just being myself. He told me my kind of input, my kind of person, was lacking in the House of Commons, so it was very important that I didn't change; that I took what I represented to Parliament and made sure that I had a voice. He was so encouraging and so knowledgeable. He was to turn out to be one of the best friends I had.

Bob was one of the most alive people I ever met – he had a superb intellect and knew Parliament backwards, but he also had an interest in a whole range of issues and his knowledge covered a vast range. What endeared him to me most was his lovely, warm sense of humour. He was very good at gently teasing people and setting them up, but never in a cruel or unkind way. I never knew Bob to be hurtful with his humour; it was always a very gentle ribbing.

The thing that always sticks in my mind is that Bob was the first MP to be televised in the House of Commons. On the first day Parliament was televised, we all knew Margaret Thatcher had been going in to the Chamber to practise and so on, and the whole place was a bit keyed up. And Bob, with typically clever use of Parliamentary procedure, got up first on a point of order. He then turned around and smiled at us all...! So a Labour member from 'below the gangway', as they call it, was the first televised MP. He said to me afterwards, "I was determined she wasn't going to get on before me!"

Bob Cryer was the first MP to speak when the House of Commons was televised.
(*House of Commons TV Archives*)

I remember talking to him at length about his time as a Minister. I got the impression he was on a huge learning curve at the time. Like many of us, he was very suspicious of the Establishment, and I think many of his fears were confirmed very quickly. He was very honest about the whole period – he couldn't stand being gagged and unable to speak out, so he resigned. Having said that, anyone you spoke to who had dealings with him at the time said he was a superb Minister, both honest and hardworking, so his resignation was obviously a big loss to the Labour Government.

Bob will be remembered as a very warm, extremely intelligent and likeable man, a stalwart for peace and for socialism.

The first televised transmission of the House of Commons. Bob Cryer standing.
(*House of Commons TV Archives*)

*Extracts from a letter to Ann Cryer from Keith Polyblank of Brixham*

Having taken a close personal interest in British politics, reading Hansard regularly and, when time allowed, watching television and the transmission of Parliament, I frequently noted your husband's regular attendance in the Chamber and his debating skills. He is going to be sorely missed in the House and particularly to the Party. It will be strange not to see him sitting next to Mr Skinner, or jumping up and down in a *bone fide* effort to catch the eye of the Speaker. Or that jacket and green party tie he wore, no longer visible. His like we shall not witness again.

## 2

## THE MENWITH HILL DEBATE

*During the course of this book several people mention the Menwith Hill Debate. This was one of Bob's last speeches in the House of Commons, and one of his best. It illustrates his commitment to peace and to Parliament's accountability to the public. The response of the Minister of State for the Armed Forces is not reproduced here.*

HOUSE OF COMMONS, 25 MARCH 1994, 2.30 P.M.

*Menwith Hill Station, North Yorkshire*

Mr BOB CRYER (Bradford, South): I am pleased to have an opportunity to speak on this subject. In a curious way, it stems from two Ministers: the Minister of State for the Armed Forces, who claimed that there was parliamentary accountability for Menwith Hill station; and the Minister for Public Transport, who found Menwith Hill station so secret that he was not even aware of it when he was a Minister at the Ministry of Defence and thought that it was a railway station. In a recent debate, he astonishingly said that his civil servants had prepared him to reply to this Adjournment debate and he then discovered that it was connected with the Ministry of Defence.

The story of Menwith Hill begins in the public area, not with a ministerial statement, debate or planted parliamentary question in the mother of Parliaments. It began on 18 July 1980 when the *New Statesman* published an article by Duncan Campbell and Linda Melvern entitled

The Billion Dollar Phone Tap – America's Big Ear in the Heart of Yorkshire.

To suggest, as the Minister has, that there is parliamentary accountability for that spy station in the Yorkshire hills is to torture the truth. Its establishment has been accompanied by lies, evasion, deceit and a persistent refusal by Ministers to provide proper information to elected representatives in this so-called mother of Parliaments. Indeed, the Minister of State for the Armed Forces has refused to allow Labour Members around the base. That is a curious change because in 1981 the former Secretary of State for Defence, Francis Pym, gave me permission to visit the base. The only qualification to that permission was a refusal to allow Duncan Campbell to accompany me because he knew something about the spying and procedures going on inside the base.

Parliamentary accountability is virtually non-existent. There is little point in asking questions when answers are refused. On 27 April 1988, I asked the Secretary of State for Defence

> if he will list the agreements authorising the use of Menwith Hill communications base, Harrogate, by the United States National Security Agency.

Mr Ian Stewart replied:

> The use of Menwith Hill by the United States Department of Defence is subject to confidential arrangements between the United Kingdom and United States Government." – [*Official Report*, 27 April 1988; Vol. 132. c. 203.]

I asked the same question on Thursday, 19 July 1990. The then Minister of State said:

> I have nothing to add to the answer which my right hon. Friend the Member for Hertfordshire, North (Mr Stewart) gave to the hon. Member on 27 April, 1988." – [*Official Report*, 19 July 1990; Vol. 176. c. 654.]

I persisted again on Tuesday 16 June 1992 and asked the Secretary of State for Defence

> if he will list the agreements governing the use of Menwith Hill by the National Security Agency of the United States of America.

The Minister replied:

> The use of Menwith Hill by the United States Department of Defence is subject to confidential arrangements between the United Kingdom and the United States Government." – *Official Report*, 16 June 1992; Vol. 209, c. 501.]

In other words, elected Members of Parliament are denied information on the appropriation of more than 200 acres of land by the United States Government, who now run a spy station in the heart of our country which is linked up to a global network. That is inexcusable. If there is parliamentary accountability, the moon is made of green cheese.

The Menwith Hill story starts with the purchase in 1955 of a 246-acre farm on rural moors west of Harrogate. On 15 September 1960, after the expenditure of $6.8 million, the United States army security field station opened. On 1 August 1966, control of the station was transferred to the ostensibly civilian National Security Agency of America. Francis Raven, who was the chief of G group of United States army intelligence until 1975, claimed that the takeover occurred because the army resisted eavesdropping on diplomatic and economic targets. That claim can be found on page 209 of James Bamford's excellent work *Puzzle Palace*. At least the Ministry of Defence is helpful in some respects. The copy of that book has disappeared from the House of Commons Library, so it secured one from the MOD library – it was the only piece of useful information that the MOD has provided on the matter.

Menwith Hill is a spy station – a sophisticated version of the man in the dirty raincoat looking through a bedroom window or the pervert spying through a lavatory keyhole. Those who defend the station's invasion of our land, which has never been approved by Parliament, are no better. There is no glory or wonderful purpose involved in Menwith Hill. That is all the more true now that the cold war is over. Ministers justified the Menwith Hill base by saying it was part of the cold war, but we understand that that has finished. What is their justification for the spy station now?

Yorkshire land has been taken from us to provide an eavesdropping centre that is virtually free from urban, electro-magnetic interference. That is why the station is sited at its current location. The station is part of a chain of such stations that span the globe. Their aim is to assert and retain United States supremacy. For example, exactly opposite to Menwith Hill, on the other side of the globe in a prohibited region in Australia, stands the twin of Menwith Hill, Pine Gap station. When Menwith Hill opened, the United States air force security service listening post at Kirknewton near Edinburgh ceased operations and a former employee is quoted on page 210 of *Puzzle Palace* as saying:

> I had to keep a special watch for commercial traffic, details of commodities, what big companies were selling, like iron and steel and gas. Changes were frequent. One week I was asked to scan all traffic between Berlin and London and another week between Rome and Belgrade. Some weeks the list of words to watch for contained dozens of names of big companies. Some weeks I just had to look for commodities. All traffic

– interception material –

was sent back to Fort Meade in Washington.

Menwith Hill took over those functions and continued to pursue military eavesdropping.

Its spying grows. The cold war has ended, but the radomes number 21 after recent expansion. About 1,200 staff, who are mainly American, are employed there – the number has grown from 400 in 1980. United States staff are ordered never to mention the National Security Agency of America and to report all outside contacts with foreign nationals – the British people who live in the region – to ensure that supervision of such contacts is maintained. The base has a few carefully controlled public relations contacts to camouflage its isolation and secrecy, but many

191

British people continue to oppose the base, for which there is no longer any justification, if there ever was.

Throughout the time of the base's existence, Otley peace action group has held demonstrations and campaigned against it. A group of women, including Lindis Percy and Anne Lee, has focused particular attention on this foreign intrusion and has repeatedly entered the base and obtained valuable information – more power to their elbow. If Parliament will not provide accountability, people outside always will. While Parliament remains inert, it is people outside this place who have pushed Parliament along the road to democracy.

Some of the information was given in a recent Channel 4 'Dispatches' programme. The fact that domestic intrusion exists at Menwith Hill station is surely shown by the fact that British Telecom has a 32,000-telephone line capacity connection from Hunter's Stone Post Office tower along the B6451 to Otley. There cannot be 32,000 telephones on the base in simultaneous use; that defies credibility. The Hunter's Stone Post Office tower happens to be a pivotal point of more than 1 million route miles of microwave radio connections installed in Britain. The cable from Hunter's Stone Post Office tower runs directly to Menwith Hill. There has never been any parliamentary authority to allow this serious and unwarranted intrusion into our telephone network.

There are two large United States firms within the military-industrial complex: Loral Space Systems Incorporated, formerly a part of Ford, and Lockheed Aerospace. They sell much of the spy equipment and they are both involved in arms sales to third-world countries. Menwith Hill gains information that would be useful to them. Lockheed and Boeing, for example, oppose the success of Airbus Industrie, which has sold many aeroplanes round the world. Can the Minister guarantee that information about commercial matters relating to Airbus Industrie and the sales of the Airbus 300, for example, has never been picked up by Menwith Hill and has never been passed on to part of the US military-industrial complex? Both Boeing and Lockheed depend for their continued existence on military contracts from the United States Government. Our Government continue to betray our people by allowing spy stations such as Menwith Hill to be dominated and operated by the United States, without any control that is visible to the people at large.

A recent 'Dispatches' programme on Channel 4 examined the matter in some detail. I shall put a few quotations on the record for Parliament. Margaret Newsham is one of the few people who have worked at Menwith Hill and spoken out. She worked there from 1977 to 1981. She says:

> From the very beginning of my employment, it became very much aware to me that massive security violations were taking place. All the programmes that I did work on were subject to these abuses.

She is referring to interference in commercial traffic.

The programme's commentary on Margaret Newsham continues:

> And that wasn't all. Inside Building 36D at Menwith, she was invited to listen in on an American Senator's intercepted phone call. After leaving, she informed the US Congress about what she'd seen.

Good on her. Can the Minister assure us that Menwith Hill never listens in to any telephone calls of United Kingdom Members of Parliament, not directly in the United Kingdom, but bounced back over the various satellite systems?

According to the programme, only one person in the world has ever got the National Security Agency to admit intercepting his messages. He was a United States lawyer called Abdeen Jabaro who said:

> It took me 18 years to get my records finally destroyed. It is like Big Brother. It's like 1984, of – surveilling people all over the globe. And if you're British, if you're French, if you're Dutch, you're any – any people, anywhere you have no rights to complain about this. You have zero rights.

What does it say for parliamentary democracy when people have no rights against these arrogant organisations which are given authority by a clique of people called the Government who have not come to Parliament to get any authority? It is a scandal and a disgrace, and I look forward to the Minister trying to explain that away, as he tried to at Question Time in a superficial and cliché-ridden manner.

A National Security Agency employee was quoted on the programme, but the words of an actor were used as a disguise. The Government know all about using actors' words to disguise someone. That employee was quoted as saying:

> Menwith Hill was responsible for intercepting 'ILC' and 'NDC' traffic from 1966 to 1976. Then came the satellite intercepts. like MOONPENNY. ILC is International Leased Carrier – basically, ordinary commercial traffic. Your and my phone calls. And 'NDC' is 'Non-US diplomatic communications'. But that job was later moved out of Menwith Hill during the 1970s, to Chicksands, where a special unit called DODJOCC was run by the NSA, direct from Menwith Hill. 'DODJOCC' stands for Department of Defense Joint Operations Centre Chicksands. Because of the high sensitivity of its work no Britons were ever allowed in.

Was that high sensitivity because they were intercepting British communications? Howard Teicher, National Security Council member from 1980 to 1986, said on the programme:

As a rule I believe that the United States government would never spy on the British government. and would never direct the National Security Agency to try to collect information on British government entities or individuals.

However, having said that that would be the rule, I would never say never in this business because, at the end of the day, national interests are national interests. And, as close as the US and the UK are, sometimes our interests diverge. So never say never. Especially in this business.

The former director of the Central Intelligence Agency, Admiral Stansfield Turner, explained how he met an American called Joe – of course – who said that there was information and that he was a CIA operator working secretly and spying in a country, the name of which is not given. Joe told the admiral that there were three contracts competing with United States firms. Admiral Stansfield Turner said:

"What did you do about it Joe?" And he said "Well, we don't have any policy on this, so I did nothing."

When Admiral Turner took over at the CIA a new organisation was set up inside the Department of Commerce. Its special function was to receive valuable information from US intelligence that the Department could use to America's economic benefit. It is the Office of Intelligence Liaison.

The programme makers were not allowed inside, so they used the American Freedom of Information Act which the United Kingdom, the home of the mother of Parliaments, does not have and they asked for the standing orders of the department. They claim that they show that the office receives some of the unique type of intelligence collected at NSA stations such as the one at Menwith Hill. It is called sensitive compartmented information. Of course, the documents that were shown on the programme demonstrated what I have already said, that Lockheed and Loral are integrated in the National Security Agency's operations. They are still involved in running the computers.

I shall quote again the words of Howard Teicher, the former head of the CIA. He said:

The United States was always concerned about the purchase of non-American advanced armaments by the government of Saudi Arabia. We were certainly aware that by preventing a foreign government from selling something that we hoped would lead to an American entity to be able to sell, it would certainly contribute to our commercial interest, but that was not the first priority.

The first priority that he spoke about was the cold war, and that has ended.

What is the first priority at Menwith Hill? Will the Minister publish the agreement that allows Menwith Hill to be operated at the base near Harrogate? Why should not the people of the United Kingdom know about these matters? In a democracy, why should they be kept from them? It is an outrage that they ever have been.

What laws govern the operation of Menwith Hill? Do the United States employees there come under United Kingdom law or does the Visiting Forces Act 1952 apply to civilians? What rights do individuals or companies have if they believe that they are being spied on by Menwith Hill? For example, can the Minister give a categorical assurance that Menwith Hill is not intercepting commercial traffic?

Finally, if the Minister is so confident about democracy, will he allow me and other Labour Members to visit the base, especially since Harrogate councillors have certainly done so?

*(Parliamentary Debates, Commons Official Report, 6th Series, vol. 240 c. 609–13.)*

© Parliamentary Copyright

# CHAPTER 14

# OBITUARY

## TAM DALYELL, MP

Bob Cryer was the first Member of Parliament, other than the Speaker, to be seen on a television broadcast from the House of Commons. At 2.33 p.m. on Tuesday, 21 November, 1989, Cryer stood up on a point of order:

> I understand that, as with the other sessional orders, this one on the Metropolitan Police is debatable. It is the right of honourable members to exercise that function in the debates of the House, whether there are television cameras here or not. I am concerned. I fully support the motion that honourable members should have access to the House, and agree that any obstructions to such access should be removed, but I can recall not very long ago when some members of the citizenry – students – wanted to come to the House and express a point of view. It is important the House considers extending these rights to the citizens and tax-payers who pay for this institution, so that they may have access to this place, and we may know that when they come to make representations, the police will help them as well, and not cause an obstruction, which is what occurred with the students' demonstration.

This was the essence of Cryer the parliamentary man. Had it been almost any other member he or she would have been muttered out of the chamber by colleagues who thought that the member speaking was simply concerned with personal publicity. Cryer was heard in silence and got away with it because he had done the same thing many times before, especially late at night, when the Press gallery was sparsely populated, and before the days when cameras were present. Cryer was recognised by friend and foe – and his extreme left-wing opinions had many foes, not only in the Government benches – as a champion of parliamentary democracy and basic values as to what the House of Commons was all about.

There was also something rather special and almost unique in Cryer's political history. Since 1945, few politicians have left Governments of their own volition on a matter of political principle or genuine differences of belief about policy. And most of the few who did so had some inkling that they were likely to be sacked or gently moved from office for other reasons such as the inadequacy of ministerial performance. One of the exceptions to this generalisation – from a group which can be counted

At the Sutton-in-Craven Labour Party rooms, 1979.
(*Keighley News*)

on the fingers of one hand – was Cryer. In 1978 he left the Callaghan Labour Government because he would not accept the Government's refusal to fund the Kirkby Co-operative. He further impressed his colleagues by not making a great song and dance about political virtue and his reluctance to injure the Labour Government. By so doing he proved what his friends had always known, that he was a man of substance. I can also vouch at first hand, having gone to him when he was Parliamentary Under-Secretary at the Department of Industry on a constituency delegation, that he was a Minister who cared about issues and the workforces in other members' constituencies.

Cryer was no mean parliamentary performer. He was an irritant to front benches, both the Government's and his own; but he was an effective irritant. He was in the tradition of the parliamentary awkward squad whom Ministers ignored at their peril. A man of impeccably good manners, he would rise time and again in a full House to challenge the

conventional wisdom. That he was heard at all, and usually with attention, in the parliamentary bear garden was due, I feel, to three factors.

First, he always put a well-informed point of view, however unpopular it
might be. Secondly, he displayed clarity of mind and diction and was
completely unflappable, even when it was quite obvious that he had
gone over the top. Thirdly, and above all, the House of Commons recognised that he was an outstanding expert on parliamentary procedure and
indeed was chairman of the Select Committee on Parliamentary Statutory
Instruments from 1979 to 1983 and again since 1987.

Cryer had enormous parliamentary stamina and was one of the late-night
sentinels of the House of Commons. No governmental shortcut, no
ministerial sleight of hand would go through unspotted when Cryer was
on duty. And he was on duty most of the time and most of the hours
when the House of Commons was sitting.

Yet as his friend Dennis Skinner said last night: "Bob Cryer was a
committed socialist and a full-time committed socialist in and out of the
House of Commons. Certainly he was one of a rare breed who could
make a relevant extempore speech at the drop of a hat." Skinner added
that whenever one needed an ally for an unpopular cause Cryer was there.
And it was my own personal experience that when I was in parliamentary
trouble, and in adversity, Cryer was a stalwart friend.

Cryer was born of a Yorkshire industrial family. After the Albert Road
school and Salt High School in Shipley he went to Hull University to study
economics, law and government. My first memory of him is of a tall,
ginger-haired, live figure striding to the platform of the Labour Party
conference in October 1962 and demanding that platform speakers and
MPs, of whom I was the most recently elected, should not make overlong speeches. In October 1964 he contested Darwen, in Lancashire, but
he had to wait until May 1971 to be elected to the Keighley Borough
Council. This was the springboard from which he was able to beat the
powerful Conservative Joan Hall in February 1974, the first of many
elections where his campaigning skills, energy and capacity to make young
people think that he was worth working for gained a seat which would
not otherwise have gone to the Labour Party. One of his first causes in
Parliament was persuading the Tribune Group to oppose the British Isles
rugby tour of South Africa in December 1974.

To the surprise of some of Cryer's contemporaries, Callaghan appointed
him to a junior post in the Department of Industry in September 1976. It
was to his credit that, while he argued inside the Government for a left-
wing approach, he did not parade his left-wing conscience in public. He

proved an extremely competent minister, well-regarded by civil servants who gave him the credit of knowing his own mind. After the Labour defeat, and only then, he criticised James Callaghan for having espoused policies which led, as Cryer saw it, to Margaret Thatcher's victory.

Losing his seat in 1983, Cryer became a member of the European Parliament, simply as an interregnum before he could fight to return to his real home, the House of Commons. His causes, in which he was greatly supported by his wife, Ann, were legion: criticism of the European Community, mandatory re-selection in the Labour Party, antagonism to cruise missiles, and endless left-wing issues. Bob Cryer was a great railway enthusiast and indeed gave technical advice on the film of *The Railway Children* (1970), in which his family appeared as extras.

Of few MPs can it be said that the House of Commons will be a poorer place without them. Bob Cryer was one such.

(Reprinted with permission from *The Independent*, 13 April 1994)

# CHAPTER 15

# PARLIAMENT, AND YORKSHIRE, CAN BE PROUD OF HIM

## THE RT. HON. BETTY BOOTHROYD, MP

### *The Speaker of the House of Commons*

Bob Cryer was one of the most tenacious parliamentarians of his day. He was also one of the most skilled. Few had studied Erskine May more thoroughly. He knew it even better than *Wisden*, the other Bible for a cricket-loving Yorkshire MP.

He was, of course, one of the stars of the Chamber, sitting as he did among like-minded colleagues in that famous front bench below the gangway. But he also used his talents to the full away from the floor of the House, where many committees had reason to be grateful for his administrative skills.

Some people must have regarded him as a barrack room lawyer. I have two comments about that. Any barrack room which contained Bob Cryer would have been a better and more civilised place for his presence. And all those who lived in that barrack room would have been made aware of their rights and he would have ensured that they got them.

For a man who was tough and never hesitated to be abrasive, Bob Cryer was liked on both sides of the House. Even his opponents recognised his sincerity – and yes, his essential decency.

He was described as a man who had a gift for holding difficult marginal seats. But he had so many more talents. As Speaker I appreciated the quality of his interventions. When Bob Cryer was on his feet it was a signal that one had to be even more alert than usual.

Parliament, like our native Yorkshire, can be proud of Bob Cryer, whose life we are celebrating tonight.

*Letter to the Special Parliamentary Meeting held on 30 November 1994.*

*Extract from a letter to Ann Cryer from the Prime Minister, The Rt. Hon. John Major, MP*

Bob and I were political opponents and often disagreed but I always had a great respect for his convictions and his qualities.

In my experience he always expressed his views fearlessly whether they were popular or unpopular; he was straight and honest in his politics; and he never took unfair advantage. These are great qualities – rare qualities – and they made him a formidable politician who earned the respect even of those he disagreed with most strongly. I am deeply sorry that he will no longer be in his place in the House to pursue his concerns.

# CHAPTER 16

# CELEBRATION MEETINGS

## 1

## FUNERAL MEETING AT ST GEORGE'S HALL, BRADFORD

### *22 April 1994*

A meeting was held on the morning of 22 April 1994 at the St George's Hall, Bradford to celebrate the life of Bob Cryer.

Speakers were:

| | |
|---|---|
| Tony Benn, MP | Alice Mahon, MP |
| Cedric Binns | Graham Mitchell |
| Jeremy Corbyn, MP | Alan Petford |
| Don Dixon, MP | Arthur Scargill |
| Mavis Giles | Dennis Skinner, MP |
| Bernie Grant, MP | Keith Thomson |
| Max Maddon, MP | Trish Walker |

and Alan Whitaker

Before and after the meeting, Alan Horsey, Organist of Bradford Cathedral played Handel's 'Water Music' and 'Music for the Royal Fireworks'. During the meeting, which was chaired by Dennis Skinner, the poem 'Adelstrop' by Edward Thomas was read by Alan Petford, Bob Cryer's nephew. At the close of the meeting everyone sang William Blake's 'Jerusalem'. The meeting was followed by a private burial at Undercliffe cemetery, where the graveside oration was given by Tony Benn, MP.

The following are some extracts from the speakers' tributes.

## DENNIS SKINNER, MP

Can I thank everybody from Bradford, from Keighley, from Parliament, all those Labour supporters up and down the country, friends of Bob's and the family, the tremendous gathering here today, who have come to celebrate the life of one of the finest socialists that entered Parliament...an activist throughout all his life.

With Dennis Skinner, April 1990.
(*Telegraph & Argus*)

Some said he was the great parliamentarian, and he was. Some said that he knew the procedure of Parliament inside out, and he did. Some people said that he was a full-time socialist, and he certainly was that. He was also an extra-parliamentarian. He knew the power of the working-class, and he knew that out of struggle, things would change. The war was going to be a long journey, but the battle had to be carried on.

I just want to tell you how I met him. I met him ... where else? at a Labour Party conference way back when Gaitskell was the 'Prime Minister' and he said he was going to "fight, fight and fight again". Bob Cryer had got other things on his mind, and he was at the back of the hall where all those people congregate who are going to move points of order. He was an expert at it, and I didn't know! I was a member of the mining delegation from Derbyshire, and I saw this flame-haired, tall man stood at the back, going to move a point of order, the finger pointing, the head on one side. I thought: "He talks different to me. Is this the modern face of the Labour Party?" But I was totally and utterly wrong. He was like me. He'd just been brought up a different way. From working class, but not in the pits, and so he broadened my outlook in that moment, and I thought: "Well, he'll not be able to move reference back." I told him how to go on. I said: "You'd better not stand at t'top o' theer because if you're not down theer for dish-out, Bob," Ah says, "they'll pull the curtains down an' you'll not move it." Because they did it like that in those days before I was the Chair, but he ran, and he was there, and he was perfect. He'd got wonderful diction. He could speak excellently. He'd got all it needed to move a reference back and to humble the establishment up on the platform. I knew from that moment on that there was a lot that we had in common, so we talked about our backgrounds and the fact I came from Clay Cross, and he said immediately: "Oh, yes, they've got a two-foot gauge Ashover light railway at Clay Cross."

Well, to tell you t'truth, I didn't know it was two-foot, but I took his word for it, and he'd got this romantic view about those wonderful wagons that used to bring the rocks from Ashover. I had to tell him. I said: "We used to run those wagons straight down into the shed, Bob," and my view about that was totally different, but I learned to understand what 'e meant, and then he told me about Bill Cockson. He said he was a cricketer. But I was a cricketer, I was a fast bowler, I thought I was, but he was a real cricketer. He used to play with Cockson, another red-haired man from Clay Cross, an ex-miner who bowled out Bradman several times, and I thought: "I'm being humbled today".

He was with Ann as well at the conference. They were together. By the time I saw him at the next conference, they were married. A perfect couple. And then I heard that he was going to be nominated for Keighley, and some of the people – by that time I was in the Palace of Varieties – and some people said to me: "Well, you know, is 'e a Left Winger?" I says: "You bet 'e is." "But will 'e be a Left Winger when 'e comes 'ere?" I says: "You bet – when a lot of others 'ave gone," ... and 'e was. He sat by me in the House of Commons. He says: "Is this where you sit?" I says: "Yes, Ah sit on the front row," Ah says, "So we can get close to the Tories." "That'll do for me," he said. He said: "When can we start speaking?" Ah said: "Today," ... and 'e did. He made his maiden speech on the first day in Parliament – an extempore speech straight from the shoulder. I've read it again this last week ... all about education ... talking about the money spent on motorways...all the sorts of things that he'd continually told us about in Parliament, and so for fifteen minutes he made his controversial maiden speech, as the Press were to say, but it mattered, and they didn't have a wind-up so I wound up for him on that first day. He never changed. He became a Minister under Callaghan, and the moment he became a Minister we walked in St James's Park to try and find ways and means of not being one. Seriously, he was a first-class Minister. Everybody saw that. He actually conveyed a Socialist message from the despatch box on those occasions that he had the opportunity, and a lot of people don't do that, but he resigned over a matter of principle, as I knew Bob would do, over the question of the failure of the Labour Government to pay out money to the workers' co-operatives in various parts of Britain, co-operatives that have been set up by his mate here today – Tony Benn. He fought and held his seat in '79 against the odds. He fought again in '83 to hold it, but the boundary changes were too much, and then he became my Member of Parliament for Europe. I could actually vote for somebody for the Common Market with alacrity.

He'd already been a founder member of the Campaign Group in Parliament, and what did he do when he got to Brussels and Strasbourg? He set up a Socialist Campaign Group amongst the Labour MEPs, and there are still quite a considerable number who are members of our group.

He's a tremendous loss to people in Bradford and Keighley and elsewhere. They always say that they can be replaced, but I don't think that Bob can be truly replaced. We'll find others that will walk in the same road that he trod, but he was a great socialist to his backbone, and his memory will live for me for ever. It's etched in my brain as I've no doubt it is in all those of you that met him. He was a wonderful friend, a wonderful socialist, and it's sad that he's left us so soon.

## MAVIS GILES

Bob Cryer was a very good and loyal friend, but I first became aware of Bob the politician some years ago through my involvement with Bradford Nuclear Disarmament Group. We were a vigorous campaigning group at the height of the Cold War, when we were witnessing the introduction of Cruise missiles and Trident and the horrifying Star Wars scenario. At that time we could always be sure that we could call upon Bob whenever a presence was needed to voice strong opposition to the nuclear arms industry. For us, his knowledge and vitality were invaluable, and his personal enthusiasm helped to motivate us.

With enlarged Parliamentary Petition against pit closures. At the bottom of
Ivegate in Bradford with Armstrong Siddeley Hurricane to the left. October 1992.
(*Telegraph & Argus*)

When you espouse a cause that at times seems to have universal unpopularity, it's very easy to become a bit despairing, and it's at these times that the Bob Cryers of this world inspire you to carry on. Last week, Ann remarked that you either liked Bob or he got up your nose, and of course, that was what Bob was about, getting up the noses of the people who did the most damage. This was never more apparent than when he'd harried the pro-nuclear propagandists, the nuclear establishment who wanted, above all, to operate in secrecy, unhindered. Bob would never allow that. He watched them, he questioned them, he monitored them, and he exposed them and held them to account. To do this, of course, you need expertise, and Bob had that in good measure. He was a careful and thorough researcher, and that's what his opponents feared. His arguments always came across as sensible and reasoned, even to the most ardent supporter of the nuclear industry, and that was hard for them to cope with. Bob dealt in facts rather than propaganda, and he didn't compromise his beliefs, nor jump to the popular trends of the day in order to gain votes, which was why his sincerity was never in question.

Bob was invaluable at public meetings, and he didn't only appear for the big crowds. He was always prepared to turn up at small gatherings, and he put as much care and effort into talking to three people as he would to three thousand. He was liked and respected among all the anti-nuclear groups in Yorkshire.

When the Bradford South seat became available, I wanted Bob Cryer to be selected because I wanted, among other things, another strong anti-nuclear voice in the House of Commons. But more than that, I and others wanted him as our MP because he was incorruptible. His reputation as MP for Keighley was outstanding. He was well-known as a dedicated and effective worker for his constituents. He wanted the job for what he could do rather than from what he could personally gain. He never used his position for self-interest. When Bob was selected to fight the seat for Bradford South, he lived up to his reputation. He and Ann worked tirelessly to make sure that Bradford South would continue to be represented by a Labour MP – and so it was – and Bob and Ann were always accessible. They had time for people. You could always contact them and, as far as the constituents were concerned, no problem was ever too small. They held surgeries every week all around the constituency and published an annual newspaper to inform the electorate of the work that he did. And of course, Bob opened a local office which provided a continual service for those who needed it.

Those of us in Bradford South enjoyed canvassing with Bob. We loved to be part of a canvassing team and to meet his electorate on the doorstep where his genuine warmth and enthusiasm came through. And the people liked to talk to him. When you were around Bob, politics were never dull or boring. He was fun to be with because he had a great sense of humour, and when things got heavy, he usually had a joke to lighten it. Even when the tension was very high at the close count during the 1987 General Election, Bob was the only one there that was relaxed and jocular. "Don't worry," he said. "Look at all those votes going into the boxes," and he was right. I think all of us have our special memories of those times.

During the past week, when so many people of Bradford have made their feelings known, I've reflected a good deal upon the changes that Bob brought about . . . the influence he had upon whatever he touched, and the line of Tennyson kept coming into my mind, and it's this:

I am a part of all that I have met.

What Bob Cryer met, he usually changed for the good.

## MAX MADDEN, MP

Comrades and friends! Today we mourn the death of Bob Cryer, but also celebrate his life and work. Bob and I first entered the House of Commons in 1974, and I was delighted when he was elected and returned to the House in 1987 with Pat Wall, whose sad death we still mourn today. And the three of us battled night and day – literally – to turn the tide, on behalf of this city, to ensure that Tories were swept from power, never to return again, and you will remember that it was in this hall where Bob and Pat spoke, when we began to turn that tide. Bob never forgot where he came from. As MP for Keighley and as MP for Bradford South, he remembered where he came from. He remembered the interests that he was sent to the House of Commons to defend, and most of all, he remembered the interests that he was sent there to promote and defend. Sometimes he'd upset a few people because he didn't like wining and dining on the ratepayers of Bradford any more than he enjoyed being lobbied by commercial lobbyists in the House of Commons, peddling influence for all the big companies and the big multi-nationals, and he spoke out against that bribery and corruption, and in some quarters it didn't win him many friends.

As has been said, Bob never regarded any issue as being too small to command his attention, or anyone too big to intimidate him from tackling. He campaigned, as you will all remember, against the closure of Westwood Hospital, demanding that those with learning disabilities should be given the quality of life, and the resources to make that a reality. And again, that didn't win him many friends in some quarters. He always

Bob and Max Madden at a Bradford Pensioners Rally
in the Tyrls, Bradford, September 1983.
(*Telegraph & Argus*)

fought for public transport, particularly for rail but also for buses, and his record will be outlined by other speakers here today, but he was also an engineer. I remember once going on a factory visit to an engineering firm here in Bradford, and for twenty minutes he and the chief engineers talked about pistons and piston rings. He never repeated himself once, and I never understood a word they were talking about. But that was Bob. He serviced those old cars of his with loving care. He really wanted to defend the textile and the engineering industry of this city, and we both have done what we can to defend that decline over the years. He wanted decent homes for people of Bradford, at rents that were affordable and at prices that were also affordable. He had an outstanding record on health and safety issues, a meticulous knowledge of the legislation which he helped to steer through the House of Commons between 1974 and '79.

He was also very keen to improve the environment. He took a genuine interest in global issues, and also a very keen interest in animal welfare. He was against the transporting of live animals and took a very deep interest in legislation, particularly over dangerous dogs, and he always said that what this Government had done was of nonsense, and so it has proved.

Bob believed in what he believed in. He never regarded his belief in nuclear disarmament, his opposition to the narrow European community or public ownership as embarrassing political baggage to be thrown over-board for reasons of electoral or political expediency, and he was dismayed at the shift of the Labour Party in recent years to the right. Bob believed that Labour councils should be different, that Labour Governments should be different, that they should help working people and their families, and he really believed that 'peace, jobs and freedom' was more than a mere slogan.

He had his differences with the *Telegraph & Argus*, and I used to share an adjoining telephone box from time to time, when he used to complain about their reporting of his speeches, or their non-reporting of debates in the House of Commons, and that still goes on today.

I just want to end by quoting two letters that appeared in the *Telegraph & Argus* in the last week, which I think summed up Bob very well indeed. One was from a lady who said his whole life was spent in serving the people, and the second wrote: "A good man, an incorruptible socialist and a friend." That will be Bob's epitaph.


## BERNIE GRANT, MP

From the very start, Bob was supportive to me, and that carried on throughout the time that we knew each other in Parliament. At one stage, I was the Chair of the Socialist Campaign Group. During that period we had a number of very sticky issues, including the Gulf War, and during that period Bob was one hundred per cent behind us, and supported everything we did.

Bob was a committed anti-racist and internationalist, and I certainly had no difficulty whatsoever in getting Bob to support the Early Day Motions and anything that I did both in terms of the fight against racism and fascism in this country and internationally.

Bob, as you know, was a member of the European Parliament, and just before he died I had a long conversation with him in the tea room, and he talked about the time when he was an MEP, and he talked about the corruption of some members of the European parliament...how they abused their position, how they abused their allowances and so on, and it was quite clear that here was a person who was totally incorruptible, and I salute Bob for all he did with regards to that.

Bob was a friend to everyone. I think that one of the most touching things that I've heard in the last few weeks was when I went into the tea room – the

Bernie Grant MP, poses with Bob Cryer on the front doorstep of his Shipley home, September 1991. Behind them is 'GNR 6', Bob's prized railway relic from Queensbury Tunnel.

members' tea room – and one of the canteen workers said to me: "I hear that Bob Cryer has died. What are we going to do now? Who's going to support and represent us now?" and the reason she said that was because, amongst other things, one of the things that Bob did was that he kept the debates going. He would get up and speak on money resolutions after the main issue was discussed, in order to take the vote past half-past ten so that the women in the canteen could get taxis to take them home, and Bob did that as often as he was able to, and when he couldn't manage it, he would raise furious points of order with a speech in order to try and stretch it out as long as possible, in order that the women could get safe transport home, and so when the canteen worker said to me: "Who's going to look after us now?" and I said: "Well, there are some of us who will attempt to take up the mantle that Bob has left behind."

And I think that one of the major things to me about Bob was his leader-ship qualities. He wasn't the person who would push himself up to be elected here and there, to the National Executive and so on, but he had a leadership quality in the House of Commons that was second to none, and Bob would attack the Tories in a way that nobody else could. He knew the running of the House of Commons, he knew the constitution of the Commons, and I remember those long months when we spent many nights arguing over Maastricht. I recall on one particular occasion when I was half asleep in my room at three in the morning and the division bell went, and I rushed down to the lobbies not knowing which lobby to vote in because I couldn't see any of the usual gang around, and I thought: "Oh well, Dennis Skinner says when you're in difficulty, always vote NO," so I went into the NO lobby, and I was waiting there very nervously, and then I saw Bob coming along and I said: "Thank Heavens! I'm in the right lobby," and that is the sort of thing that Bob did for everybody, and especially at times like the Maastricht debates.

I feel not only sad today, but I feel a great loss because socialists are few and far between, and at a time when there are huge changes in the world, when there are changes in the Labour Party. When some of us don't recognise which way the Labour Party is going, I think that people like Bob were there as real beacons of hope for the likes of us, and I think that he will be sorely missed. And I know that where he's gone, it can't be a bad place, and I hope that we'll meet again there some day. Thank you.

## CEDRIC BINNS

Comrades, I suppose it was the 1966 General Election when a tall chap stooped in through the committee room door in Oakworth and said he was a Labour Party member who'd just moved to Keighley, and how could he help to make sure that Keighley was won for Labour. So he and I were despatched down to Goose Eye to collect the four votes that existed in that hamlet, and from that point on, Keighley was never the same, because Bob took a principled stand on all sorts of issues. He was outspoken, not only about Johnson's murder in Vietnam but also about Wilson's sycophancy, and he feared nobody, in putting the case when he believed that case was correct. And of course it was then no surprise that in 1972 Bob got the selection for Keighley. By the time of the Election in 1974, the Tories daren't debate issues with him. They walked off platforms when he came in because they knew they'd no answer, and in '74 he won Keighley.

He started to hold surgeries. He took up the cases of many people. I know from Bob and Ann that the surgeries that were due to start at 10.30 in the morning, and finish at 11.30 and 12, used to go until 1 or 2 because people wanted the support of their MP, and Bob unswervingly gave that support to thousands of ordinary working people around Keighley.

His support for the Asian community was second to none. I know that he would be rung up and asked for help when some pettifogging bureaucrat had attempted to incarcerate an Asian at Heathrow, and it would be Bob

With Trade Union banner in front of the Bradford war memorial, November 1988.
(*Telegraph & Argus*)

that made sure that those Asians who'd been incarcerated were released to their families in Keighley and elsewhere.

His support for the Labour Party in Keighley was unswerving. Thanks to Bob and Ann, we have our own Labour rooms in Keighley. He supported them and did absolutely everything that was legally possible to ensure that the Labour Party benefited from his duties as an MP.

His support for ordinary workers was outstanding. I was reading the other day the minutes of the Standing Committee for the 1974 Health and Safety at Work Bill, and it's quite clear, when you read those minutes, that the reason that there was a seventh sitting of that Committee was that Bob was pushing the points for the protection of ordinary working people, and they needed to have a seventh meeting to consider the things that he was raising. Of course this all got up the Tories' noses, and they tried to unseat him in 1979, and when we expected Keighley to go Tory, it didn't – it stuck with Bob.

By 1983, they decided that the real answer was to sling into the Keighley parliamentary constituency something like 15,000 Tory votes, and yet, despite that, Bob stood by Keighley. He stood there, not merely because he represented the best chance of winning Keighley, but also he knew that if he had taken a seat elsewhere – and there were many offers on some with majorities in the five thousand/ten thousand bracket – if he'd have taken one of those offers, then whoever had fought in Keighley would have had an even more difficult time 'cause the Tories would attempt to abuse it and, of course, we know what happened . . . he lost, and Keighley lost the finest MP that it has ever had and is ever likely to have. But that wasn't the end of Bob's commitment to Keighley because in the 1984–85 pit dispute Bob and myself were on the streets of Keighley every month, collecting money for the miners.

The same was through the Silentnight dispute. Bob and Mike Hindley – a fellow-MEP of his – collected thousands of pounds. He got Dennis to come along to a rally, and I can remember Dennis and Bob speaking through a P.A. system on top of the mini van, and the moment they got up to speak, the bosses turned the music up in the factory so the scabs couldn't hear, but it didn't have much effect 'cause the scabs came to the window to listen and watch what was going on, and Bob's support for the workers in their struggle was absolutely second to none.

We had Bob back to Keighley last year, to speak in a miners' rally, and we had him back to a General Committee meeting because some moderniser had the idea that proportional representation was a good idea, and Bob came and spoke to the Keighley General Committee and he had a few words with the comrades there. He'd no time for spin doctors, new realists, modernisers, bedfellows to the Liberals. He gave them short shrift, and I want to leave you with Bob's closing words of that speech. What he said was that "What this country needs are good, sound, socialist remedies."

## TONY BENN, MP

Comrades . . . it has all been said, and more will be said before the end of the meeting, but what impresses me in a way most is the number of people who have come – from all over the country. I've had letters of condolence about Bob's death, which I've never had for anybody else, because people knew we shared the sense of loss.

Coming up on the train, a retired head teacher from Norfolk . . . "Where are you going?" . . . "Oh, I'm coming to Bob's memorial service." "Why?" "Well, Bob was always ready to come to our meetings." Somebody else on the train – a retired cabinet maker from Wakefield: "Oh, I wouldn't miss it." And people from the South Coast, and I think that is an indication of the impact that he'd made.

Now, many people in politics are remembered by the offices they held, and although Bob held many very important offices he's not really remembered, I think, primarily for that. He was a councillor in Keighley. He was a Member of Parliament, of course, for Keighley as well, although I didn't first meet him then. I first saw him when I saw *The Railway Children*, which I've seen many, many times, and I've got the video at home and I've watched it again and again, and I shall watch it more. He was a Member for Keighley, then he stuck by the constituency when the boundary commission tried to get rid of him, a thing the voters hadn't wanted to do, then a member of the European Parliament as has been said, then a Member of Parliament and, of course, a Minister, and he'll be remembered for what he believed in and what he stood for, and what he fought for, and what he did for the people who represented him. And no one worked harder – as has been said by everyone – than Bob, and he was quite untainted by the temptations that come with office. I had one letter, which I am going to pass on to Ann and the family, from Jack Spriggs from KME 'cause Eric and I went up to Liverpool and we saved one of those engineering companies. We set up the co-operative there – and then after the referendum I was sent to Siberia . . . by Harold Wilson. Rather like Malinkov who was sent to a power station in Siberia, I was sent to the Department of Energy – it was actually a very important job – and Bob went into the Department of Industry, and he kept me informed. "Would you believe, Tony," he'd say, "what's going on!" and then in the end he resigned because the support was not forthcoming for them.

He suffered a lot of setbacks, and many attempts were made to modernise him and his opinions and so on, but there never about Bob was any trace of personal bitterness or disappointment. Indeed, he was a very cheerful

Bob Cryer and Tony Benn (as Secretary of State for Energy)
on a 'walkabout' in Keighley in 1976.

and amiable man in all his dealings and his arguments, and the arguments were very penetrating and very clear, but they were entirely free of malice or personal abuse, and that's why so many Conservative members joined in the tributes that were paid to him in the House of Commons. Indeed, when the news came through, I do recall a sense of shock, among members of all parties. He had very wide-ranging interests because he was a great believer in the whole culture and traditions of our society, and at a time when Socialism is under attack everywhere and the media trying to persuade us it will never return, Bob's life proves how false it is.

He was popular at Bradford because he was a left-wing socialist and he cared for people because he was a socialist, and people cared for him because he was a socialist. The inspiration that comes from the life of somebody like Bob Cryer is what creates new socialism, and we must never, ever believe that socialism will only survive so long as its more famous advocates are still alive. Socialism is made up of two flames that are burned in every generation in every country – the flame of anger against injustice and the flame of hope that we can build a better world, and in Bob those two flames burned brightly, and because they burned brightly, they will never be extinguished.

## ALICE MAHON, MP

I think it would be impossible to pay a tribute to Bob and his life-long commitment to justice, socialism and peace without mentioning Menwith Hill. Bob's last major debate in the House of Commons was about Menwith Hill*. With typical humour, he opened the debate by revealing that the Ministry of Transport thought he would be replying to a debate and he had one of his civil servants searching for a railway station called Menwith Hill, only to learn that Menwith Hill is a secret communications centre run by the Americans, so secretive in fact that the same Minister of Transport, who'd been a Minister of Defence, didn't even know of its existence! Little wonder that Bob, in summing up the Minister's complete ignorance of both transport and defence, was able to conclude this whole revealing episode reflects a Department of Transport devoted to road interests and restricting their knowledge of trains to go straight, and I think that was typical of Bob's humour.

In that very good debate on Menwith Hill, Bob went on to expose the real nature of the billion-dollar phone-tap up there, placing on record the purpose of this secret station where the United States use the most

* The Menwith Hill debate is reproduced on pages 189–195.

Ann Cryer and Alice Mahon MP, with the Otley Peace Action Group
at the memorial tree planting, Menwith Hill, 1995.

sophisticated listening equipment to help their defence industries gain confidential commercial secrets about their competitors, and no doubt to listen in to the rest of the trouble-makers in the Labour Party and the Trade Union movement. In Bob's words – and I think it was such a good debate, I do hope people read it – our Government continue to betray our people by allowing spy stations such as Menwith Hill to be dominated and operated by the United States without any control visible to people at large. He was very good at exposing the Government and its unaccountable way of carrying on business.

In this debate, Bob paid tribute to the peace campaigners who for years have kept a constant vigil on Menwith Hill, and he asked the Minister how many MPs' phones were being tapped. Not surprisingly, he didn't receive an answer to that one. But this was vintage Bob Cryer, probing, exposing, holding Parliament to account, and I was very proud to be his friend when I heard this debate. I really do think it was one of his finest.

Bob, of course, will be remembered most for his superb support for peace and the peace movement, and we all remember the inspiring speeches he made against the obscenity of the arms trade and nuclear weapons, but I remember especially when I came under pressure from a hostile media proposing the Gulf war. Bob was just simply a tower of strength of faith and hope, and advice, to those of us who were having a bad time.

He was an incredibly brave and principled comrade, he had a lovely sense of humour, and the way he used to speak out and use his voice put me in line with W. H. Auden who, just before the start of the second world war, used his great gift with words to warn the world on an impending crisis, and he said: "Who can reach the deaf? Who can reach the dumb? All I have is a voice to undo the folded lie." I think Bob certainly used his voice to undo the folded lie speaking for socialism and peace.

## ALAN WHITAKER

I'm grateful to have this opportunity to say a few words about some of Bob's other interests, those which his family good-naturedly described as his eccentric side.

Second only to his passion for socialism was his love of railways which played an important part of his life over many years. In particular, he was noted for his unfailing enthusiasm for the railway heritage in the Bradford and Keighley area. Our great mutual interest, and the catalyst for what was to become a lasting friendship, was a somewhat obscure system of branch lines which linked Bradford, Halifax and Keighley, and converged at a triangular junction at the hill village of Queensbury,

Driver Bob Cryer at the controls of 2-6-2 tank engine number 41241
on the Keighley and Worth Valley Railway, 1973.
(*Bishop Eric Treacy*)

which is the home of the famous Black Dyke Mills. It was the closure of
these former Great Northern Railway lines in 1955 which determined Bob
to found the Keighley and Worth Valley Railway, as he was keen to
ensure that the same fate did not befall the branch to Oxenhope.

But while the Worth Valley lines flourished in private hands and became
internationally famous with its starring role in the feature film *The
Railway Children*, the remnants of the old Queensbury lines began to
fade away largely unnoticed. In later years, Bob and I were to ensure
that this was put right, and today there's more interest in these obscure
routes than there ever was when they were operating lines.

I first met Bob in August 1964 as a boy of 12, when he turned up with a
cine camera to film the track-lifting trains between the village of Thornton
– where I lived, and my father had been station master – and Cullingworth. The footage that Bob shot during that month eventually formed
the basis of a film which he updated in later years by re-visiting the old
track-bed. He entitled the film *The End of Enchantment* – a wonderful title
– and showed it regularly to enthusiasts and local community groups
along the route of the old line. It was always well received.

I myself actually travelled on some of these track-lifting trains in 1964, and on one occasion clearly remember a tall, lean, bespectacled man in a tweed jacket, clambering down from a steam loco footplate, beaming, after we arrived at Cullingworth. It was none other than Bob, who'd persuaded the crew to let him have a go at driving. He was very proud of that, and he never let me forget it. In later years Bob actually completed regular driving turns on the Worth Valley line and became an experienced footplateman, something he very much enjoyed.

## GRAHAM MITCHELL

Thirty-two years ago, following the closure of the then seemingly insignificant branch line to Oxenhope, I first met Bob Cryer at the public meeting which created the Keighley and Worth Valley Railway Preservation Society. He was the inspiration, the driving force, the 'man of vision' who saw what might be. Without his energy, his eternal optimism and his unshakeable belief that the branch line could, and would be re-opened, it's extremely doubtful whether that fledgling society would have survived to create a nationally and internationally recognised independent railway, but Bob believed, and he made everyone else believe, in the seemingly-impossible dream. He was re-elected annually as Society chairman for ten years, creating a unique system of railway management: open government of the railway by a council of twenty-four democratically elected members.

There's no other railway in Britain where the ordinary workers enjoy such direct control. It was Bob's most precious gift to us and we guard it very jealously.

He remained active in the Society as a qualified steam locomotive driver until the late 1970s, and thereafter he remained a vice-president, a regular speaker at the Society AGM, and someone who was enormously proud of all that the railway had achieved in a quarter of a century of unpaid volunteer operation.

Now, the Worth Valley Railway has always been a sort of neutral territory, a truly classless society where a person's age, sex, income, race, religion or politics has never really mattered very much. But integrity has always mattered, and no one could ignore or fail to admire Bob's total sincerity – always completely honest and straightforward, a man of boundless optimism and enthusiasm, a lifelong supporter of public transport.

Five thousand Society members have lost a great man, a true friend and a loyal champion. We owe him an enormous debt. I hope that the Keighley and Worth Valley Railway will be seen as one of Bob Cryer's lasting memorials.

## ALAN PETFORD

My own earliest memories of Bob are connected with being swept up to the entrance to Exchange Station in Bradford on a rather foul, dark November day, in an ageing green Armstrong Siddeley car. Of course, the circumstances and the setting of this memory are apt; we were here in Bradford, a town he was very proud to belong to, we were heading for a railway, and we were in an Armstrong Siddeley. Although, as he said, he bought Armstrong Siddeleys at first because they were a big car for a little money, and of course that's partly the truth, there was more to it than that. They were not just very good value, they were also very

Campaigning in the 1987 General Election with his
Armstrong Siddeley 'Hurricane'.
(*Telegraph & Argus*)

good engineering, and Bob valued good-quality things wherever he found them. He spent a lot of time with his old cars, proudly maintaining them himself, relentlessly searching at auto-jumbles for elusive spare parts, and taking enormous pleasure in simple tasks that some of us might consider dull, such as the patient dismantling of a derelict specimen in order to increase his own stock of spare parts.

To take a journey with Bob – and Bob was much concerned with transport – was a liberal education. I think of a journey taken not so long ago. We went over the Pennines to Manchester, a journey which was punctuated by exhortations to look at this or that picture palace, now regrettably turned into a bingo hall, the happy cry of recognition when former Co-operative Society premises were seen, and all the while of course, the commentary, the running commentary, on every railway line we passed, its history, its rise, and all too often its demise. His knowledge of these things was vast, and the detail was impressive, and he loved to share these things with us all. Obviously, he was a good talker, a brilliant raconteur, a witty man, and yet he was also a good listener. He could listen, and he could learn from what he heard, and he could bring to your own enthusiasm, the enthusiasm which he'd brought to his own interests.

One Bank Holiday we set off for Morley and spent a fascinating afternoon discovering the churches and the chapels, enthusing about the civic architecture of that rather neglected town. Bob liked northern towns. He liked their intimation of the past, he liked their people, and he liked their buildings. And he did a great deal to ensure that their buildings were not swept away – witness his enthusiasm to find an alternative use for the Upper Independent Chapel at Heckmondwike, and his rejoicing when this building that we're in now was saved from the dead hand of ring road re-development. Re-development was not something that appealed very much to Bob. A re-development too often means the advance of concrete, the corporate image, the strategic plan, and that usually involves the sweeping away of the little man, the removal of the corner shop, the closure of the local industry, and all these things he held very dear.

You know, the most remarkable thing about Bob was that in the midst of an incredibly busy life, he never seemed to be very hurried. He always had time. He had time to visit his relations, time to entertain them, and time – most important of all – time every weekend, time to enjoy his family.

And so today we celebrate this great, good, genial man who strode across our lives, sharing with us his wit, his knowledge and his enthusiasm, leaving us the better and very much the richer for having known him.

## DON DIXON, MP

Bob knew the rules of the House down to the smallest detail. His knowledge of its procedure was unbelievable. He operated non-stop, day and night, and often late into the night. Bob and I had this joke ongoing. As Deputy Chief Whip, Bob used to refer to me as the Establishment, and late at night when most MPs had gone to the places that they go to late at night, Bob, Jimmy Hood, Billy Etherington, Dennis Skinner, Derek Foster, and one or two more, would be sitting there in the corner of the tea room plotting and planning how we were going to distribute the business the following day. If I went to the counter and asked for a coffee Bob used to say, "I'm not going to be bribed by the Establishment." And when Bob went to the counter and offered to buy me one, I used to say, "Well, you're kow-towing to the Establishment now, Bob!"

To give some idea of the work that Bob did on a normal day, one morning we visited a film studio, because Bob, along with all the other things, was chairman of the Labour Party Film Group. We would meet the trade unions and the employees and discuss with them how we could help the members and the industry. Then we'd rush back to the House of Commons. Bob would go into the tea room. After that he would rush round to the Table Office and put a question in, and after that he would nip into the Chamber. He'd generally have a question in the frame, and if he didn't, then he would ask a Supplementary. He would, after Question Time, in all probability raise a point of order, then rush off to chair the Statutory Instruments Select Committee, or the Member's Interests Committee, or the Liaison Committee. Even later on he'd make a speech on whatever Bill he was wanting to raise at the particular time. And then call a vote if he didn't agree with it – invariably he didn't.

Bob made an art form of speaking on Money Resolutions. Last parliamentary session he spoke almost eight hours on Money Resolutions and he spoke on every one. He used to speak on Money Resolutions for two reasons. First of all he said that whenever the Government spent money it should be challenged, and that's what he did. Secondly, as Bernie mentioned, the girls in the tea room, if the adjournment debate started before half-past ten, had to make their own way home by public transport. Bob used to keep the business going so that those girls could get taxis back home. We have a saying in the north of England: "Tough as old boots and as soft as clarts" [clarts = soft mud]. That typifies Bob. When it came to attacking the Establishment, he was as tough as old boots. When it came to representing the people he came from, he was as soft as clarts.

Since I was first elected in 1979, I've always enjoyed my job as a Member of Parliament. There were only two occasions when it wasn't so enjoyable. One was when Dennis fell off his bike and was missing from the House of Commons for a considerable time. The second was when Bob lost his seat at Keighley and went across to Europe. I remember during that period I went to the Labour Party Conference and was at one of the CND fringe meetings and I said to Bob, "How are you finding it in Europe? What's it like over there?" He said, "Don, politically it's a cemetery, financially it's a bonanza." And that's the way Bob always considered the European scene.

His enthusiasm for a cause never flagged. Whatever, or with whomever, he associated, his hatred of oppression and tyranny never waned. I think, unquestionably, Bob was incorruptible. I take comfort that I've been associated with Bob Cryer, a person who did so little for himself, and so much for others.

## Councillor KEITH THOMSON

I don't know what the relationship between ward councillors and MPs is in other districts but I do know that it would have to be remarkable if it was to improve on the excellent performance that Bob gave – the contribution that he gave to us at the ward level. Not only did he help us whenever we needed it, to keep us informed about what was happening, but he used his power, he used that voice of his, he used the knowledge that he had to overcome the smaller problems that all of us at the ward level might have.

Some examples: a year or two back, a lot of people were having difficulty getting a Disability Living Allowance, but a quick phone to Bob and it was done within the week. And there were many people in Bradford who got their benefits from the DLA, not because of work that people like me do, but because of work that Bob could do, and the way that he could cut through red tape.

We had a local school which had the temerity to think that it would be useful to opt out from local democracy – to secede. We talked to Bob about it. Now, normally when you talked to people like that, they'd give a list of addresses and some suggestions about what you could do. Bob didn't do that. Three days later – just three days later – there was an Early Day Motion on the order paper signed by the good and the mighty here. The exposure that that gave helped us to enable folk in the area to take that matter seriously. That school is now still part of the local community. Thank you, Bob.

And sometimes, when we were looking for support on wider issues, when the Council was looking to make sure that environmental matters were taken seriously – not an easy matter these days – when we were looking for support for energy conservation, we asked for the support that Bob could give us. Again order papers, again Early Day Motions, again speeches from him, and again the Bill that's dealing with this is still there and it's still making progress. Thank you again, Bob.

It was not just those areas, it wasn't just those matters, it was also to do with the practical help that Bob and his family could give. It was only two Sundays ago that Ann and Bob were in a windy, high-altitude bit of Bradford, on the Buttershaw Estate, making an impact, an impact for me. It wasn't the impact caused by an Armstrong Siddeley noseying round a corner where normally Armstrong Siddeleys aren't seen, it was the way that Bob canvasses.

Now you all know there are various types of canvassers. Two mainly, there were those that tiptoe up the garden paths with temerity, they knock on doors that have been freshly painted and soon as no one answers they are off to the next one, with having stuff shoved through the letter box. And then there are people like you and me who give a fairly hefty thwack, you wait for someone to come, or not come, and then we are off to the next one, normal canvassing.

But there is a third type, there's Bob's type, and it was a sight to behold. Just one Sunday back. There was Bob, it was cold and the wind was blowing, and he had that mac on. That mac that we all know, that mac that Bob loved and it was flapping, his hair was bouncing and he strode up those paths, and he knocked and he knocked on the door. Now that knock was something to behold. It was not a normal knock, it was an announcement, and it stirred the area, and that knock was twice as loud as anybody else's, and it was more than that because it went on three times as long as everybody else's, and the rest of us there knew where Bob was. You did not have to look at what number he was at, you could tell by the knocking, and so could the people living in the houses. You could hear them thundering down the hall. The door would be opened, a strangled, "What the . . . ! Bob, it's you!," and then a very pleasant discussion would take place. Bob would make sure the message was well received, and he was then down that path and then he was coming to the next one.

That was the sort of practical help that people like me needed, and the practical help that we didn't have to ask for. I didn't know that Ann and Bob were coming out that afternoon. The Armstrong Siddeley came round the corner, and there they were, our numbers had doubled in one fell swoop. But the impact that he made, was far more than double.

That area, in fact, is still talking, as they all do, that Bob's been, and then we all follow on behind, and it's that sort of support, Bob, that I am grateful for and I know that all Councillors in the area say the same. So Bob, on behalf of all the local Councillors in South Bradford, I stand here very pleased and very humbled to record our support, and our thanks and our gratitude for all the help that you gave us in the fullest measure. We will miss you. Thank you.

## JEREMY CORBYN, MP

Bob was a great man and a great socialist, and there's three things I want to say about him.

Firstly, Bob saw it all. He was an MP, he was an MEP, he'd been a councillor, and in all those positions there are lots of temptations put our way. We are sent into public office to represent the people who put us there, and to represent those socialist ideals and socialist principles that saw us elected in the first place. Tragically, many stray on the way-side. They're tempted by power, they're tempted by privilege, they're tempted by money and by corruption. Bob was tempted by none of that. He was a man of absolute integrity and exposed the corruption and hypocrisy that surrounds so much of what goes on in Westminster, in Brussels, in Strasbourg and so many other places. He was brilliant in exposing the corruption of power that exists there, because he recognised that if we are to be effective socialists, then we have to act effectively, act with principle and, above all, not take for ourselves what others cannot get. That was Bob, and Bob's life, and he never failed anyone in his job as a representative or spokesperson for them... individual constituents, friends or anybody else.

He and I passed, if you like, in 1983. In that dreadful 1983 Election, when both he and Tony Benn lost their seats. A number of us came in, and whilst Dennis was there to help and guide us, we missed people like Bob and Tony. Tony came back in the Chesterfield by-election, and Bob came back somewhat later for Bradford South. He was brilliant all the time that he was in Parliament, with his help, with his advice, with his support, and his standing firm on principles.

Bob passionately wanted a peaceful world. He joined CND because he believed in unilateral nuclear disarmament, because he believed nuclear weapons were immoral and wrong. Nothing, nothing on earth would change his view on that. Nothing would distract him from that view. He opposed the Maastricht Bill because of its implications, because of

John, Ann, Jane and Bob: the Cryer family above Heaton Woods,
Christmas 1990.

its narrow Eurocentrism, because of its failure to appreciate the need for
an interdependent and peaceful world. That's why he voted in every single
division on Maastricht, that's why he was there for every second of those
debates. He was a person of principle. Just as he opposed the Vietnam
war, he opposed the Gulf war. Just as he stood for peace for the people
of Vietnam, he stood for peace for the people of the Middle East, as he
stood for peace for the people of Yorkshire and this country and the whole
world. He was a true internationalist, and by God! the Labour Party needs
some true internationalists.

And he had other interests. I got a very moving letter from a constituent
a couple of days ago who said: "Please tell Bob's family and his friends
that those of us who work in what remains of the British film industry
appreciated his support for our work, our industry and our trade union",
and I've heard so much about Bob's interest in cricket and railways. I
once made a mistake of saying to Bob I was interested in cricket and railways. I wish I'd never opened my mouth because he exposed my lack of
knowledge on both subjects within the first five minutes and I was forced
to have some corrective tuition for the following 35 minutes. Bob always
had time for everybody, and I was always amazed on these occasions
when somebody like Bob, so active and so prominent and so helpful
and so supportive, had time for so many issues. How he had time to
change the piston rings on an Armstrong Siddeley, and play cricket,

and be interested in the film industry, and be a brilliant MP, I don't know, but I'm going to find out because I really do admire the way he lived and worked.

In Parliament he understood the need for an absolute understanding of parliamentary procedure, not for its own sake, not because it was some kind of academic interest, not because in his retirement he was going to write some worthy work on parliamentary procedures, but because he understood how you could get under the noses of Tory MPs, and I thought it was great. When I was a Teller late at night on these odd votes that Bob and Dennis would call, standing next to some Tory MP also counting, who's come along with his dinner jacket because he was expecting just to vote and go home – and this is three o'clock in the morning – he'd say: "What's the matter with Cryer? Does he not want to go home?" And they were just so angry about it, and it gave me pleasure. It gave me pleasure to see these people – well-fed and well-dined – forced to stay up all night and listen to socialist speeches from Dennis and Bob and others about the evils of Maastricht and other things. He will be sorely and sadly missed for all that he did there.

But he also recognised that what happens in Parliament and what changes things isn't just what goes on in Parliament, it's what goes on outside Parliament, and that's where the *Guardian* got it wrong in what they said about Bob. There is no criticism of Bob from any of us for his obsession with parliamentary procedure. We admired it and we appreciated it. We also appreciated the way that he wanted a network of supporters developed outside Parliament – a network of people to bind Socialists together to give us strength and give us that common feeling and common understanding. For Labour to succeed, as Bob said so often, you don't do it by spin doctors, press releases and instant appearances. You do it by long-term dogged work, explaining to people that the only way of achieving a decent, reasonable society is a society based on socialist values which you talk about, preach and act throughout your entire life. That's what Bob did, and we are deeply grateful for everything Bob did in his life. And this huge meeting today is a testament to all those who loved Bob so much during his life, and we thank him very much indeed.

## TRISH WALKER

I started working for Bob, as his secretary, in 1987 when he first became Member of Parliament for Bradford South. In those six and a half years, I saw Bob work untiringly for his constituency in Bradford South. He opened a constituency office soon after being elected. The office was opened in Bradford, for which he was immensely proud. It was open five days a week. 22 Edmund Street, our office, was a very, very busy place. Bob provided accommodation there for various organisations... the National Union of Teachers, the Socialist Book Shop, and a recent one, Yorkshire and Humberside CND. He took great pleasure in lending the meeting room to the many Labour Party and voluntary groups. It was a very, very busy office. No letter nor call remained unanswered. Bob replied to every issue that was addressed to him, regardless of the politics of the author. In addition, he was fiercely proud of his Saturday morning advice surgeries – forty last year – and he never missed one. He held these surgeries so that his constituents in Bradford South had access to him. Indeed, he held the surgeries around the whole of the constituency to make it as easy as possible for people to come to see him. The response to his tragic death bears testimony to that work. Of the many cards, letters and telephone calls received in the office over the last ten days, one particular phrase remains with me. It is: "There was no such thing as a lost cause for Bob, no problem too big or, more importantly, too small."

In all the many tributes paid to Bob over the last week, my three-year-old daughter paid one of the best. Out of the blue, she said: "Bob, he made us laugh, didn't he?" He did, and we should remember that. Thank you.

## ARTHUR SCARGILL

It's more than twenty years since I first met Bob and Ann Cryer. It was in the Yorkshire Television studios, when Bob was being interviewed, and as I listened before it was my turn, I knew then that I was witnessing a truly remarkable human being. And whilst we gather today to mourn his untimely passing, it's right that we also take this opportunity to celebrate his life and his achievements. During the two decades since I first met Bob, I've come to regard both Bob and Ann as friends and as comrades, and I'm privileged at the participation of so many people in this memorial service and celebration of a life of a truly remarkable human being and an outstanding Socialist.

Both the National Union of Mineworkers and I have known Bob as a comrade and as an unswerving supporter in our long fight against pit closures and Tory Government policies, and their determination to destroy our organisation. And from our National Executive Committee and from the magnificent women support groups whom he supported completely, I bring their sympathy to Ann.

I can never forget Bob's solidarity. Not only during the 1984–85 miners' strike, but throughout the difficult years since – and speaking personally – both Peter Heathfield and I will never forget Bob's unswerving support throughout the witch hunt against both of us in 1990. It was this kind of support from Bob, Dennis, Tony and others which helped us to give us the strength to fight back and overcome that particular attack. He gave us class support because always he gave us socialist commitment. Bob gave himself with a struggle against depression of all kinds. He fought with total commitment against the tyrannies of unemployment, racism, religious bigotry and war. His solidarity was with the dispossessed and the disenfranchised, and it seems to me that is the way that we should remember his life, because it provided all of us with an inspiration.

He was an outstanding socialist who had an international as well as national perspective and vision. He detested sectarianism and the forced nationalism which has always led to division and human suffering. It was a privilege to work alongside him in the struggle to end apartheid in South Africa – a goal soon to be achieved – against racism and fascism, and, of course, in the ongoing campaign for world peace and nuclear disarmament. Bob cared deeply for his fellow human beings and was truly committed to the welfare of others. His personality was in tune with his principles. The warmth of his kindness radiated from the heat of his class feeling. He waged his own battle against the new realists of recent years, rejecting any compromise with basic socialist principles. There was never any danger that Bob would lose the visionary gleam that built our movement and will help to see us through difficult times ahead.

In every respect of his life and work, Bob beckoned to us all and wanted to see all of us join the fight for world peace, to free the world from poverty, injustice and inequality, where people, through the common ownership of the means of production, distribution and exchange, are able to control their own destinies and make the world a better place in which to live. His great political skill, his wonderful oratory and total commitment was sustained by his happiness with his loyal comrades, Ann his wife, his pride in Jane and John, and his enormous network of caring friends and colleagues.

We should also celebrate his magnificent achievements and commit ourselves to achieving that socialist vision of which he was so proud. We owe it to all, but more important, we owe it to an outstanding comrade and friend, to carry forward the banner towards the vision of socialism that he fought for so hard, and make it become the socialist reality that he so desperately needed.

*Extract from a letter by John Smith, leader of the Labour Party, read by Dennis Skinner at the close of the meeting*

"I will always think of Bob as a proud and fearless parliamentarian determined to use his office as an MP to fight against privilege and for justice in every day that the House of Commons sat. He was often disarming when with a twinkle in his eye he would reflect the ironies of politics in the many discussions among the Labour MPs in the tea room. He could of course, and this was one of his great strengths, be scathing and contemptuous of those on the other side of the House, who pursued heartless policies towards the poor and under-privileged in our community, and who use their parliamentary positions to pursue their own vested interests. He was, in Parliament, an acknowledged and respected expert on checking the abuse of secondary legislation by the Government. Bob was a man of courage and of principle, never hesitant about being in a minority if he thought the cause was right. All this, in the forefront of the battle. He was a great socialist, a valued comrade and a fine man. While his own family will miss him most, the whole of the Labour Party shares their loss, but they like us, can be proud of his life and of his work and his intense commitment to the values of socialism, by which he lived his life.

---

## 2

## SPECIAL PARLIAMENTARY MEETING HELD IN MEMORY OF BOB CRYER, MP

*on 30 November 1994, in the Grand Committee Room, Westminster Hall*

Chaired by ALICE MAHON, MP

The text of the following contributions was transcribed by Diane Tempest from a video made of the meeting, and edited by Bob Duckett, both of Bradford Libraries. The publisher wishes to thank the speakers for giving their permission to use this material. The following are some extracts from the speakers' tributes.

### RT. HON. GREG KNIGHT, MP

*Minister for Industry and Former Deputy Government Chief Whip*

Many of you will think I am the last person you expected to see here, and with good reason. Apart from one or two notable exceptions, Bob Cryer, above all, gave me more headaches than any other backbench Member of

TPW 370, a 1955 346 Sapphire saloon, was the longest serving of
Bob's Armstrong Siddeleys. Purchased in 1964 and photographed
in New Palace Yard in May 1991.

Parliament. Night after night he caused me to keep a hundred or more
Conservatives in the building in case there was going to be a vote when
he decided to speak at length on money resolutions, orders, motions,
and ways and means resolutions; even though these items had been agreed
as being non-controversial and matters which could go through without
debate by the usual channels. Indeed, on many occasions, he spoke
*because* they had been agreed by the usual channels! Time after time he
caused the Government's business to slow down and proceedings to
drag on by talking at length, being one of only a handful of MPs who
could speak for an hour, an hour and a half, on a very narrow motion,
and yet always remain within the rules of order. He used the rules of
procedure, he did not abuse them. For that reason he made few enemies,
and gained respect. We will miss him on the Government side; in fact he
will be missed in all parts of the House.

Bob also played a very important role, the media would probably call it a
backroom role, but it certainly was not, as Chairman of the Joint and
Select Committee on Statutory Instruments, a job that requires a keen
eye for detail and a lot of stamina. And the fact that he did that job for
so long speaks for itself.

I have to say I was rather surprised reading some of the obituaries in the newspapers which referred to Bob as a champion heckler. Well, champion heckler he certainly was, but he was also much more than that. He was a serious and intelligent politician, and those that knew him well also knew that he had a softer, passionate side. When the political debate was over he was always fun to be with. I first saw this passionate side of Bob Cryer before I was a Whip, in 1988, when I was waiting to speak on a debate on a British Railways' Bill. Bob rose to his feet and I, and I think most of my colleagues on the Government side, expected a political tirade against Government policy. But instead he made a quiet, thoughtful and passionate speech, not only about the state of railways generally, but particularly about a line he was interested in on which he felt action should be taken.

The other passion in his life was classic cars. It was in May 1991 when I first realised that Bob had an interest in classic cars. I had entered into the RAC classic car run, which is the largest event of its kind. It starts at eight different points around the UK, and finishes at a race track. This particular year it was taking place during the Whitsun recess, and the rally finished at Donington Park in Leicestershire. And from each of these eight points the contestants were started at one minute intervals, and at the end cars were arriving at ten second intervals. I thought I was the only MP taking part. I arrived quite early and noticed some five or six seconds later an Armstrong Siddeley Sapphire pulling up alongside. Bob was behind the steering wheel and his navigator was Ann. I think for the first few minutes Bob thought that this was some intricate Government Whip's ploy to try and get some dirt on him. What was a Government Whip doing sitting in a car next to his at the finish? After a few minutes of lively political banter we started to talk about his Armstrong Siddeley Sapphire and his Armstrong Siddeley Hurricane convertible cars, and from that moment on a behind-the-scenes friendship between us developed.

About a year later I was due to take part in a rally. I had paid the fee, but my car was off the road, I couldn't get a part for it. The rally organisers said they wouldn't give a refund, it was too late, I would have to lose my fee. I happened to mention this to Bob, that my normal supplier hadn't got the part in stock, and I was going to have to pull out of the rally. He said nothing, but about an hour later, on the internal message board, there was a note from him giving me the name of a supplier who had this part, giving me the price and the telephone number. I got the part, ordered it over the telephone, and started to look for Bob to thank him. I found him later on in the evening going into the Chamber with a huge pile of papers. I said "I would like to thank you, Bob, for giving me the name

Bob Cryer with Senator Patricia Giles and Senator Rosemary Crowley of the Australian Privy Council, delegates to the 1989 Commonwealth Delegated Legislation Conference, at the Queen Elizabeth Centre, Westminter.

and address of that part supplier." He said "You can't buy me off with flannel, the Government are going to be here all night!" He always put his beliefs first, and that is how it should be.

The last occasion I met him was on the last Thursday he was at the House. He was leaving and we bumped into each other in New Palace Yard. We started to talk about his two cars and he said "Are you interested in playing a part in an all-party committee?" I thought, to start with, he was having me on because I knew he had a healthy disregard for all-party consensus, but he said "No, I actually think people who care about classic cars and try to keep them on the road should get together. I think we should have an all-party parliamentary classic car club. Would you be interested in taking part?" I said I would. He said that to be effective we would have to make sure the chairman of the group was someone who passionately believed in the subject and was actually going to take action to get the group up and running. And he said to make sure we got the right person "I think we should have a rule that the chairman has to be someone who owns two cars of the same make!" "Bob," I said, "I will gladly propose you as chairman." We agreed to speak on the first day back after that weekend and set about putting this idea on the all-party whip. Unfortunately it was a journey he never made.

The Labour Party has lost a superb parliamentarian; someone who was an effective campaigner for causes he believed in. But the loss goes wider. We miss him in all parts of the House.

## LORD DORMAND OF EASINGTON

*Former Chairman, Parliamentary Labour Party*

Bob Cryer knew more about the film industry than anybody I have known during my fifty years' interest in films. I was going to say 'as an amateur', which he was of course, but I suspect that he knew more than many of the professionals in the industry. He knew about films, their actors and actresses, their producers, their directors, when the pictures were made, how much they cost, the problems associated with particular pictures, and many other matters. There was much more to it than that. He knew about the whole background of the industry. Some of us had a bit of a tease with him over the years. The group was always called the Films Group. If you talked to Bob about it, it was always the Film Industry Study Group. Of course, he was absolutely right about that, because the people who knew about the group thought that we were only concerned about the merits of movies. In fact we seldom discussed the merits of particular pictures. The topics we discussed were the economics of the industry, the making of films, the technicalities of making them, the training of film makers (which was a particular interest of Bob's – he got us to the training school on more than one occasion), problems of distribution, and so on. Bob knew a great deal about all these aspects; he gave us the lead when we wished to pursue them with Ministers (who had very great respect for him indeed), with the money men of the industry, and with particular individuals.

In this respect it was Bob who realised that a visit to the studios could play an important part in the work we were doing in the group. There had been very occasional visits in the early years. I remember making one to Shepperton, and the occasional visit to Pinewood, but Bob set it up on a regular basis. In doing this, of course, we were meeting film actors, famous people, that attracted quite a few people into the group. They were enjoyable experiences and not only attracted members to the group, but they were invaluable in increasing our knowledge, those of us who were interested in movies, on everything that was associated with the industry, and they really brought the work that we were doing alive.

Bob and I were having lunch one day in the cafeteria, and he said "Let's go to Hollywood!" I said "Great, fix it up for next week!" Needless to say, I

A discussion with Benezir Bhutto at the House of Commons, 1990.
(*Coun. Ghazanfar Khaliq*)

thought no more about it. Some time later he came to me with that great enthusiasm of his; "Jack. Hollywood. I think I've got some concessionary travel for both of us. And not only that, I've got a contact in MGM. Great stuff!" I was stunned. He actually meant it. But I had a problem, I didn't think I could afford to go, apart from other things, but with Bob Cryer's enthusiasm and determination it was going to be a very difficult thing to say "Well, Bob, I thought you were kidding!" He was still talking about it when I last saw him.

Some months ago he was invited to join the Board of the British Film Institute. I have to say that that was long overdue. He ought to have been on that Board a long, long time ago. He had already made an impact in the short time that he was on the Board. He had a number of interests, and one of them was the railways. So it is fitting and proper that he should be the railways adviser for that wonderful film *The Railway Children*. I still get a kick, as I did recently, when I saw that picture for the umpteenth time, and on the credits it had: Railway Adviser – Bob Cryer. The British film industry has had some severe and serious problems for some years now, but more recently it appears that things might be improving. Attendances in cinemas have been going up significantly. We could have done with Bob at the present time. His leadership would have been critical. His knowledge, enthusiasm, his drive, would have made a vital contribution to that change which is now taking place. The respect he had engendered, not only with Ministers, but in the industry itself – and he was highly respected in the industry – would have been of enormous help.

Bob had a way with him which is difficult to describe. I mentioned his proposal to visit Hollywood. Looking back on it, it demonstrates what I mean. It was the most natural thing in the world that the two of us should traipse to the other side of the world to do something about the British film industry. Similarly, when I was forming the Parliamentary Humanist Group some months ago, I said to him, "You're not a religious person, Bob, are you?" He gave me the most withering look and response I have ever had. Very coolly he said, "Jack, who do you think you are talking to? I am an atheist as any fool should know." But he said it in that very open, generous way which was his trademark.

We had a number of unusual things in common. We were cricketers, film buffs, atheists, and republicans. It was not only a joy to do so, but a stimulating and refreshing experience to get his attitude and views on all these things. If ever I wavered a bit, and we all do occasionally, there was only one thing to do – go and have a chat with Bob. He would put it right. It was not possible to put him into compartments. Even if he and I had no common interests, he would still have been for me one of the most remarkable personalities I have ever known. He was open, frank, honest, and I am not sure he would have liked this word, but he was charming. He was a charmer. My lasting image of him is of him walking into the Member's Cafeteria. He and I used to eat about the same time. There was always a smile on his face, and I knew I was going to get the real story of whatever was happening. There were no ifs and buts about Bob. He was black and white, and you got the whole story, there and then. What he told you was *it*. No other version would do. If ever I chose to question anything, which I did very seldom, I would get some disarming response which made me feel that I should have kept my mouth shut. There was no malice, no nastiness, just humour and tolerance, and sheer niceness. We are missing him and shall continue to do so for a very long time.

## THE RT. HON. TONY BENN, MP

*Former Secretary of State for Energy*

They say you know people by their friends, and looking around me at the people who have come tonight, where else in the world would you find two Speakers of the House of Commons, a former General Secretary of the Labour Party, a former General Secretary of the Communist Party,

Bradford's Temple Bank School visit Parliament, June 1991.

Alan Clark!, former Conservative Ministers, the Sergeant-At-Arms, and Clerks of the House? It really is an indication of the enormous affection that Bob had for people.

The first time I ever saw Bob was at *The Railway Children*, and I introduced him to my children and grandchildren. We watch it every year, and I burst into tears every year at the end. I had the great privilege of visiting Ann and the family in Keighley, and he took me to the railway station, the actual one. What I always felt about Bob's feeling about railways, was that he really respected the skill of the people who made the railways and who ran them. It wasn't just the mechanics, but the people. That skill is not very much respected nowadays, although it was on skill that we built the industrial revolution.

Tonight we are celebrating a life, though it is hard not to remember the moment we heard the news of his death. It was a shock that went round the House of Commons for which I know no parallel in my life, and I have been here for forty years. The funeral service in Bradford was immensely moving. There were crowds of people there, and at the lovely cemetery I was asked to do the most difficult thing of my life, I was asked to say the words at the graveside. But tonight we are celebrating his life and that's different from mourning his death or attending his funeral. We remember him more every day. It's not that you remember he died, that comes to everybody at some time, but you actually wish he was here.

The thing that interests me about Bob was the enormous range of his experience. He was a teacher; he was a local councillor; he served as a Member of Parliament – and a very good one; he was a Member of the European Parliament; he was a Minister; and he was the chairman of a select committee which included Peers and Members of the House of Commons. He know more about the House than anybody else. I cannot think of anyone who has served in so many capacities in what was really a fairly short period of his life, because he wasn't very old when he died.

What made him special was that none of the many temptations that tend to corrupt people in public life ever touched him. He wasn't pompous. He wasn't ambitious. I never knew Bob do anything for himself. He was always out for his cause. He wasn't manipulative, you never found him in a back room organising anything that would do anyone any harm. He wasn't jealous. He wasn't sectarian. He was never looking at some-body else and saying, "You have let us down." And he didn't do it for fame or money. And he didn't, throughout the whole of that period, ever give up his faith in socialism. Now it is true that some people do move from the left to the right, you'll have heard of them, but Bob dee-pened his commitment as a result of his experience. Everything that hap-pened to him made him realise more of the relevance of what he believed in. It strengthened, it didn't weaken his faith. He was not in any way ashamed of his socialism; he was proud of it. He never deserted the people who put him there.

Bob did have a lot of charm, and a capacity to have a rapport with every-body he met. You only had to see Bob in his constituency to realise that people knew he was on their side. They would talk to him and he picked up their experience. He learned all his life. He encouraged people and he taught.

The people who hold office do not always make the greatest difference. The people who are remembered are the people who have contributed their experience and their knowledge and their skills to an understanding of a period of history. Bob was a great teacher in that sense. Everything that he touched, he dealt with, but also out of it, he explained. Above all, he was very well trusted.

Bob and Ann Cryer on the House of Commons terrace with Bill and Mrs Dobson and friends, 1991.

I hope that the sharing of the grief will lighten the burden, because with the passing of the years it is the memory that will be alive.

## THE RT. HON. ALAN CLARK

*Former Conservative MP and Minister of State for Trade*

How tiresome it was for Bob not to believe in God. Yet how also very characteristic it was of him. It showed exactly the measure of his integrity that he would not in any way compromise his beliefs and enter into some of the cosmetic appearances that we are all prone to, but I didn't know of any other parliamentarian who was so replete with Christian values in his character. You could never catch him out in any way compromising his beliefs or his values. When I first came into this place I sat exactly opposite Bob, and I thought "Who is this dreadful fellow, smart-arsing around, making trouble, getting in the way all the time, keeping us up late at night and always getting up on his feet." If he had been called every time he got up he would have filled the index of *Hansard*. Then, slowly, and very grudgingly, I realised that there was something going on there that was extremely important for the integrity of the House of Commons, and the whole democratic process. Often single-handedly, Bob was committed to and proselytised particular values which ought, certainly, but very seldom are, to be in the minds of every person who is elected to the House of Commons. I used to watch him many times in his duels with the clerks. Often he'd get the better of them, and as a card-carrying and inherited member of the establishment, I had to be opposed to anyone who tries to undermine it. But I was often uneasily aware that Bob was right, and the reason he was being opposed by the clerks was because they somehow saw themselves as having a vested interest in maintaining the status quo by preventing too high a level of destabilisation, and that they had lost sight of the basic principles they should be guarding. Sometimes Bob had typically taken the party line, and I never knew, and would liked to have probed him deeply, when he was doing that because he really believed it, or whether he was just using it as a tool in a party conflict. Many, many times he was fighting single-handedly on behalf of people outside and away from this place; people who think, in their innocence, too often, that this is how all MPs behave. And how very, very few of them actually do. With his departure the Commons is very much poorer. I do not know if it will ever recover in our lifetimes. I should also say that it is my belief that the Labour Party is very much poorer too.

## THE RT. HON. TONY BLAIR, MP

*Leader of the Opposition*

I was very keen to come along this evening, not because I knew Bob tremendously well, I didn't – we came from different parts of the Labour Party and from different traditions in it – but for three reasons. The first is that in any decent political system or society you need people who are prepared to be thoroughly difficult and awkward, and to be so because they understand that unless the political system is challenged from time to time, then it breaks down. When you are sitting there, or standing, as leader of the Labour Party, then sometimes you want everything to work like clockwork, and someone like Bob can make it work not like clockwork at all. The day everything just goes through in the way that leaders, or anyone else, wants it to, endangers the whole political system. That was what he used to do, not just in the House of Commons, but in the Labour Party. He would speak consistently as to what he believed, and that would come out in every single part of his political life. Bob was the type of person who, you felt, it didn't matter if an entire room was against him; he would still get up – enjoyed getting up – and saying what he actually thought. So this is one thing that I remember about him very clearly. I remember those late nights in the House of Commons when the money resolutions would come on and he used to go across and say there were points that have to be raised here and they were going to be raised. Up he would get, and it didn't matter that people were waiting

With Rosa Wilkinson of Baildon on the House of Commons terrace, 1991.
(*Ginny Wilkinson*)

to go home, the points would be made. It was a great tribute to him that he
would always do it because he thought it was right, and he would conduct
the fight wherever it needed to be conducted, and however hard it needed
to be conducted.

The second thing that I remember about him was his absolute and total personal courtesy. He was always courteous to me even when he was completely disagreeing with me. Indeed, I remember one of the many times when I was in some slight conflict with other parts of the party, and things were going extremely badly, and he actually sought me out in the tea room and said, "You are going through a difficult time, but lots of people do, don't worry about it, you'll come through." He did not need to have done that. I always found him as having total and unfailing courtesy, which is a very big tribute. There was never any personal bitterness or rancour in anything that he ever did. Politics, in the end, should be about principle and belief, and doing what you think is right, but it should never be by hatred. It is people who have strengthened their principles that can behave like that, and he did, always courteous and always decent.

The third thing about him was that he was totally and completely Labour Party. Not in the sense that everything the Labour Party did he always agreed with, but he was completely loyal to the political principles of the Labour Party, and understood that that was always important to me. I don't know of anybody who had a greater appreciation of what the proper values of the Labour Party were than him. A lot of the time I did not agree with everything he said on policy, but the fact is he understood what it was that made people Labour and want to support the Labour Party. There are not that many people that you can say this about in politics, or in any walk of life for that matter. And he had a complete and total inner integrity. Some part of his character was very strong, something that kept him going and made him respected.

There must be an enormous sense of pride for his family to know that people miss him and believed in him. Even when they didn't agree with him, they still miss him and still believe in him. We do miss him, very much indeed. There is a part of the House of Commons that will never be the same again, and there is a part of the Labour Party that will never be the same again. I'm delighted to be here.

## BILL McKAY

*Clerk Assistant, House of Commons*

I can share and recognise a lot of the words which have been used about Bob Cryer this evening. Words like trust, integrity, and awkwardness. And I say this as a duellist on various occasions. And enthusiasm. I was one of the clerks to the Statutory Instruments Committee; a committee

Bob Cryer chairing a meeting of the Britain–Vietnam Committee at the House of Commons, 1992.

which, for the average Member of Parliament, there is no political payoff of any kind. It was a job which he did supremely well; a job which involved more paper than is environmentally sensible and which involves work delving into the middle of instruments made by obscure civil servants in obscure departments, and bringing to light all sorts of unpleasantness in all sorts of ways. He did all that without either complaint or reward for many years.

The second thing I shall always remember Bob for is something which everyone remembers him for, the money resolutions. These can very often be a spill-over for those who did not get in on a second reading. It was never this in his case. He was always 'ornery'; you always twitched in your seat as you saw him heading beyond the scope of the money resolution, and then you sat back because he saw the boundary, drew back, and he was off for another ten minutes. That is an art practised with skill by scarcely any Members of Parliament, but it was practised with supreme skill by Bob Cryer.

The third duelling episode which I remember very specifically was in the Table Office. Bob came in with an adjournment subject which was disorderly. We had a discussion about how it could be got in order. I thought I had got it in order for him and wrote it down, and just as I was giving it to him I suddenly realised I had drawn him one from one set of disorderliness into another set of disorderliness. I said "I am sorry. I have made a mistake. I don't think we can accept that." He grinned and said "Yes, I wondered when you were going to realise that!"

# CHRIS MONCRIEFF

*Former Press Association Chief Political Editor*

It has been known for some members of the Press who have moved a vote of thanks at the end of Labour Party Conferences – a daunting task – to have occasionally been greeted with something just a smidgen less than sheer unadulterated warmth from some sections of the audience when they have mounted the rostrum. Bob Cryer was never among that minority which justifiability may have felt aggrieved at the way some parts of the media were treating the Labour Party. Bob Cryer was always a great friend of the Press gallery, but he was not one of those MPs who are constantly besieging you with dossiers and documents, and unfathomable explanations to go with them, usually about some minutiae concerning an abstruse order surfacing among the oceans of paper in Brussels. He was not pro-active towards the national Press, but he was, which was his great virtue from our point of view, highly receptive to any overtures made to him by us. Bob Cryer, who I was constantly ringing up at home, morning, noon and night, was my ideal in that respect. He was that splendid thing: a broad-brush man. I am sure it's accepted that he had a great mastery of the detail as well, but simple souls like myself have spent a lifetime ignoring the small print, largely because we never understood it. Bob Cryer always knew that when you rang him up for a quote on some issue of the day. And he responded in exactly the way you invited him to without any of the nudging or pressure which often has to be exerted in other cases. He invariably delivered the goods in dramatic, fluent language. Bob Cryer was doing that long before anyone had ever heard of soundbites, and whenever Bob Cryer commented 'off the cuff' you could guarantee it would get all over the papers throughout the land. You never had to ask Bob, as you did most other MPs, for that little extra important bit: "Would he be so kind as to give the story a peg by tabling a Commons question, or even tabling an early-day motion." Bob's final sentence of any passage he gave you, no prompting required, always began "And therefore I shall be putting down a question to the Secretary of State...". Always when this conversation was about to finish he would ask "Is that all right?" as though it might not have been up to scratch. But it was always absolutely brilliant. Whenever I finished a telephone conversation with Bob there was always a spring in my step, because I knew that, thanks to him, the story was on its way.

Bob Cryer was not only a great friend of the Press gallery, he was obviously of massive value to the Labour Party that he loved. With Dennis Skinner he was easily the most frequent attender in the Commons Chamber, sitting there in that honourable place, the front bench below the

Daughter Jane, Bob, son John and grandson Conor in Bob's tiny
House of Commons office, November 1992.

gangway, the natural home of the habitually unruly. But he had no need to
be unruly, and he never was. His sniping at the enemy, the Tories, was
always vitriolic, but never unfair. It was not unknown, either, for him
to let off an occasional salvo at his own party leadership if he thought
that was necessary. Can you imagine his reaction now to the current
furore involving lobbyists in Parliament? They were his *bête noire*. He
would be in his element attacking what he considered to be an insidious
misuse of Parliament by outsiders. Some years ago I was asked to write
an article for a big posh designer magazine on the subject of lobbyists.
In the end the article was 90% quotes from Bob Cryer. A related
campaign of his was the so-called junketing by MPs and MEPs at
taxpayers' expense. He used to do Micawber-like calculations to demon-
strate what he considered to be an outrage. He once reckoned that a trip to
Strasbourg cost £150, but that the person travelling used to receive a "useful £500 tax free". That generates, he used to say dryly, "a considerable
surplus", and he had nothing but scorn for the former Tory MEP (who
lost his seat last June) who sought to explain it like this: "Our allowances
are large because our expenses are large." Bob Cryer might as well have
said, "Thank you very much, you made my day for me!" He would certainly endorse the Dennis Skinner school of thought that you never found
MPs going on fact-finding tours to Greenland in the middle of winter.

A reception in the Speaker's House prior to the Rugby League final in 1974 for
MPs representing rugby league constituencies.
(*United Agencies*)

Then of course there was the case involving the fifty pieces of silver. These
were fifty pieces of silver cutlery and tableware from the House of
Commons which should have been melted down, but which, in fact,
were sold at an auction in America, all bearing the portcullis, for a mere
£109. The items were resold for up to £250 each. Naturally the auctioneer
was overjoyed at this easy money and he actually, and innocently from his
point of view, telephoned Bob Cryer of all people, to ask if he could get
any more of this stuff. Needless to say, the matter was on the floor of
the House within a trice and the practice was stopped forthwith.

One of his traits which did not necessarily endear him to the Press gallery,
but certainly generated their admiration, was that he was one of the
few members assiduous and bold enough to tackle, late at night, the
perilous minefield of the money order. To get through that without being
challenged by the Speaker was an achievement of which the most
knowledgeable parliamentarian would be proud. But then he was a
knowledgeable, indeed a masterly, parliamentarian. He knew how to
exploit, legitimately always, the myriad of rules and regulations which
encompasses the place.

Bob Cryer threw his entire energies into whatever he pursued. There were
no half measures about him inside, or outside, Parliament. That applied
particularly to his much loved Keighley and Worth Valley Railway. I

believe he possessed five ten pound shares in that, but insisted he received no dividends. Bob was also an accomplished cricketer and a lover of the cinema. I am sure the term antique films is wrong, but he expressed a passion for cinematography and film appreciation. He once teamed up with Tony Banks, Jeremy Corbyn and Tony Benn to protect the good name of Laurel and Hardy. He was leading a protest that his heroes were being used to advertise Martini, and he tabled a Commons motion, no less, complaining about this assault on Stan and Ollie's integrity.

We all want to support the family in the loss of a man who, as this meeting visibly demonstrates, shows he had friends and admirers all over the House of Commons. He was a favourite of the Press gallery. Labour, also, have lost someone who could deliver the message dramatically, fearlessly and selflessly in a way that few others could do. On behalf of the Press gallery I would like to say that Bob Cryer was our best asset on the Labour back benches, and although occasionally the Labour leadership may have sometimes been a little rattled by his tactics, those tactics were always in the best interests of his party. And he will always he honoured for that.

## ALAN SIMPSON, MP

### *Chairman, Campaign Group of Labour MPs*

Bob was the first secretary of the socialist Campaign Group and I am the current one, and it is at times like this that you realise what a large pair of shoes he left behind. I am very conscious as well of a piece of advice that I was given by my mother when I was small, which was that whenever you are talking to a mixed audience avoid talking about sex and politics. I am going to try to do that tonight and just talk about Bob and cricket. There are some cricketers who can only perform before a big crowd, bowling downhill with the wind behind them. Bob wasn't that sort of cricketer. He would bowl uphill, into the windbags, in the dead of night, for as many hours as Parliament would continue to sit. He was in there when everyone else was wanting to up stumps and go home. Bob would be the first to rise to his feet, glower across the Chamber at whichever hapless Minister happened to have the responsibility for moving that night's money order, and immediately launch his own assault from the socialist end of the field. There was a deftness as well as a belligerence about the way in which Bob delivered his assaults. If you stood or sat close to him, you realised how much care and thought had gone into his own preparations. And his deliveries would curl through the air, they'd dip late, pitch into the rough, and rise sharply off the pitch into that region

Bob Cryer bowled as the Lords and Commons team is defeated by the
Home Office at the oval cricket ground, 1975.
(*Nicholas Scott MBE, MP*)

somewhere between the political groin and the ribcage. Invariably there
were howls of anguish, either when stumps got scuttled, or Ministers
got clobbered as a result. If they did, or if they were bruised rather than
bowled, well, that was life. Bob was doing his part of a job that he set
about doing religiously and devotedly, and professionally, during the
whole of his political, as well as his cricketing, career. He did this because
he knew he was bowling for a Labour movement that had shaped his
heart and trained his eye and taught him lessons throughout the whole
of his life.

He came into Parliament with a commitment, not only to follow that
through, but to share those lessons. And that's the other thing that was
really a strong and huge influence on me, because Bob came in here as a
teacher and as a learner. I don't think that he ever stopped learning
throughout the whole of his life, nor did he ever stop teaching and sharing.
He was an incredibly generous person in his willingness to show those of
us who had only just entered the institution, how it was that you needed to
play, why it was, reminding us what it was we were playing for, and

sharing the lessons he himself had learnt throughout his period, not only in Parliament, but within the Labour movement.

I don't think there are many who would doubt that Bob had become a real expert in relation to Commons' procedures. His knowledge of these was unparalleled, and he knew in many ways that an institution that was actually going to work properly, democratically, in ways that were acceptable and defendable, also had to be held to account by its own rules. He did that more religiously than anyone else that I have come across. Up to the moment that Bob died, he was a defender of Parliament and parliamentary processes, and a staunch opponent of any whittling away of parliamentary rights in favour of the executive. He was a believer in the integrity of parliamentary democracy, as long as it was made to work and made to be held to account. I think that in that sense, Parliament as a whole is much the poorer for his dying.

Another thing was that Bob wasn't just an anchor man at one end resisting things, he also knew what he was bowling and batting for. He was a life-long champion of open Government, and a lifelong champion of the underdog. He was a lifelong champion of honesty and decency. He was the scourge of corruption and of the closed society. In many ways he had a natural gift for bowling into the rough of political impropriety, whether this happened to turn out to be in the region of members' interests, or of Menwith Hill and the unaccountable role of the intelligence services. But he also knew who he was bowling for. In many ways I got to know Bob better when he was on his long run up around the country than from his short run up in Parliament. I joined him on numerous occasions as part of my own learning curve in the peace movement, and it was his unstinting commitment to go out, irrespective of the political weather, and argue a cause that he knew in his heart to be absolutely right, that impressed me. He was never apologetic. He was never fearful of taking the criticism of the established line on the chin, because he always knew that his own beliefs would stand up to whatever criticism and assault would come his way.

He made it phenomenally easy for other people to stand alongside him and share those commitments. He knew throughout his life that he was bowling for the poor, for the peace movement, for industrial democracy, for full employment, for social justice, and yes, for socialism. I think Bob at this point, would simply want it noting that he bowled with his left. No one would ever have accused Bob Cryer of ball tampering. Why, after all, should he think of using his nails on the ball when he could get his claws into the Government? No doubt there were times when he was equally assiduous at putting his claws into the conscience of the Labour establishment. Again, he would probably have wanted it simply noting that if, either today or in the years to come, we continue to feel the pinch of conscience from him, its only Bob and his claws reminding the party of what it should actually stand for.

Bob's death has robbed us of a kind and honest man, a courageous champion of socialist virtues, a fierce defender of parliamentary democracy and public accountability, and of an unselfish teacher. What would he say to us now? Would he say "Play up, play up, and play the game"? I don't think so. I think he would be saying "Play up, play up, and pray for the ball that curves in the air, dips into the rough, rises sharply off the ground, catches them under the ribs, and brings the buggers to their knees." Because that is what he was here for. He was here to stand for a set of values that shone through in everything that he did. And if there is a tribute that we can pay to him, it is simply for the rest of us to pick up the ball that he has left, to stick to the line that your heart tells you is right, and wait for the lift which, when it comes, Bob Cryer will certainly be a part of.

## DENNIS SKINNER, MP

We were big friends, and we were competitors. We hatched all kinds of plots on that front bench, and some of the best quotes were never made, because we dare not risk them. We tried a few, and I usually got chucked out for it! It's hard to follow on from what everybody has said because what they have said is true. He *was* like that, except that he was harder than what some of the people said tonight. He was totally and utterly committed, and we were reminded of that every single day.

In 1976, when Jim Callaghan took over, Bob rang me up and said "Dennis, I think I had better tell you. Jim Callaghan's offered me a job." I said "Christ, Bob. What is it?" He said "I'm not sure yet." I said "For God's sake don't become a whip!" Anyway, he finished up in the Department of Trade and Industry, as it now is. When I read his comments in answer to questions, he was very forthright. He didn't leave anything out. He went on to the attack every single chance that he had when he was answering on the front bench. He stayed there for about two years and then we started walking round St James's Park, trying to find excuses for him to pack up. Eventually they decided to ditch the co-operatives, and the one in Liverpool in particular. He realised that that was time to go. He got back to the front bench below the gangway.

He always had a marginal seat. When you think about where he stood on all the major issues and he hardly had a majority! At Keighley I don't

Dennis Skinner making a point, with Bob Cryer as chair at 'First Past the Post',
a Labour Party Conference fringe meeting, Brighton, October 1991.

think it ever got to a thousand, and at Bradford, in the first place it was
about the same. He managed to improve it towards the end, yet he was
a committed unilateralist through and through. On all the other issues
he was on the left, on the committed left. That's why he became the
secretary of the Campaign Group; because we all knew that we could trust
him to carry out that job.

In all his Supplementaries in Parliament, he never failed to get Bradford
in. It was an art form. He always talked about unilateralism and the
Common Market, but nine times out of ten he would finish up mentioning
some school or other thing in Bradford. Because of the marginal seat, he
was very disciplined as well, and organised. He was no fly-by-night.
Hardly anything he did was off the cuff. In his lifestyle he was disciplined
as well.

He was a socialist to his fingertips, and throughout all his campaigning
outside Parliament, and inside, he had got a set of principles from which
he never shifted. He believed in first past the post. He'd got no time for
proportional representation. He also had a lot of courage. I remember

Bob Cryer (chairman) with the Lord Mayor of London hosting an event for the 1989 Commonwealth Delegated Legislation Conference, Westminster.

when the De Lorean thing was in the air. He said "This thing's a racket, there is money pouring down the drain here." So he started raising it. He then got a request to go out into the central lobby to meet a group of trade unionists from Northern Ireland. He came back and said "They've sent trade unionists to see me and they reckon they are going to get in touch with the AEU and the T&G and all the rest in my constituency to try and unseat me." But he never shifted. He, more than anybody else, was responsible from a parliamentary point of view, for exposing the De Lorean scandal in Northern Ireland.

We worked as a team, as everybody knows. It was so easy – we agreed on nearly everything. There were odd little things, I suppose, but we always knew that if somebody was going to start the ball rolling late at night, then the other one would be able to follow on. You have heard it all from others, about his procedural expertise. He knew everything inside out, and he knew the Standing Orders. He also knew about those orders that went before his committee, or didn't go before his committee. He used to say to me "It's not been before our committee." He knew everything. They couldn't touch him whenever he got up on points of order.

I will always remember him, and I think we all will, here. I look for him now, whenever I'm sat on that front bench below the gangway. I always think that he could make a difference. I am absolutely convinced that there have been at least five possible votes that we have missed since he died, because we weren't sharp enough to get those two tellers in and do the shouting at the appropriate time. And one of them was very important. He wouldn't have allowed us to miss those chances.

A lot of people knew exactly where they were when Kennedy died. I knew where I was when Bob Cryer died. I shall never forget the moment when Don Dixon came into the Commons on that Tuesday after the holiday and said "I want you out." I wasn't keen to leave question time, but I knew that his ashen face was telling me something important. Then he told me the sad news, the tragic news. It was hard to believe. It was a haunting experience to think that a man who seemed so strong before the holiday, had gone. A haunting experience that will live with me forever. All that we can do in return is to thank Ann and the family for letting us have part of him, and to remember that the least we can do is to try and continue to live by all those wonderful ideas and ideals that Bob had.


## GINA COOK

*Supervisor, Members' Cafeteria*

I'd like to say something on behalf of the evening staff. Bob was very good at doing things for the evening staff. He was someone we held in very high regard, especially by the Refreshment Department staff. He was always polite and courteous, even after an all-night sitting. If the House was likely to go out before the staff could officially get taxis, he would raise points of order so that the House would go on later and we could all get taxis home. For this reason, as well as being a genuinely nice man, Bob Cryer will always be remembered fondly by the staff.

He was a comedian. He really was. He gave me a time. He really did. He was a teaser. Alright, I knew him from '74, but when we got new staff in that didn't know him, he would get them. He'd come up, put his hand on the counter and he would ask for a pot of tea. And while they where getting his pot of tea he would keep saying, "If it's not too much trouble." Every time you bent down he would ask "Are you sure it's not too much trouble?" "What's the matter with that guy?" they would say, "I bet he doesn't do that at home!" I would say to them "Just look into his eyes, he's so full of devilment."

We were discussing him this evening, and one of the things was his hair. He was always fond of his hair. He came in one evening and his hair was everywhere, like he'd been pulled through a bush backwards. "I do like it like your hair," I said. "It makes you so beautiful and boyish looking." "Do you really?" he said. "Takes years off you," I said. Of course it was a wind up. "Is it the red curls?" he said. "What red curls?" I said. "Do yourself a favour," I said. "The only red that that's seen comes out of a bottle!"

When men have to work away from home, it's so difficult. Families are split up, wives have to bring up the children on their own and make all the decisions. Ann was a real credit to him. All the family was. She was a pleasure to know. And so was he. I'll really miss him.

*Bradford Playhouse & Film Theatre presents*

# A TRIBUTE TO BOB CRYER

### Saturday 18 February 6pm

In memory of the late Rt Hon Bob Cryer MP, Bradford Playhouse & Film Theatre will present two of his favourite films -
*Brief Encounter* and *The Third Man*. The evening will be introduced by the Rt Hon Dennis Skinner MP and all proceeds from
ticket sales will go to charity, to be nominated.

The evening will begin at 6pm with
*Brief Encounter*, the famous story of
a short-lived love affair directed by
David Lean, who used as a setting
the railways - one of Bob Cryer's
main interests. *The Third Man*
follows at 8.15pm - directed by
Carol Reed, this classic dark
thriller features Orson Welles.

Both films are certificate PG.
Tickets are £3 full price and £2.50 for concessions
for both films or one film alone.

**CHAPEL ST,
OFF LEEDS RD
BOX OFFICE:
(0274) 820666**

# CHAPTER 17

# PLAQUES

## 1. BRADFORD CITY HALL

In Memory of

## BOB CRYER, M.P.

### 1934–1994

A good man, fine socialist and distinguished
parliamentarian, who fought tirelessly
to build Jerusalem in this his beloved
City of Bradford

The wording of the brass plaque unveiled at the City Hall, Bradford, by
Tony Benn, MP, following a memorial lecture on the first anniversary
of Bob's death, 12 April 1995.

### JERUSALEM

by William Blake

AND did those feet in ancient time,
Walk upon England's mountains green:
And was the holy Lamb of God,
On England's pleasant pastures seen!

And did the Countenance Divine,
Shine forth upon our clouded hills?
And was Jerusalem builded here,
Among those dark Satanic Mills?

Bring me my Bow of burning gold:
Bring me my Arrows of desire:
Bring me my Spear: O clouds unfold!
Bring me my Chariot of fire!

I will not cease from Mental Fight,
Nor shall my Sword sleep in my hand:
Till we have built Jerusalem,
In England's green and pleasant Land.

Jerusalem was sung at the end of the funeral service held in Bradford's St. George's
Hall.

## 2. BRADFORD SOUTH CONSTITUENCY PARTY

This tree was planted in fond memory of

### Bob Cryer

Member of Parliament for
Bradford South Constituency

From
1987 to 1994

Who died tragically on
12th April 1994

### Bradford South Constituency Party
1st Oct. 1994

This tree and plaque were first located alongside Bradford Magistrates' Courts, but they were later transferred to the new Centenary Square in front of the City Hall.

Tony Benn, Ann Cryer, and members of the family laying a posy of red roses at the Bradford South Labour Party's plaque, Bradford, April 1995.
(*Telegraph & Argus*)

## 3. HAWORTH STATION

In Memory of

# GEORGE ROBERT CRYER MP BSc (Econ)

1934–1994

K & WVRPS Chairman 1962–1972

whose idea it was...
If you seek his memorial, look around you

Jane, Ann, Conor and John Cryer at the unveiling of the plaque at Haworth
Station, November 1994.
(*Telegraph & Argus*)

## 4. THE ELMS MENTAL HEALTH RESOURCE CENTRE

The Elms Mental Health Resource Centre

was opened on

14th November 1994

by

Mrs Ann Cryer

in appreciation of the service
to the community by Bob Cryer

Member of Parliament for Bradford South
from 1987 to 1994

Bob was invited to perform the opening ceremony, and accepted, just
before he died.

# CHAPTER 18

# PARLIAMENTARY PROFILE

## ANDREW ROTH

Reprinted from *Parliamentary Profiles*, by Andrew Roth. Parliamentary Profile Services Ltd., 1994.

'Bob' (George Robert) CRYER dcd   Labour   BRADFORD SOUTH '87–94

*Majority*: 4,902 (9.27%) over Conservative 4-way.

*Former Seat*: Keighley '74–83.

*Description*: The marginal Bradford seat with the most council estates (22%) and the fewest Asians (1%); it contains 70% owner-occupiers.

*Position*: Chairman: Joint Select Committee on Statutory Instruments '87–94, '79–83;
on Liaison Select Committee '87–94, '79–83;
Chairman, PLP's CND Group '90–94;
Governor of British Film Institute '92–94;
on CND National Council '85–94;
on Select Committee on Members' Interests '89–92;
MEP for Sheffield '84–89;
Under-Secretary for Industry '76–78;
Chairman, PLP Defence Group '88–92;
PLP Employment Committee '87–90, '75–76;
Defence Group '80–83, Industry Group '82–83, '79–80.

*Outlook*:
Very able, hyper-assiduous, hard-Left retread whose accidental death evoked fulsome tributes;
long the 'Sundance Kid' to his 'Butch Cassidy' partner, Dennis Skinner;
one of "those two splendid trouble-makers" (Ian Aitken, *Guardian*);
was "a guerilla fighter: he passed ammunition to Dennis Skinner, but he's also effective when he fires it off himself" (Julian Critchley, MP);
second only to Skinner as an assiduous attender;
a sectarian critic of any Labour MP more moderate or willing to serve on Labour's front bench;
"could be described as Dennis Skinner without the charm" (Ian Aitken, *Evening Standard*);

"a humourless but conscientious, full-time constituency MP", "a
  Parliamentary purist who disapproves of two-job MPs" (Michael
  Jones, *Sunday Times*);
had "an almost unrivalled knowledge of the procedure of the House
  and that knowledge [was] greatly respected" (Attorney General Sir
  Nicholas Lyell);
he willingly used this as Chairman of the Joint Committee on Statutory
  Instruments;
was such a hard-line Campaign Groupie that – despite his considerable
  abilities – after '89 he lost a third of his backing from Labour
  colleagues;
was a CND activist who also sharply opposed the Gulf War ("might
  see himself as a friend and ally of Saddam Hussein" – Defence
  Secretary Malcolm Rifkind);
a puritanical critic of the corruption of Parliament by outside interests
  ("Labour's scourge of private lobbyists – David Hencke, *Guardian*);
self-described "unremitting critic of the Common Market" after having
  been an MEP;
had a fine line in political invective, initially as the "Keighley Jacobin"
  (Michael White, *Guardian*);
"one of the foremost conspiracy theorists in the House and an
  acknowledged expert at muckraking" (PM John Major);
had a talent for winning and holding difficult marginal seats;
a rooted northerner, was an opponent of positive discrimination for
  women;
was the Convenor of the Campaign Group in European Parliament
  '84–89, in the Commons '82–83;
anti-nuclear (power and weapons), anti-EEC (full withdrawal);
pro: full-scale nationalisation, siege economy (import and exchange
  controls).

*History*:
He became a conscientious objector against nuclear weapons, joining
  CND and the Labour Party '58, the Co-operative Party in '60;
contested the West Yorkshire County Council and Shipley Council May
  '61, and Shipley Council again May '62;
at annual conference he objected to overlong platform speeches Oct '62,
  Oct '63;
contested hopeless Darwen Oct '64, West Riding County Council May '66;
was elected to Keighley Borough Council May '71;
captured Keighley from Joan Hall Feb '74;
joined the Tribune Group Mar '74;
opposed the Lions' tour of South Africa Dec '74;

was named Under Secretary for Industry with responsibility for small
businesses Sep '76;

resigned as Under Secretary over Government secrecy and the refusal to
continue funding the Kirkby Co-operative Nov '78;

retained Keighley with a majority of 78, May '79;

helped launch the Labour Co-ordinating Committee to push substantive
constitutional reforms in the Labour Party Mar '79;

with Arthur Scargill attacked James Callaghan for having supported
Rightwing policies which, they claimed, contributed to Labour's
defeat June '79;

complained that all the members of the Select Committee on Members'
Interests had outside interests themselves July '79;

attacked Shirley Williams for her doubts about mandatory reselection
Sep '79;

again opposed subsidies to Press Gallery Dec '79;

helped launch a new CND campaign Dec '79;

introduced a Bill to curb phone-tapping Feb '80;

criticised a civil servant for taking a job at GEC Apr '80;

introduced Bill for referenda on having A-power stations within 30
miles June '80;

introduced a Bill for referenda on having Cruise missiles nearby June '80;

the anti-Left Social Democratic Alliance threatened to field a candidate
against him July '80;

urged James Callaghan to sack Bill Rodgers as Labour's Defence
Spokesman for his support of Cruise missiles July '80;

complained of the divisive way in which magistrates were chosen Mar '81;

warned of danger of a "computerised police state" May '81;

demanded an investigation of the 'Yorkshire Ripper' hunt June '81;

his fiery attack on Dennis Healey was part of his campaign backing
Tony Benn, for the Deputy Leadership Sep '81;

accused the Labour "Rightwing" (including Dennis Healey, Austin
Mitchell and Jack Straw) of trying to purge undemocratic
"extremists" to end Labour's commitment to "unilateral nuclear
disarmament, withdrawal from the Common Market and the
Alternative Economic Strategy" Dec '81;

introduced his Registration of Commercial Lobbyists Bill Feb '82;

attacked witch hunts (against Militant) July '82;

criticised Michael Foot for nominating four "working peers" to the
Lords Dec '82;

lost marginal Keighley, largely because of adverse boundary changes
June '83;

was mentioned for Chesterfield, where Tony Benn became the hard-Left
candidate and MP Nov '83;

was elected to the European Parliament for Sheffield June '84;

was selected for marginal Bradford South – to succeed Tom Torney – from a shortlist of five on the third ballot by a majority of 36 to 32 May '85;

as part of a "small clique" (Barbara Castle) of hard Leftwingers in the European Parliament, he attacked soft-Left MP Stan Newens for accepting Britain would remain in EEC Aug '85;

at fringe meeting said "if a Labour Government controlled the movement of capital, it would have to withdraw from the EEC" Sep '85;

denied being "hard Left", threatening to sue Conservative Chairman Norman Tebbit over the allegation May '87;

narrowly retained Bradford South June '87;

on the Campaign Group slate for the Shadow Cabinet, received 35 votes July '87;

endorsed Jeremy Corbyn's right to secure access to the Commons for his researcher, an imprisoned-but-cleared ex-IRA supporter Nov '87;

again urged that bribing an MP be made a criminal offence Nov '87;

asked Mrs Thatcher whether she would set up a register of lobbyists Jan '88;

voted against Licensing Bill to ease pub hours Feb '88;

again opposed closing of Settle–Carlisle line May '88;

backed Tony Benn's effort radically to rewrite the constitution July '88;

voted against Defence Estimates, instead of abstaining as requested Oct '88;

received 42 votes for Shadow Cabinet Nov '88;

was elected Chairman of PLP Defence Committee Nov '88;

voted against Prevention of Terrorism Bill instead of abstaining as requested Dec '88;

opposed extra pay for Ministers, who gained lots of perks Dec '88;

claimed "the Philistines in the Government are destroying the cinema from within by their tax policies" Mar '89;

with other unilateralists, rejected Neil Kinnock's multilateralism May '89;

was named to Select Committee on Members' Interests June '89;

backed televising the Commons but rejected a dedicated Commons TV channel as an "electronic ghetto which would be seen by everybody for about five minutes in their lives and then switched off" June '89;

told local Council of Mosques that but for their "singularly ill-judged and misguided campaign" against Salman Rushdie, sales of *Satanic Verses* would have continued to plummet July '89;

was re-selected unopposed Sep '89;

was rated as having been the second most frequent Parliamentary intervener after Dennis Skinner in the 1987–89 sessions Nov '89;

voted against EC broadcast directive June '89;

received 42 votes for the Shadow Cabinet Nov '89;

predicted, "if Michael Heseltine had the guts to stand against Her, she would be swept from office and dumped" Nov '89;

opposed Bill to develop Immingham Port, partly because it was a Government Bill disguised as a Private Bill Nov '89;

opposed auction system in Broadcasting Bill which would give money to the Treasury but take money out of broadcasting Dec '89;

voted against EC Jan '90;

backed miner-MPs in opposing Bill to improve Immingham port fearing increased import of cheap foreign coal Jan '90;

said it was "outrageous" if lobbying organisations "can actually buy influence in Parliament" for "multinational corporations and the well-heeled" Jan '90;

attacked globe-trotting select committee's over-expensive trips: "the budget for these trips next year is going to be half-a-million pounds of taxpayers' money" Jan '90;

urged renewal of Multi-Fibre Agreement to protect local textile workers; "I was brought up in Saltaire, a textile village" Jan '90;

with neighbouring Trotskyist MP Pat Wall, refused to support call for ban or withdrawal of *Satanic Verses* as demanded by many constituency Muslims, despite narrowness (309) of his majority Jan '90;

backed fund-raising by *Morning Star* to help provide "diverse political opinion" Feb '90;

was teller in vote against EC policy on agriculture Feb '90;

was listed as a supporter of the Militant-organised Anti-Poll Tax Federation Mar '90;

urged a register of lobbyists Mar '90;

said the 20-day suspension of John Browne, including the unprecedented withholding of his salary, indicated the seriousness of the offence of the Tory MP in concealing his interests Mar '90;

introduced Bill to abolish the offence of blasphemy Mar '90

introduced Bill to make security services democratically accountable Mar '90;

opposed embryo research Apr '90;

complained about Government's sale of skill centres May '90;

said "I remain an unremitting critic of the Common Market";

"the EC has been a burden on our backs" June '90;

opposed "unfair, unjust and onerous" student loans as "probably the only Hon Member who had to go to university with a loan in 1953, when it was very difficult to obtain a grant, the local authority refused me one; had I known that I would have to go through university on an annual loan, I would not have entered in the first place"; "I had to work week after week in a part-time job to eke out my university existence; the loan was a millstone round our necks ... because it continued well into my married life – and I was married at 29"; "the burden of those repayments was still there in my early 30s; I would not wish to impose such an onerous duty on any other student" July '90

said, "the scrutiny of delegated legislation is unsatisfactory; bringing that fact to the attention of the Chamber is an important way of seeking improvements which, I judge, is part of my task as Chairman of the Committees on Statutory Instruments" July '90;

again urged UK to dump its nuclear weapons July '90;

as a former Bradford League cricketer, backed tax concessions for amateur clubs July '90;

scorned Defence Secretary Tom King's "pompous and arrogant" "decision not to cancel the Trident programme" as "immoral and outrageous" July '90;

voted against the Gulf War Sept '90;

received 30 votes for the Shadow Cabinet Oct '90;

co-urged peaceful negotiations with Saddam Hussein Nov '90;

after Mrs Thatcher failed to defeat Michael Heseltine, urged dissolution of Parliament Nov '90;

backed Jonathan Aitken's anti-EC amendment Dec '90;

voted against Gulf War Dec '90;

asked PM John Major whether the Government would "make serious efforts to develop an arms embargo to curtail the wretched trade in arms ... or do the Government put profit before peace?" Jan '91;

his amendment in the PLP – saying "sanctions [against Iraq] will be effective independent of any military threat" – was heavily defeated on a show of hands Jan '91;

tried to amend Government motion supporting the Gulf War by calling for "a halt to hostilities to provide for a peaceful settlement" Jan '91;

voted against Gulf War Jan '91;

co-deplored bombing of Iraqi civilians Feb '91;

decried low flying as "a tactical failure in the Gulf War" Jan '91;

complained that opponents of Gulf War were excluded from debate Jan '91;

claimed that the "dreadful" Gulf War was illegal because of China's abstention in Security Council voting Feb '91;

urged more effective legislation against dangerous dogs May '91;

claimed Ministers were planning to bail out 62 bankruptcy-threatened Tory MPs who were Lloyd's 'names' June '91;

urged Lloyd's 'names' be banned from voting on Finance Bill June '91;

launched Labour Campaign for First-Past-The-Post June '91;

urged a disqualification for Ministers "holding any office of profit other than under the Crown" July '91;

urged stronger regulation of offshore banks like BCCI July '91;

sought to modify rules of Committee on Sittings of Commons July '91;

opposed cutting Parliament's working week to four days, saying it would make it difficult for a Labour Government to get legislation through against a determined Tory Opposition July '91;

urged democratic control of telephone tapping July '91;

in anti-PR meeting on fringe of annual conference, warned adoption of PR would mean there would never again be a majority Labour government that was not dependent on Liberal Democrats Sep '91;

helped secure report urging lobbyist registration by Select Committee on Members' Interests Sep '91;

after a local child-mauling, urged inclusion of dobermans and rottweilers in dangerous dog legislation Sep '91;

co-sponsored motion urging assistance for defence industry diversification and re-training and re-housing of ex-servicemen Oct '91;

received 29 votes for Shadow Cabinet Oct '91;

backed motions blaming US for Indonesia's invasion of East Timor and killings in El Salvador Dec '91;

expressed concern that Transport and Works Bill might repeal railway safety regulations Dec '91;

claimed that a "serious error" had been made in expelling Dave Nellist MP from the Labour Party for having links with Militant Tendency Dec '91;

was rated as having the second best voting record after his partner Dennis Skinner, with 216 votes to Skinner's 217 in the '90–91 session, Jan '92;

after he complained of "misguided" and "selective" actions against Iraq, Defence Secretary Malcolm Rifkind said Cryer "might see himself as a friend and ally of Saddam Hussein" Jan '92;

again urged withdrawal of Polaris and scrapping of Trident Jan '92;

opposed development of King's Cross, fearing it would mop up funds for rail links to the North Jan '92;

congratulated campaigners against US National Security Agency ("international phone tapping") at Menwith Hill Feb '92;

retained seat with majority up from 309 to 4,902, a swing to Labour of 4.33% Apr '92;

was re-named to Joint Committee on Statutory Instruments June '92;

urged fair trade for Bradford's textiles with no dumping June '92;

received 29 votes for Shadow Cabinet July '92;

introduced Firearms (Amendment) Bill to bar replica guns (which he later dropped) July '92;

said, "consensus in this Chamber is the worst aspect of Parliament at work" July '92;

tried to prevent Commons rising a fortnight early July '92;

was ousted from office on PLP Defence Committee with fellow hard-Left members of Campaign Group, Harry Cohen and Dennis Canavan Nov '92;

in his *Morning Star* column lashed the "lavish allowances" picked up by MEPs such as he had been Nov '92;

complained that Chancellor Lamont has extracted an undisclosed £18,414 from Treasury for legal costs of evicting "sex therapist" from his house Nov '92;

co-sponsored motion attacking Royal Family for not paying for Windsor Castle fire Nov '92;

was named to Liaison Committee of Commons chairmen, and again to Select Committee on Members' Interests Nov '92;

urged a posthumous pardon for Derek Bentley Nov '92;

was named a Governor of the British Film Institute Dec '92;

criticised Prince Charles for his "ignorance" and "insensitivity" in praising French rural life Dec '92;

attacked wheelclamping on private land Feb '93;

was rated as the second most active rebel against Maastricht Feb '93;

complained that Caravan Sites Bill would increase illegal camping by travellers who were not "guitar-strumming Romanies" Feb '93;

co-urged retirement of costly and obsolescent royal yacht *Britannia* Feb '93;

complained that the Railways Bill (Ways and Means) might make life difficult for hobby railwaymen like him Keighley and Worth Valley line Feb '93;

with Dennis Skinner forced votes on every motion for technical orders and called "I spy strangers" to delay debate and disrupt business Mar '93;

was teller against National Lottery Bill, protesting its effect on small charity lotteries; he tried to amend it to provide more money for British Film Institute Apr '93;

claimed the 14,000 contracts in BR's semi-privatisation would create a bonanza for lawyers May '93;

complained that British Waterways Board were being given too many powers which could be misused against 12,000 houseboat owners May '93;

urged bar on air strikes in ex-Yugoslavia to protect UK troops May '93;

voted against 3rd Reading for Maastricht treaty May '93;

strongly supported further tightening of registration of Members' interests June '93;

complained that expansion of European Parliament was meaningless since it was still consultative while "legislative powers in the Common Market are still in the hands of the Council of Ministers, which meets in secret" July '93;

urged an inquiry into Ministers with undeclared directorships, like Sir Wyn Roberts' Professional Secretarial Services July '93;

received 14.248% of vote for Treasurer of Labour Party Oct '93;

again voted against Defence Estimates Oct '93;

asked PM John Major "to clear out the cesspit of the present Government by sacking all those Ministers who conspired to pervert the course of justice in the Matrix Churchill case in order to cover up a Government policy encouraging the sale of machinery to Iraq" Nov '93;

contrasted the derisory sentence for fraudster Joseph Levitt with "the zeal with which [the courts] pursued poll tax defaulters" Nov '93;

voted for a lesser increase in pay for MPs earning over £2,000 a year from outside interests Nov '93;

urged cuts in Government hospitality Nov '93;

was renamed to Standing Orders Committee Nov '93;

was teller against European Economic Areas Bill '93;

was rated the second best attender after Dennis Skinner, with 97% attendance Dec '93;

claimed NATO's role had "disappeared – if it ever existed" Jan '94;

urged a debate on GATT, since "I have 11,000 textile workers in my constituency" Jan '94;

in Campaign Group amendment to Finance Bill, co-demanded publication and debate on Memorandum of Understanding on Royal Taxation Jan '94;

attacked Deregulation Bill as giving too much power to ministers and risking ending safety regulations Feb '94;

despite being an agnostic, he treasured "the beauty and the majesty of churches in the townscape" Mar '94;

died in road accident en route to Commons after Easter recess Apr '94.

*Born*: 3 December 1934, Bradford.

*Family*: S John Arthur Cryer, fitter, and Gladys Evelyn Cryer; m '63 Ann (Place) ex Darwen Labour Councillor, who worked part-time as one of his assistants; 1s, 1d.

Last rally. Reform of the Child Support Agency at Leeds, April 1994.
(*Telegraph & Argus*)

*Education*: Albert Road School, Shipley; Salt High School, Shipley;
Hull University (in the absence of a grant, ran up student loans
which were difficult to pay off; BSc Econ).

*Occupation*:

Author: *Queensbury Lines* (1984), *Steam in the Worth Valley*, Vols I and II (1969), (1972);

Governor, British Film Institute (no remuneration) '92–94;

Shareholder, five £10 shares in Keighley and Worth Valley Light Railway (no dividends; he founded the railway and was Chairman of this 5-mile branch line for 10 years); '66–94;

ex: MEP (contributed a third of his salary to Leftwing causes) '84–89;

Lecturer in Law and Government: Keighley Technical College '65–74, Dewsbury Technical College '63–64;

Personnel Officer: Blackburn College of Technology '64–65, Hull '58–59;

Teacher: Keighley '62–63, Hull '61–62, Bradford '59–61;

Director, Keighley and Worth Valley Light Railway Company Ltd '66–74.

*Traits*: Tall; lean; ginger-haired; specs; persuasive;

"I am not a drinker of alcohol";

"an instinctive Puritan, spurning the Commons bars" (*Times*);

agnostic; railway buff; film buff;

cricketer (formerly with Yorkshire Universities XI and in the Aire/Wharfe League);

"thorough, tenacious, censorious, a real craftsman" of legislative devices (Michael White, *Guardian*);

"full of his own cleverness" (*Sunday Express*);

"strives manfully for the title of the rudest MP" (Jim Naughtie, *Scotsman*);

"a walking collage of Leftwing slogans" (Edward Pearce);

had an open-top Armstrong Siddeley.

# CHAPTER 19

# POST-SCRIPT

## JANE KILDUFF
### *Daughter of Bob Cryer*

Sudden death, for a time, overshadows the life that went before it. We remember, as if it were yesterday, the dreadful message to phone Watford hospital, the appallingly urgent journey on a busy M25 to a rather sparse and impersonal chapel of rest to say goodbye to someone we knew had already left us. All of these memories are fresh, but this collection of other peoples' memories of my father gives me, his only daughter, a chance to reflect upon what he had achieved in a life cut short.

At the funeral meeting, held at St George's Hall, I turned whilst 'Jerusalem' echoed around me, and the hall was full to the Gods. Why had so many people come to say goodbye to my father? I think it was because he made everyone who ever met him feel as though they mattered. And

Grandpa Bob Cryer with Conor James Kilduff, one week old,
October 1992, Ashford, Kent.

One of the last photographs taken of Bob Cryer at his Shipley home at Easter 1994. Ann holding Conor, son John, son-in-law David, daughter Jane, and Bob. (*Photo taken by daughter-in-law Narinder*)

Bob holding Conor, Narinder and husband John,
Jane at back with husband David on right.
(*Photo taken by Ann Cryer*)

in a world where there is little opportunity for the common touch to triumph, that is a remarkable achievement.

Private memories of Dad should remain just that, but I have a recurring image of my father that I should like to share. That of a tall, lean figure, dressed in dark green sports jacket, moss green cavalry twill trousers, brogues, a pale green shirt and dark green Labour Party tie. Never ever changing his sartorial direction; and even in the most ferocious heat refusing to remove his tie. Under his (usually) unkempt hair and through his Autumn Tint glasses he looks at me with a twinkle in his eye and a boyish grin and says "Really! Jane, you do say the most appalling things!" – his way of acknowledging in me the same instinctive disobedience and lack of respect for convention that drove him.

Our children will never know their grandfather, and perhaps this is my keenest sense of loss. But in spirit, I believe, he will live on. And when our three boys get into trouble for disobedience, talking too much, asking too many questions, breaking too many rules, I know I have my father to thank, and I will secretly hope their fearlessness, like that of my Dad, is never, ever, conquered.

# INDEX OF CONTRIBUTORS